D0507329

99 ANSWERS to QUESTIONS about ANGELS, DEMONS & SPIRITUAL WARFARE

B. J. Oropeza

InterVarsity Press
Downers Grove, Illinois

©1997 by B. J. Oropeza

All rights reserved. No part of this book may be reproduced in any form without written permission from InterVarsity Press, P.O. Box 1400, Downers Grove, IL 60515.

InterVarsity Press® is the book-publishing division of InterVarsity Christian Fellowship®, a student movement active on campus at hundreds of universities, colleges and schools of nursing in the United States of America, and a member movement of the International Fellowship of Evangelical Students. For information about local and regional activities, write Public Relations Dept., InterVarsity Christian Fellowship, 6400 Schroeder Rd., P.O. Box 7895, Madison, WI 53707-7895.

All Scripture quotations, unless otherwise indicated, are from the HOLY BIBLE, NEW INTERNATIONAL VERSION®. NIV®. Copyright ©1973, 1978, 1984 International Bible Society. Used by permission of Zondervan Publishing House. All rights reserved.

Cover illustration: Scala/Art Resource, NY. Beccafumi, Domenico. Last Judgement. S. Maria del Carmine, Siena, Italy, Rodi.

ISBN 0-8308-1968-1

Printed in the United States of America ♾

Library of Congress Cataloging-in-Publication Data

Oropeza, B. J., 1961-
    99 answers to questions about angels, demons, and spiritual
    warfare/B. J. Oropeza.
        p.   cm.
    Includes bibliographical references.
    ISBN 0-8308-1968-1 (alk. paper)
    1. Angels—Biblical teaching—Miscellanea.   2. Demonology—
    Biblical teaching—Miscellanea.   3. Spiritual warfare—Biblical
    teaching—Miscellanea.   I. Title.
    BT962.O76   1997
    235—dc21   97-14368
                                                                CIP

| 19 | 18 | 17 | 16 | 15 | 14 | 13 | 12 | 11 | 10 | 9 | 8 | 7 | 6 | 5 | 4 | 3 | 2 |
| 12 | 11 | 10 | 09 | 08 | 07 | 06 | 05 | 04 | 03 | 02 | 01 | 00 | 99 | 98 | | | |

To my wife, Cathie,
whose faith through her battle with cancer
has been an inspiration to many

ABBREVIATIONS —— 8

1 THE ANGEL & DEMON CRAZE —— 9

2 QUESTIONS ABOUT ANGELS —— 17

3 QUESTIONS ABOUT THE ACTIVITIES
OF ANGELS —— 33

4 QUESTIONS ABOUT FALLEN ANGELS —— 50

5 QUESTIONS ABOUT SATAN —— 79

6 QUESTIONS ABOUT SPIRITUAL WARFARE —— 113

7 QUESTIONS ABOUT THE OCCULT —— 140

APPENDIX: LIST OF QUESTIONS —— 173

NOTES —— 176

SCRIPTURE INDEX —— 210

Abbreviations

b.	from Babylonian Talmud
KJV	King James Version of the Bible
LXX	Septuagint (Greek translation of the Old Testament)
MT	Masoretic Text
NIV	New International Version of the Bible
RSV	Revised Standard Version of the Bible

Dead Sea Scrolls and Related Texts

CD	Cairo *Damascus Document*
1QapGen	*Genesis Apocryphon* from Qumran Cave 1
1QH	*Hôdāyôṭ* or *Hymns of Thanksgiving* from Qumran Cave 1
1QM	*Milḥāmāh* or *War Scroll* from Qumran Cave 1
1QS	*Serek hayyaḥad* or *Rule of the Community, Manual of Discipline* from Qumran Cave 1
1QSb	Appendix B, *Rule of Benediction*, to 1QS
4Q400-407	part of *Songs of Sabbath Sacrifice* or *Angelic Liturgy* from Qumran Cave 4
11QPs	*Psalms Scroll* from Qumran Cave 11

1

THE
ANGEL &
DEMON CRAZE

It was Christmas Eve when twenty-one-year-old Tim's car broke down, stranding him in a blizzard. Suddenly a tow truck appeared out of the storm. The driver towed Tim's car and drove him to a friend's house in Fort Wayne, Indiana. When Tim went outside with money to pay the man, he found no one there. The only tire tracks in the snow were from Tim's car. After he described the incident to his mother, journalist Joan Wester Anderson, she called the highway patrol and area towing services, only to find no record of the call. She believes an angel visited her son that day. His experience inspired her to write *Where Angels Walk,* a book about angels that made the *New York Times* bestseller list.[1]

Anderson's bestseller on angels is not unique. Five out of the ten religious paperback books on a recent *Publisher's Weekly* bestseller list focused on angels.[2] "Angelmania" describes the prevailing mood. A poll conducted by *Newsweek* magazine revealed that "13% of Americans have seen or sensed the presence of an angel."[3] A poll conducted by *Time* magazine found that 69 percent of Americans believe in the existence of angels, and 46 percent believe they have a guardian angel.[4]

These days various bookstores feature angel sections that display a wide range of angel books. Angel boutiques, angel newsletters and angel seminars are on the rise. Top schools such as Harvard Divinity School and Boston College offer angel courses. In the performing arts arena, Tony Kushner won a Pulitzer Prize for his sentimental *Angels in America,* a Broadway play about a benevolent angel who helps an AIDS victim.[5] On the silver screen, movie blockbusters like *Angels in the Outfield* and *Michael* demonstrate Western society's current fascination with heavenly visitors.

But angels do not hold a monopoly on things spiritual. The occult, the traditional breeding ground for demons, is also drawing a lot of interest. Recent successful movies such as *Independence Day* and *Phenomenon,* as well as television programs like *The X-Files,* play to society's interest in the paranormal. One Gallup poll found that 75 percent of Americans read their horoscopes occasionally, while 25 percent read them rather devotedly. Another 25 percent believe they have had at least one extrasensory or psychic experience, 25 percent believe in ghosts, and 10 percent claim either to have seen or to have been in the presence of a ghost. One out of six believe they have contacted someone from the dead. Do superstitious beliefs still scare us? Fourteen percent of all Americans fear having a black cat cross their paths, and 12 percent are afraid to walk under a ladder.

A recent *Newsweek* poll discovered that 48 percent of Americans believe in UFOs and 29 percent believe that we have contacted space aliens.[6] Occultism has even reached the White House, with Nancy Reagan consulting an astrologer and Hillary Clinton "imagining conversations with Eleanor Roosevelt."[7] More startling, a Gallup poll discovered that between 19 and 24 percent of Catholic, Protestant and born-again Christians believe in reincarnation—the rebirth of the soul into a new body.[8]

Question 1: Why Are So Many People Intrigued by Angelic Beings?

It doesn't take a rocket scientist to recognize the impact that the spirit world exerts on our society. Why has a postmodern, secularized Western culture like ours resurrected the medieval topic of angels and demons? Here are a few possible answers.

1. Many people in Western society are rediscovering their spiritual roots. Hard scientism, which insists that everything has to be proved by the five senses, no longer holds sway. The Newtonian "closed universe" that seemed to exclude God and spirits is being eclipsed by the newer sciences of an "open universe" and quantum mechanics. It has become politically correct to tap into your spiritual side. Just don't insist that your spirituality is right and someone else's is wrong!

Spirituality has taken on new meaning in recent times as people pursue self-awareness. In the 1960s many "found themselves" by tapping into Eastern mystic ideas. Hindu terms such as *karma, guru, transcendental meditation* and *reincarnation* have become household terms in the West since the New Age movement breathed new life into them. But when baby boomers, baby busters and Generation Xers dig deeper than the 1960s counterculture,[9] they often find that their spiritual roots take them back to principles found in the Bible. As recent news magazines have shown, many from the baby-boom generation are going back to church.

Can a frivolous, faddish spirituality lead us to authentic spirituality? Perhaps the stress of living in the modern world—including family discord, job pressures and financial uncertainty—has something to do with drawing people back to a power higher than themselves. (And let us not forget the prayers of the saints.) God has a way of speaking to us through life's experiences. The 1960s and 1970s showed many that drugs and dropping out of society did not provide the answers they were looking for. Many who did not drop out had their faith in the system shattered by Vietnam and Watergate. Thus the search for order, sanity and spiritual sustenance in the 1980s and 1990s seemed a reasonable way to go.

But heightened interest in spirituality has not led everybody to the portals of the church. Many have found spirituality through paranormal venues. As one recent *Newsweek* article reports regarding the current neospiritualist movement:

Boomers approaching their golden years are sill searching for Meaning in their lives, something more transcendent than an old Grateful Dead record. Disillusioned Gen-Xers, prone to conspiracy theorizing, are convinced they have a better chance of encountering an alien than they do of collecting Social Security. It's a substitute religion for people who haven't got one and a supplemental one for those who already do. . . . "I want to believe" is the movement's (and the moment's) mantra.[10]

Awareness of the spirit world raises multiple questions. If I believe in God, must I also believe in the devil? Do I go directly to God with my prayers? How does God relay messages to people? This leads to the second point.

2. Angels serve as nonthreatening mediators between God and humans. Another reason for the angel craze centers on the angelic role of mediator. Some people are afraid to pray directly to God. Images of God as a white-bearded Father Time figure holding a lightning bolt in his uplifted hand persist in the Western world. Earthquakes, floods and other natural disasters are still classified as "acts of God," and the mindset of rebellious youth remains the same: "God is an old meanie who doesn't want me to have any fun."

But some do pray to Jesus. The Bible identifies him as the only true mediator between God and humankind, and many do turn to him. But others would rather turn to angels, perhaps because Jesus expects obedience and holiness. Turning to Christ involves confession of sins and complete commitment. There's less commitment involved in communicating with angels, and less accountability. New Agers claim they can channel their own angelic guides with little fear that their celestial friends will want them to turn away from their sins.

3. *Angels are almost universally recognized.* Angels appear in almost every culture and religion in the world, from ancient Sumeria, Egypt and Assyria to contemporary civilizations. From the dawn of the Hebrews' tradition-history, when Adam and Eve were banished by the cherubim (angels) from the Garden of Eden (and even before that if the serpent is understood as a fallen angel), angels are said to have interacted with humanity. As one Catholic theologian affirms, "The angels are taken for granted; they are simply there, as in all the religions of the world surrounding the Bible, and are simply known to exist."[11]

Not only do angels appear in the Old and New Testaments, but they also appear in the literature of Judaism, Qumran (the Dead Sea Scrolls community), Islam, Zoroastrianism, Buddhism and Hinduism. And let's not forget the role they have played in Western art and literature. Who isn't impressed by Michelangelo's cherubs or Milton's elaboration of the demonic entourage in *Paradise Lost?*[12] Angels, therefore, are easy nominees for a politically correct "spiritual" age of networking, globalism, religious ecumenism and "all religions lead to God anyway"-ism.

Some religions also recognize another set of spiritual beings whose object is to cause evil, disaster and chaos. These are commonly known as evil spirits, jinn or demons. On April 5, 1991, Americans stared wide-eyed at an exorcism performed live on the ABC television program *20/20.* This viewing prompted Barbara Walters to ask, "Is the devil real?" Demonic forces are mitigated in some Eastern-oriented religions that ignore or play down evil, suffering and sin. But do demonic forces vanish simply because some no longer believe in them?

Charlatans aside, could it be that some of the spirit beings religious channelers converse with are deceptive spirits?

4. *Many religious people see themselves in a battle between the forces of good and evil.* Angels and demons serve as the chief rivals in this conflict. Where does this battle mentality come from? Ancient Zoroastrianism and prophetic Jewish literature often portray such a battle. Of course, biblical scripture confirms a conflict between good and evil, as it does the existence of angels and demons. The book of Revelation describes this cosmological battle and predicts that goodness will prevail over evil. Bestsellers like Frank Peretti's *This Present Darkness* and *Piercing the Darkness* have captured the imaginations of Christians by giving them a creative and dramatic glimpse of how angels and demons might "duke it out" in the spirit world. More extreme thrills and chills abound in Christian bestsellers such as *Pigs in the Parlor* and *He Came to Set the Captives Free,* which claim that not only unbelievers but even believers can suffer from demon possession.

How This Book Addresses Angels and Demons
What is the need for another book on the current spirit craze? In a word, discernment. We need discernment regarding supernatural beings such as angels and demons. Is the New Age correct when it portrays angels as nice creatures who are always willing to assist us? If early Christian and Jewish literature are correct about malevolent spirits, then how do we distinguish between angels and demons? Are the bestsellers correct when they assert that demons are behind all our problems? This book addresses these and other related issues through an in-depth study of biblical Scripture, where we find that angels and devils appear many times. We will also refer to literature from ancient Jewish sources and the church fathers because these materials often shed light on how the biblical writers may have interpreted the spirit world.

This book is divided into three sections. Chapters two and

three focus on the subject of angels. In chapter two we will probe questions about the creation and the character of angels. What is an angel? How were angels created? How many angels are there? Chapter three examines the work of angels. What do angels do? Is it wrong to call on them for help? We will answer these and other questions through biblical insights.

Chapters four through six focus on demons and Satan. Chapter four answers questions about the creation and character of demons. Chapter five looks at the figure of Satan. How do many arrive at the conclusion that he was once a beautiful angel called Lucifer? Where do we get the notion that he is red and carries a pitchfork? In chapter six we will examine the works of both Satan and his minions. What does biblical literature say about their agenda in relation to humans? How do we know when a supernatural event is from God or from some other source?

Finally, chapter seven answers questions about the occult. We will tackle issues of the paranormal, from astrology to astral projection, from reincarnation to psychic powers, from UFOs to witchcraft, and many things in between.

Some readers may wish to jump right into the section on the demonic, while others may be afraid to go beyond the benign angels of chapter three. Others will want to read the book from cover to cover. Still others will simply want to use this book as a reference tool to answer specific questions they may have. Whatever your approach, let me add this one caveat. As a writer on discernment issues and a former researcher on new religious movements and paranormal questions, I have tackled issues like these on numerous occasions. When we engage in discussions about the nature of supernatural spirits, we also seem to open the door to a spiritual dimension that can be either a blissful or a horrible experience—many times it's both.

Some readers may not like being exposed to the spirit world. If you feel you are not ready to handle this subject, then do not read the book. I do not like to water down the issues. On the other hand, I feel that everyone who is interested in this subject needs the information and discernment this book provides. Above all, let's not overestimate or underestimate the angelic forces of good and evil. Having said this, let's move on.

2

QUESTIONS
ABOUT ANGELS

Modernists often consider angels a fictional product of our superstitious past. In the nineteenth century, Friedrich Schleiermacher, often considered the father of liberal theology, questioned the purpose of having a doctrine of angels. In the twentieth century, New Testament critical scholar Rudolf Bultmann essentially denied their existence altogether. So what does it profit us, as we look toward the twenty-first century, to study the archaic subject of angels? Theologian Millard Erickson lists five benefits for the spiritually minded:[1]

1. It comforts us to know that numerous powerful beings exist who are available to help us (2 Kings 6:17).

2. Angelic worship shows us how to worship God (Rev 4:8-11).

3. That some angels fell away cautions us to watch out that we do not fall away from our faith (1 Cor 10:12).

4. The reality of fallen angels alerts us to the ways that we can be tempted (Mt 4:1-11).

5. As powerful as Satan and his minions are, it comforts us to know that they are limited in what they can do (Job 1–2).

The current fascination with angels takes less interest in deep questions about angelic essence and nature and more interest in angelic activities. We "postmoderns" are more interested in what angels can do for us than in what they are. But this focus can fail to distinguish the difference between good and evil angels. Before we study what angels do, we must understand who and what they are. And that is the focus of this chapter

Question 2: What Does the Word *Angel* Mean?

The Old Testament Hebrew word for angel is *mal'āk,* meaning "messenger" or "representative." The word appears in the name of the prophet Malachi, "my messenger," indicating a messenger sent by God. In Greek mythology, the word translated "angel," *angelos,* was used of the god Hermes, who functioned as a messenger for the other gods. A messenger can be either a human (Gen 32:3; Eccles 5:6) or a spiritual being (Gen 28:12; Dan 6:22).

In Mark 1:2 John the Baptist is the messenger *(angelos)* who prepares the way for the Lord. In Luke 9:52 Jesus sends his disciples as messengers to prepare the way for him in Samaria. The word *angelos* appears 175 times in the New Testament.[2] The context of a passage often determines whether the messenger is a human or a spirit. In Matthew 28:2, for instance, the messenger is a supernatural being, an angel from heaven who rolled back the stone from Jesus' grave. The angel's action was beyond the natural capability of a human being.

The first time angels appear as supernatural messengers sent from God is in Genesis 3:24: "After he [God] drove the man [Adam] out, he placed on the east side of the Garden of Eden cherubim [angels] and a flaming sword flashing back and forth to guard the way to the tree of life."[3] These messengers could not have been human beings, since in Genesis Adam and Eve were the first ones. This account leads us to a crucial point regarding angels. They first appear after Adam and Eve fell into sin, after they put on fig leaves and hid from God's presence, and after God had pronounced judgment on them. It was only after sin ended Adam and Eve's intimate relationship with God that angels come into the picture.

Thus the word *angel* commonly identifies *a supernatural being who plays a mediating role as a messenger between God and humans.*[4] But we should recognize from the outset that angels are not mediators of salvation—the Bible affirms that Christ is the only mediator in this sense (1 Tim 2:5). Christ reconciles humans to God and makes them God's children; angels assist and minister to humans at God's direction.

Question 3: What Are Angels?

Perhaps the greatest speculations on the nature of angels came from a Dominican monk, Thomas Aquinas (1225-74), who earned the title Doctor Angelicus. Aquinas answered 118 questions about the character and attributes of angels and provided a basic definition of angels: "purely spiritual, intellectual and non-corporeal creatures, with 'substances.' "[5] Let's break down this definition to note several aspects of the nature of angels.

1. Angels are spirits. Like God, angels are spirits (invisible and immaterial essences) who are not limited by the physical constraints put on humans (Heb 1:14; compare Job 4:15-16).[6] For one thing, angels never die (Lk 20:36). Thomas Aquinas claims that angels are able to take on the physical appearances of eating, talking, and so forth, even though they are not actually fulfilling such activities (*Summa Contra Gentiles* 50.5; 51.3; cf. Tobit 12.19; Philo *Quaestiones in Genesin* 4.9; Josephus *Antiquities of the Jews* 1.11.2). If they are spirits, they probably do not have physical digestive systems. Nevertheless, angels can interact with the physical world. The angel at Christ's resurrection had no problem removing the heavy stone that sealed Christ's tomb (Mt 28:2; Mk 16:3-4).

2. *Angels are superhuman beings.* Angels are superhuman in the sense that they have greater abilities than humans. They can open prison doors to free captives (Acts 5:19; 12:5-11), they reveal messages from God (Acts 10:3-4; 23:9; 27:23), and they bring physical judgment on the wicked (Acts 12:23). In Genesis 19:10-11 they blinded the men of Sodom who were trying to molest them.

In Revelation 7:1, John depicts four angels that hold the four winds of the earth. This perhaps implies a Jewish belief that angels have power over nature (*2 Enoch* 5.1). We do not know, however, whether the angels perform superhuman feats by their own power or whether they are specially empowered by God for the occasion. Whatever the case, good angels act in harmony with the will of God.

3. *Angels are personal beings.* Unlike earthquakes, tornadoes, radar and other impersonal forces, angels are persons. They are not merely God's chesspieces or spiritual robots; they have intellect, emotion and will. Regarding intellect, they have wisdom and can discern between good and evil (2 Sam 14:17-20; 19:27). They long to understand the complete plan of God's redemption (1 Pet 1:10-12; Eph 3:10). Regarding emotion, they rejoice over God's creation and over any sinner who repents (Job 38:7; Lk 15:7, 10). We might assume therefore that they grieve over those who reject the message of salvation (Pseudo-Philo 19.12-16).[7] Regarding volition, they willfully choose to obey God's word (Ps 103:20; Rev 22:8-9), although some who are called fallen angels have chosen to disobey God (Jude 6).

4. *Angels are holy beings.* Angels are sometimes called "holy ones" (Dan 4:13, 17; 1 Thess 3:13; Jude 14; Rev 14:10; 1QH 3.22; 4.25; 11.12; 1QM 1.10-11; 14.15-16). Although they can clothe themselves with glory and splendor (Lk 2:9; 24:4-5) and they have access to heaven (Gen 28:12; Lk 2:13-15; Jn 1:51), their holiness comes from God. Angels do not possess perfect holiness; they worship God alone as the absolutely holy one

(Job 4:18-19; 15:15).[8] The seraphim angels cry "holy, holy, holy" before the throne of the Almighty (Is 6:2-3; Rev 4:8). The Jews understood God as being so holy that if the angels forgot to say "holy," God would consume them with fire and create new ones (*3 Enoch* 40:3-4)!

5. *Angels are not gods.* Angels are not minor deities like the ones in Greek mythology. Such a view of angels would amount to polytheism—belief in many gods. The Bible declares that there is only one God (monotheism) and that there are no other gods but him (1 Cor 8:1-5; Gal 4:8; Is 41:10-11). Angels are inferior to God and do not have God's attributes of eternality, omnipotence (all-powerful), omniscience (all-knowing) and omnipresence (everywhere present).[9]

Question 4: When Were the Angels Created?

Before we can determine when the angels were created, we must first establish *that* they were created. If they had no beginning, then they would be eternal like God. In John 1:1-3, we read that all things were created by Jesus Christ, the Word of God, including the angels (compare Neh 9:6; Ps 148:2-5). Colossians 1:15-16 states that all things were created by Christ, "things in heaven and on earth, visible and invisible, whether thrones or powers or rulers or authorities; all things were created by him and for him." Thus angels did not exist with God from all eternity; they had a beginning.

But the Bible does not state when the creation of angels took place. They already existed when God created the world. God questions Job, saying, "Where were you when I laid the earth's foundation? Tell me, if you understand . . . who laid its cornerstone—while the morning stars sang together and all the angels shouted for joy?" (Job 38:4-7). Both Scripture and certain Jewish traditions imply that angels existed from the first day of creation; thus they would probably have been included in the creation of "the heavens" in Genesis 1:1 (see *Jubilees* 2.2-3; 11QPs *Hymn to the Creator* 26:13).

Why did God create angels? If we assume that the primary function of angels is to minister to God's people, then some might think that angels were created in view of God's foreknowledge regarding humanity (Heb 1:14). But this does not adequately explain why God created angels first and humans second.[10] As we read in Job 38:7, the angels rejoiced at God's creation. Perhaps their primal purpose was to glorify God in reference to God's mighty act of creation.

Question 5: What Do Angels Look Like?

Angels are not limited in attire to the halos and white garments that they usually wear in classic paintings. Since they are spirits, they can take on various forms and appearances. They can assume the appearance of humans, as did the messengers who ate with Abraham and were later mistaken for men by the Sodomites (Gen 18—19; compare Heb 13:2; Ezek 9).[11] They also appear in other forms. The cherubim angels that Ezekiel saw had wings with many eyes, and four faces representing the faces of a man, a lion, an eagle and a cherub (Ezek 10:12-14).[12] On other occasions they have wings, which may signify that their true abode is in heaven, not on earth (Is 6:2; Zech 5:9). They wear white garments or bright, shining clothes (Mt 28:3; Mk 16:5; Acts 1:10; Lk 24:4-5; Acts 10:30). Sometimes they wear golden sashes (Rev 15:6; compare 2 Maccabees 10:29-30). Such clothing represents their purity, holiness and glory.

Angels appear in different sizes. Some angels are human sized, while others are gigantic enough to place one foot on land and the other in the sea (Acts 1:10-11; Rev 10). In one Jewish tradition, an angel named Metatron (who in the text seems to be Enoch from Gen 5:24) is said to be the size of the earth, having 365,000 eyes and 72 wings—each wing large enough to cover the entire world (*3 Enoch* 9)! Another angel, Hayli'el, could swallow the earth in one gulp (*3 Enoch* 20:2), while the angel 'Opanni'el is so tall that it would take a twenty-five-hundred-year journey to cover his height (*3 Enoch* 25:1-4). Such exaggerations seem to stress symbolic meanings. In these cases angelic power is emphasized.

There are no tiny angels or fairies in the Bible. Although cherub angels are often portrayed in art as naked, pudgy babies, we find no such description of them in Scripture. But since angels are spirit beings, they could appear in any size, shape or form that God allows.

Question 6: Are Angels Gendered?

One prominent Jewish tradition claims that the "sons of God" who married the "daughters of men" in Genesis 6 were angels called the "Watchers" (*Jubilees* 7.21-25; *1 Enoch* 6). Obviously the implication is that the angels in this account were all males. One tradition even claims that angels get circumcised on the day of their creation (*Jubilees* 15.25-27).[13] This once again assumes that the angels are males. Indeed, Scripture usually has angels manifesting themselves as males (for example, Gen 18—19; Zech 1:10-12). Yet angels can also manifest themselves as females (Zech 5:9-11).

The passages that depict angels, however, have little to say regarding gender-related issues. That angels manifest themselves to us as males or females does not mean they are by nature males or females. As spirits, they are genderless. Since angels do not marry, their gender is irrelevant. By nature, the angels are sexless and do not reproduce themselves (Mk 12:25).[14]

Question 7: What Position Do Angels Occupy in the Scheme of Things?

In the Middle Ages, many Christians felt themselves unworthy to communicate directly with a holy and transcendent God. The philosophy of Neoplatonism, which regarded the physical world as a lower level of existence far away from God (or "the One"), influenced the thought of Augustine (354-430) and other church fathers. This outlook complemented religious practices such as confessing before a priest and praying to the saints and the Virgin Mary. In the same era, Pseudo-Dionysius the Areopagite (c. 500) wrote a treatise about angels called "Concerning the Celestial Hierarchy" *(De Hierarchia Coelesti).* Dionysius affirmed that since the law of Moses was mediated through angels, humans could not receive divine revelation except through the mediation of angels.[15] Medieval metaphysics tended to emphasize the superiority of angels over humans.

Although angels are mediators in that they relay messages from God to humans (Gal 3:19; Acts 7:53; Heb 2:2; Deut 33:2 LXX), the Scriptures do not emphasize their superiority over humans. They are of a higher order than humans in the present era (Heb 2:5-8; 2 Pet 2:10-11), but they are not so high that people must communicate to God through them, and God does not always need to go through them to get to us. In the future Christians are said to judge at least some of the angels (1 Cor 6:3).

The unfathomable gap between God and humans has been bridged by Jesus, and angels serve as ministers to the saints (Heb 1:14; compare Jn 14:6; 1 Tim 2:5). Both God the Father and Jesus Christ have a far greater status than the angels (Ps 89:5-7; Rom 8:38-39; Eph 1:19-20; Phil 2:9-11; Col 1:16; 2:10; Heb 1:3-14; 1 Pet 3:22; Rev 5:1-7). And angels, along with Christians, worship the Father and the Son (Neh 9:6; Ps 148:2; Heb 1:6). Thus angels currently have higher status than humans, but God reigns supreme over all.

Question 8: Do Humans Ever Become Angels?

Are humans elevated to the status of angels after death? Although we read earlier that Enoch was transformed into an angel, this viewpoint comes from a fifth- or sixth-century Jewish document, not Biblical scripture. Christ said that in heaven people will neither marry nor be given in marriage, but "they will be like the angels in heaven" (Mt 22:30). However, becoming like the angels does not mean actually becoming angels. In heaven humans will be "like the angels" in the sense that we (1) will not marry and (2) will never die again. Scripture gives us no indication that we will ever become angels.

Prior to Christ's second coming, believers' bodies remain in the grave, yet their inner person seems consciously present with God (Lk 23:39-43; Phil 1:21-23; 2 Cor 5:8). When Christ returns, according to the New Testament, their bodies will be raised from the dead and will be transformed to a state of incorruptibility (1 Thess 4:16-18; 1 Cor 15:12-57; Rev 20:4). Unbelievers will be raised from the dead too, but they will suffer eternal punishment (Jn 5:28-29; Rev 20:11-15).

Question 9: Are There Different Classes of Angels?

Since God is a God of order, we would expect God's angels to exist in a state of order. Perhaps order in worship lies behind the meaning of 1 Corinthians 11:10: "For this reason, and because of the angels, the woman ought to have a sign of authority on her head." As the angels conduct orderly worship, so the Corinthian women should worship in an orderly way. Disorderly worship might offend the angels. A study of 1 Corinthians 11—14 shows that Paul is attempting to correct a problem with disorderly worship in Corinth.[16]

How are the angels organized? Identifying clearly distinct classes or ranks of an angelic hierarchy is a difficult and speculative task. Yet if God created varieties of shapes, sizes, colors and functions within the domains of the human, animal, insect and vegetable kingdoms, why would God not create variety on a higher level with angels? Scripture does suggest several possible types of angels.

1. Archangels. One angelic class is the "archangel" (the term *archē* meaning "chief" or "prince"). The one Scripture specifying the status of Michael (translated "Who is like God?") as an archangel is Jude 9. We recognize Michael's authority in Revelation 12:7-9, where he and a host of angels battle and defeat the devil and his angels. We also find him breaking through the power of another spiritual being called the "prince of Persia" in Daniel 10:13. But Michael is not the only archangel. In the same verse he is called "one of the chief princes," implying that there are others like him. Michael watches over the children of Israel (Dan 10:21; 12:1).

2. *Cherubim and seraphim.* The cherubim and seraphim make up another class of angels.[17] The cherubim are often associated with clouds and transportation; they accompany God in a heavenly entourage (Ps 18:11; compare 80:1; 99:1; 104:3; Is 19:1; 1 Kings 7:29-36; Ezek 1:10). The Hebrews set two cherubim figures on the lid of the ark of the covenant (Ex 25:10-22). The cherubim having four faces in Ezekiel chapters 1 and 10 are probably the same as the "four living creatures" of Revelation 4. In both cases, they are said to have four faces depicting a lion, a man, an ox and an eagle.[18]

The four living creatures in Revelation 4 have six wings and cry "holy, holy, holy" before the Lord God Almighty, as do the seraphim angels that Isaiah saw in Isaiah 6. Perhaps there is no real distinction between cherubim and seraphim angels—the two different names may indicate different roles for the same creatures. Some even argue that they are not real creatures at all. Augustus Strong, for instance, asserted that cherubim and seraphim are not actual beings, but are mere "symbolic appearances" that represent "redeemed humanity, endowed with all the creature perfections lost by the Fall, and made to be the dwelling-place of God."[19] The Bible, however, records that cherubim protected the way to the Garden of Eden after Adam and Eve were banished (Gen 3:24). This would indicate that the Hebrew writer considered the cherubim as more than merely "symbolic" figures.

3. *Elect angels.* In 1 Timothy 5:21 Paul mentions "elect

angels." Some identify these angels with the spirits that did not fall away with Satan. In what sense does this make them elect? Were some angels predestined not to fall, as opposed to the ones that God permitted to fall? Did all angels deserve damnation prior to their fall so as to make God appear merciful by giving grace to some but not others? We should avoid the assumption that angels are elect in the same way humans are; God does not seem to have a plan of redemption for the angels (see answer 55).

An alternative explanation for the word *elect* has nothing to do with the fall of nonelect angels. First Timothy 5:21 suggests that God selected a special group from among the benevolent angels to serve as witnesses of the coming end-time judgment (Rev 14:10; Mt 25:31; Lk 9:26; 1 Thess 3:13).[20] This interpretation fits the context of the passage, for Paul charges Timothy to keep his pastoral instruction "without partiality, and . . . do not share in the sins of others. Keep yourself pure" (1 Tim 5:21-22). Paul is exhorting Timothy to make sure he is conducting his affairs in righteousness, for God, Christ and a special group of angels observe his conduct and will be involved in judging his works in the last day (2 Cor 5:10; 1 Cor 3:11-15).

The elect angels might indicate what the Dead Sea Scrolls call the "angels of the Presence" (1QSb 4.25; 1QH 6.13; compare *Jubilees* 1.27–2.2; *1 Enoch* 9.1; 20.1-7; 40.1-10; *Testament of Levi* 3:4-8). These are "angels of a special higher rank who stand before the face (glorious presence) of God [that is, they are in some higher state of glory than other angels]; this term is also known from the rest of Judaism"[21] (*1 Enoch* 39.1; *Odes of Solomon* 4.8; *Testament of Twelve Patriarchs* 19; 4 Ezra 16:66; compare Dan 4:13, 17; Zech 14:5). This group of angels might also be connected with the idea of heaven as a royal court with an angelic "council" (Ps 58:1; 89:6-9; Jer 23:18; 1 Kings 22:19-22; Job 15:8; Lk 9:26; compare *1 Enoch* 14.21; 1QH 3.35; 1QM 12.7-8). Then again, since we are speculating, these angels of

God's presence may function in the same way as the cherubim and seraphim.

We have not covered all the various classes of angels. We have yet to discuss the different classes of fallen angels, or demons, as well as Satan. Moreover, we have yet to mention the greatest "angel" of all, the angel of the Lord. There are other possible classes or ranks of angels about which we know very little. The "heavenly host" may be a class of angels that wage war (Ps 148:2; Jas 5:4); the "Watchers" may be another distinct class (NIV "messenger," Dan 4:13, 17, 23; compare *1 Enoch* 6-16; *Sibylline Oracles* 1.95; *Testament of the Twelve Patriarchs* 5.5-6). Apart from the ones that are mentioned in Scripture, there may be angelic groups of which we know nothing at all (compare Deut 29:29).[22]

Question 10: What Are the Archangels?

In Scripture certain high-ranking angels are referred to as archangels (Jude 9; Rev 12:7-9; Dan 12:1). We have already learned that Michael is the only archangel identified as such in Scripture, yet Daniel 10:13 implies other archangels. Many identify Gabriel ("hero of God") as another archangel, perhaps because, like Michael, he has a proper name (Dan 8:16; 9:21; Lk 1:11-19; 26-38). The proper name Raphael appears in the Apocrypha (Tobit 5.4).

Some suggest a case can be made for identifying seven archangels, Michael, Gabriel and Raphael being three of them (*1 Enoch* 20.1-8, 21; 40.9-10; 81.5; 90.21-22; Tobit 12:15; 1QM 9.16; *Testament of Levi* 8.1; compare Rev 8:2). The names of the other archangels vary from list to list, but the names of the other four are usually Uriel, Raguel, Seraqael (Zerachiel or Araqael) and Haniel (Remiel or Anael). In later Jewish history, Phanuel was substituted for Uriel; in church history, Pope Gregory the Great (540-604) listed the seven as Michael, Gabriel, Raphael, Uriel, Simiel, Orifiel and Zachariel.

There is no consensus limiting the number of archangels to

seven. According to Gustav Davidson, Jewish literature of antiquity also gives other names such as Barachiel, Jehudiel, Sealtiel, Oriphiel, Sabrael, Arael, Iaoth, Adonael and Zadkiel. Michael or Raphael is usually named as the leader. Other chief angels include Azrael, the angel of death, and Israfel, the angel of music who sounds the trumpet on judgment day.[23]

Question 11: Is Jesus Michael the Archangel?

In an effort to deny the deity of Christ, Jehovah's Witnesses affirm that Jesus is really Michael the archangel. According to *The Watchtower*, Jesus is a high-ranking angel, even a little god, but he is not God the Son, the eternal second person of the Trinity. An excellent way to refute this false belief is to ask the Jehovah's Witness to show you the Scripture that identifies Jesus as Michael. The Bible nowhere declares this.

Jehovah's Witnesses often cite 1 Thessalonians 4:16: "For the Lord himself shall descend from heaven with a shout, with the voice of the archangel, and with the trump of God" (KJV). This verse claims that the voice of an archangel will accompany Christ at his Second Coming.[24] It does not mean that Jesus is the archangel or that this archangel is Michael.

There are other reasons for rejecting the assertion that Jesus is Michael the archangel. First, Scripture states that Michael is "one of the chief princes" (Dan 10:13). If Michael were Jesus, then we would have to assume that other Christs exist! Unlike Michael, however, Jesus' status is unique—he shares it with no one else (1 Cor 8:1-5; 1 Tim 2:5; Jn 14:6). Second, no angel receives worship from humans, but humans are allowed to worship Christ (Mt 8:2; 9:18; 14:33; 20:20; 28:16; compare Col 2:18; Rev 19:9-10). Third, Jesus receives worship from all the angels, which means that even Michael worships Jesus (Heb 1:6; Rev 5:11-14). After all, good angels do not worship other good angels—good angels worship God alone. For these reasons, we conclude that Jesus is not Michael the archangel.

Question 12: Is Jesus the Angel of the Lord in the Old Testament?

The angel of the Lord is the most prominent angel in the Old Testament.[25] Unlike other angels, this particular messenger sometimes appears to be God (Gen 22:11-18; 32:24-31; Hos 12:2-4; Gen 48:15-16; Ex 23:20-21; Judg 2:1-5; 6:11-24; 13:21-22). After Hagar, Sarah's nurse, meets this angel, she "gave this name to the LORD who spoke to her: 'You are the God who sees me,' for she said, 'I have now seen the One who sees me' " (Gen 16:7-13). When God meets with Moses in the burning bush in Exodus 3, the text refers to him as the "angel of the LORD" (Ex 3:2; compare Acts 7:30-38).

J. M. Wilson makes three suggestions regarding the identity of this angel: (1) the angel of the Lord may simply be an angel with a special commission; (2) the angel may be a momentary descent of God into visible reality (a theophany); (3) the angel may be the preincarnate Christ, the Logos (Word) of God.[26] Wilson's first suggestion seems hard to reconcile with the direct way Scripture sometimes equates this angel with God.

The second suggestion seems more plausible, since a theophany is an indirect manifestation of God that veils God's transcendent nature. Unlike the incarnation of Christ, which is a permanent revelation of God, theophanies are temporary manifestations. One scholar writes, "God is understood by Israel to be a reality different from the world and unlimited by it (1 Kings 8:27; Amos 9:2-4; Psalm 139). Yet in theophanies God is revealed by self-limitation to specific places and particular forms within the world itself."[27] Since no one could look on God in God's true essence and live (Ex 33:20-23), the angel of the Lord would be an indirect manifestation of God to humans. The only problem with this view is that sometimes the angel of the Lord seems to be someone *other* than the Lord from heaven (2 Sam 24:16; Zech 1:11-13; Ex 23:20-21; Num 20:16).[28]

Wilson's third suggestion is that the angel of the Lord is an appearance of Christ before his incarnation. This view reconciles the paradox between some of the passages that describe God as the angel of the Lord and other passages that make a distinction between the two. Nevertheless, we need to refrain from any dogmatism,[29] because it is always possible that none of the above meanings entirely captures the term "angel of the LORD". Sometimes it may refer to God's very presence, while other times it may designate a mere angel sent by God. One theologian puts it this way:

> The God who reveals himself in the *mal'āk* [angel] is in no sense present in a human body or as a permanent personal being, but appears only during a limited period of history, namely the era of the early Israel, and in a variety of forms, now in a flame, now in human lineaments, now in a dream, now in auditory experiences.[30]

Question 13: Who Is the Commander of the Army of the Lord of Hosts?

In Joshua 5:13-15, right before the Israelites conquered the city of Jericho, Joshua meets a peculiar figure who describes himself as the "commander of the army of the LORD." When Joshua bows down to the commander, he declares, "Take off your sandals, for the place where you are standing is holy." The angel of the Lord said the same thing to Moses in the burning bush (Ex 3:2-6).

Like the angel of the Lord, the commander of the army of the Lord paradoxically appears as *both* the Lord *and* the Lord's messenger. It seems to be the Lord speaking to Joshua in Joshua 6:2 (the text of Joshua 5:13—6:5 should be taken as one literary unit). In all likelihood, the commander of the Lord's army is the preincarnate Christ or a theophany of God (see answer 11) In favor of the formers when we compare God's name as the great "I AM WHO I AM" in the burning bush with John 8:53-59, we find that Jesus also claimed to be "I AM." He is also the commander of the armies of heaven in Revelation 19:11-14.

Question 14: How Many Angels Are There?

We do not know the exact number of angels that exist. From the most ancient times, people from different cultures believed in an enormous number of heavenly beings. Before Newton discussed gravity, ancient and medieval cultures thought that angels controlled the forces of nature and moved the stars in their orbits (cf. *2 Enoch* 4:1-2).[31] Hence angels were considered as innumerable as the stars in the sky. Even today many believe that at least one guardian angel watches over every human, implying the existence of at least five billion angels. (But this number depends on the questionable hypothesis that every person is assigned a guardian angel—more on this in the next chapter.)

In Revelation the number of angels worshiping before the throne of God numbers "thousands upon thousands, and ten thousand times ten thousand" (Rev 5:11-13). Since Revelation is a highly symbolic book, we doubt that the number of angels literally stands at a little over 100 million.[32] John's count in Revelation may be simply a figurative way of asserting an uncountable number of angels (Job 25:2-3). The Greek word for "ten thousand" *(myrios)* that appears in this passage most likely indicates a number of angels that is too great to count by ordinary means (Heb 12:22; compare Mt 26:53; Jude 14; Dan 7:10; Deut 33:2; Ps 68:17).

Early Christian and Jewish literature gives us a diverse sampling of the nature and characteristics of angels. They appear in different ways to different people, and some seem of higher rank than others. If different classes of angels exist, it follows that not every angel does the same thing. They all have particular roles or tasks to perform, and this will be our focus in the next chapter.

3

QUESTIONS
ABOUT
THE ACTIVITIES
OF ANGELS

In the movie *Grand Canyon,* actor Kevin Kline, alias Mack, recalls a time when a woman saved his life. As he was about to cross Wilshire Boulevard in Los Angeles, a woman pulled him back to the curb as a city bus zoomed by, missing him by a few inches. He never got her name as she went on her way through the crowded street. He noticed that she was wearing a Pittsburgh Pirates baseball cap. The Pirates happened to be Mack's favorite team. He wondered if she was an angel.

In the movie the business of angels is to assist humans, and Scripture often shows them protecting God's children. What are the activities of angels? Do they still intervene in human affairs? Do we have guardian angels? In this chapter we will explore the works of angels.

Question 15: Do Guardian Angels Exist?

There are many accounts of supernatural protection from

guardian angels. One inner-city counselor claimed a seven-foot angel protected her from a gang of thugs.[1] On the other hand, Wolly Tope established a ministry to other disillusioned Mormons. In April 1992 he had an appointment with destiny. When he heard about riots breaking out in Los Angeles, Tope took to the streets and preached to the rioters. A gang of hoodlums beat him so severely that he fell into a coma. Tope died the following year, never regaining consciousness after his beating. Why didn't angels protect Wolly Tope during the riots? If everyone or at least every Christian has a guardian angel, where was Tope's guardian angel that night?

Belief in guardian angels is nothing new. Ancient thinkers of the Greek and Roman world such as Plato, Menades, Plutarch and Plotinus believed in spiritual guardians, as did Babylonian and Assyrian writers.[2] Ancient Jewish traditions suggested that guardian angels were assigned to everyone (*Jubilees* 35.17; *Testament of Levi* 5.3; Philo *De Gigantibus* 12; compare Tobit 5.4; 2 Maccabees 3:25; 10:29; 11:6; 15:23).[3] According to one interpretation of the children of Israel in the wilderness, God commanded Israel's guardian angels not to intercede anymore on Israel's behalf, for they had become too rebellious (Pseudo-Philo 15.5; compare 11.12; 59.4). In the Dead Sea Scrolls angels watch over the meek, the despised and the orphaned (1QH 5.20-22; compare Mt 18:10).

Many of the church fathers believed in guardian angels, but they disagreed on their function. The Shepherd of Hermas (fl. 140-155) records that guardian angels were appointed to everyone (*Mandate* 6.2.1-3), but Jerome (342-420) believed that sin prevents these angels from assisting the wicked (*In Jeremiam* 30.12; compare Basil *Homilies* 33.5; 1 En. 100.5). Ambrose (339-397), on the other hand, believed that the righteous did *not* have guardian angels. The saints were to struggle through life without celestial help in order to obtain a greater future glory (*In Psalmos Davidicos* 37.43).[4]

Peter Lombard (1100-1160) believed that every guardian angel was assigned several persons to watch (Sentences 2:11). Conversely, some have argued that certain individuals have more than one guardian angel (compare Mt 18:10-13). Roman Catholics still consider belief in guardian angels to be in keeping with the "mind of the church," even though it is not an article of faith for Catholics.[5]

The Bible in some places supports a belief in personal guardian angels (Ps 90:11; 33:8; 34:5-7; Mt 10:18; Acts 12:15; Heb 1:14). It may be comforting to think of an invisible angel standing next to us, but why should this be more comforting than knowing that the omnipresent God always watches over us (Mt 10:29-31; compare Heb 4:13; Ps 139)? In what sense do guardian angels protect us more than any other angel that God could send to protect us?

Some of the church fathers, such as Hermas and Gregory of Nyssa (330-395), believed that everyone was assigned both a good and an evil angel (*Mandate* 6.2:1-3; *De Vita Moysis* 12-13).[6] A strong belief in guardian angels can easily lead to such conclusions. If each one of us has an invisible angel always protecting us, why do so many calamities befall us? Wouldn't this imply that Satan also assigns a "guardian" demon to constantly harass every one of us? We must dig further to arrive at a feasible conclusion about guardian angels.

The term *guardian angel* never appears in the Bible. Many biblical passages cited to support the idea only affirm God's general providence in protecting his saints by sending angels.[7] But two Scriptures tend to support guardian angels: in Acts Christians mistook Peter for "his angel" (Acts 12:15); in Matthew Jesus said, "See that you do not look down on one of these little ones. For I tell you that their angels in heaven always see the face of my Father in heaven" (Mt 18:10).

The Jews believed that guardian angels could take on the likeness of the person under their protection.[8] The early Christians assumed this about Peter in Acts 12:15. However, the book of Acts is a *descriptive* narrative, not a *prescriptive* epistle. Since almost everyone in the church of Jerusalem grew up listening to folklore, is it any wonder that they had misconceptions about guardian angels looking like those to whom they were assigned? (The saints didn't believe it was Peter who was knocking on their door, even though they had been praying constantly for his release from prison [Acts 12:3-15].)

Yet assigned angels do exist, for Jesus teaches about them in Matthew 18:10.[9] The passage, however, does not refer to these angels as "guardian angels," neither does it give the number of angels God appoints to each person. And it does not assert that God appoints at least one angel for every person on earth. Moreover, if these angels reside "in heaven" and are "always" in the presence of God, how can they constantly assist us here on earth? If they reside in heaven, then their primary function may be to watch God's elect and request judgment against those who harm them (compare Rev 8:4; Job 5:1 MT/LXX; Tobit 12.12-15; *1 Enoch* 9:3; 15.2; Testament of Dan 6.1; Pseudo-Philo 15.5; 1QS 2.9; Origen *Stromata* 5.14; 7:12; Augustine *City of God* 7.30; 10.25).[10] Occasionally, if God so chooses, he can send these or other angels to assist or protect us on earth.

So what can we say about guardian angels? They do exist, but not as commonly described in popular and religious culture. There is little biblical evidence that invisible angels guard our paths on a daily basis. Matthew 18:10 describes angels who watch and perhaps intercede for us in heaven, but we find no evidence that these angels invisibly stand in front of us to protect us continually. Ultimately, we should remember that angels assigned to us submit to the sovereign will of God. Sometimes, due to his unfathomable purposes, God refrains from having angels physically protect us. He never promised that he would protect us from all physical harm in this present age; he does promise that he will work all things out "for the good of those who love him" (Rom 8:28).

Question 16: Do Angels Protect the Nations?

Do angels protect entire cities or countries? Biblical scripture calls Michael "the great prince" who protects the children of Israel (Dan 10:21; 12:1). In Revelation Christ sends seven messages to the angels of the seven churches in Asia Minor, possibly implying that these angels watch over entire congregations (Rev 1:20; 2:1, 8, 12, 18; 3:1, 7, 14). The book of Daniel mentions the "prince of Persia" and the "prince of Greece," who seem to be angels that watch over these two countries (Dan 10:13, 20-21; compare *Sirach* 17.17; *Jubilees* 15.31-32). Since they fight against Michael and Gabriel (who are good angels), the princes of these countries seem to be fallen angels.

Deuteronomy 32:8 reads, "When the Most High gave the nations their inheritance, when he divided all mankind, he set up boundaries for the peoples according to the number of the sons of Israel." Some scholars suggest this passage refers to the Tower of Babel incident (2400-2000 B.C.E.). All people spoke one language, but God scattered the nations by diversifying their languages (Gen 10—11). We can supposedly count a total of seventy nations in Genesis 10 and compare this with the seventy children of Israel who entered Egypt (Gen 46:27; Ex 1:5; compare Num 11:16).

Thus some understand that God apportioned the seventy nations according to the seventy children of Israel, suggesting the world dominion of God's elect over the nations. But we run into a few difficulties with this interpretation. If in Israel's tradition-history the Tower of Babel precedes the birth of the nation of Israel, how could God apportion the nations after the number of Israel's children when Israel did not exist at the time?[11] We would have to conjecture that God numbered the nations based on his foreknowledge of Israel, but the context of these passages does not seem to adequately support this interpretation.[12]

The Septuagint (LXX) version of Deuteronomy 32:8[13] substitutes "angels of God" for "children of Israel." The Dead Sea Scrolls substitute "sons of God" for the former phrase (4QDeut). These versions agree *against* the traditional Masoretic Hebrew text, which is rendered "children of Israel." The Dead Sea Scrolls normally interpret the "sons of God" as angels who play the same role as the "sons of God" in the book of Job (chaps. 1–2). They are described as the "Sons of Heaven," "Holy Ones" and the "Heavenly Watchers."[14] God seems to have permitted angels to superintend the nations, but the evidence tends to suggest that most of these angels were wicked (compare Dan 10:13 and answer 66).[15]

Question 17: Do Angels Attend Church Services?

We know that angels worship God (Ps 29:1; 103:20-21; 148:1-2; Lk 2:13-14; Rev 4–5), but do they worship unseen with humans at church services? Are angels present whenever two or three Christians are gathered together (Mt 18:20)? Some testify that angels have visited them in their worship services (see answer 23). Although angels have occasionally appeared in the Lord's sanctuary (Lk 1:11), there is no biblical evidence that angels invisibly attend every church function, but there is also no evidence that they do not.

Jesus said, "In the same way, I tell you, there is rejoicing in the presence of the angels of God over one sinner who repents" (Lk 15:10 compare 15:7). Some therefore argue that if a person converts at a church service, angels must be present. But Luke 15:7 states that this angelic rejoicing takes place "in heaven," not necessarily at a church service. Still, this passage assumes that angels do have knowledge of human affairs and church services (compare Heb 1:14).

Question 18: Is It Wrong to Communicate with Angels?

It would not be wrong to communicate with a good angel that

manifested itself to us. But how many of us have ever had such an experience? In most cases people who claim to communicate with angels are the ones initiating the conversation. Some misinformed people, for instance, pray to angels. The church father Ambrose (339-97) influenced the later Roman Catholic idea of communicating with angels. He taught, "We should pray to the angels who are given to us as guardians."[16] But this action is unbiblical for several reasons.

When John bowed down to worship the angel who showed him prophetic revelations, the angel said, "Do not do it! I am a fellow servant with you and with your brothers who hold to the testimony of Jesus. Worship God!" (Rev 19:10; compare 22:8-9).[17] Paul seems to warn against a communion with angels when he writes, "Do not let anyone who delights in false humility and the worship of angels disqualify you for the prize" (Col 2:18).[18] Some would argue that they are not worshiping the angels but are merely asking angels to intercede before God on their behalf. We find no biblical warrant, however, for praying to anyone other than God (compare Mt 4:10). Believing that angels intercede for humans is one thing; praying to angels as mediators is quite another.

The Bible identifies Jesus as the only mediator we need before God the Father (Jn 14:6-14; compare 1 Cor 1:1-2; 1 Tim 2:5). If we pray to angels, we are implicitly declaring that Christ's mediatorship is insufficient. (It is interesting that our sinful desires, as well as the devil, tend to draw our prayers and attention to everything *but* Jesus, our only real mediator.) If we pray to other mediators because we think Christ is too holy and we are too unworthy to address him, we are exercising a false humility. God sent his Son to die on the cross for our sins, and thus we have the privilege, despite our shortcomings, of approaching God through his Son, Jesus.

If we prayed to an angel and our prayer were "answered," isn't it likely that our future prayers would be directed to that angel rather than God? This is one way we could be diverted from praying to the Lord. Some New Age channelers communicate with "angels." If these channelers are communicating with real entities, such powers are not good angels. No spirit that comes from God would lead us away from the teaching that Jesus Christ is the only mediator we need (Gal 1:8-9; 1 Jn 4:1-6).

Some faith preachers teach that they have the spiritual authority to address angels and charge them to do our bidding. Is such a belief biblical? Nowhere in biblical scripture do we find that humans have the right to order benevolent angels around; if anything, we find passages that lean toward the opposite conclusion by warning against speaking presumptuously to angelic beings (1 Pet 2:10-11; Jude 8-10).[19] In Scripture it is the angels who give orders to human beings (for example, Acts 10:3-6; 12:7-8).

Commanding angels is not much different from praying to angels as intercessors on our behalf. Both activities involve initiating a communication with angels, and both are unbiblical. Such communication would be more akin to magic than prayer—the angel functioning as a genie or a talisman. Good angels do God's bidding, not ours. We cannot manipulate them.

Question 19: What Are Some Works That Angels Do?

Angels perform a number of activities in reference to humans, in addition to protecting them. Here is a short list of some of their other activities.

1. Angels reveal the will of God to humans. Angels revealed the future to prophets like Daniel. In the New Testament they revealed God's prophetic revelation to John. Not only did angels reveal the future, but in a more general sense, they revealed the will of God to the saints (Num 22:31-35; 2 Kings 1:3-4; Job 33:23; Acts 27:23-25; compare 1 Kings 13:18; *Testament of Reuben* 5.3; *Testament of Issachar* 2.1; *Testament of Joseph* 6.6; *Joseph and Asenath* 14). In Acts 10:3-5, an angel revealed to the Gentile centurion Cornelius that God recognized his religious works. This event resulted in the first outpouring of the Holy Spirit on Gentile believers (Acts 10:44—11:18).

Angels mediated messages from God to humans in the Old Testament. The angel of the Lord appears to have been the primary mediator in the Old Testament (Ex 3), and the New Testament affirms that angels mediated the law of Moses (Gal 3:19; Heb 2:2; Acts 7:53). Although the Old Testament law was fulfilled in Christ (Heb 7:12-25; 8:7-13; 10:1-10), angels still delivered divine revelation in the New Testament (Rev 1:1). They will not, according to Scripture, reveal any contrary information about gospel or the end times (Gal 1:8-9; Rev 22:18-19).

Angels can manifest themselves in the physical world, but they can also communicate to humans in dreams or visions. The angel that visited Cornelius came by means of a vision (Acts 10; compare Zech 1:8). Angels have also appeared to humans through dreams (for example, Gen 28:12; Mt 1:20; 2:13; 2:19-20), while at other times they appeared in the physical world (Acts 12:7-11).

2. *Angels minister to humans.* A primary function of angels is to serve God's people (Heb 1:14). One way they do this is by providing guidance. When Abraham commissioned his servant Eliezer to find a bride for his son Isaac, he told Eliezer that God "will send his angel before you so that you can get a wife for my son" (Gen 24:7). The angel providentially led Eliezer to Abraham's relatives and specifically to Rebekah, who became Isaac's wife. In the New Testament an angel led Philip the evangelist to convert the Ethiopian eunuch (Acts 8:26).

God often sends angels to strengthen, encourage and protect his people (1 Kings 19:3-7; Lk 22:43; compare 1QM 17.5-8). Elisha's assistant became afraid when the king of Aram sent an army to seize the prophet. Elisha responded, " 'Don't be afraid . . . Those who are with us are more than those who are with them.' And Elisha prayed, 'O LORD, open his eyes so he may see.' Then the LORD opened the servant's eyes, and he looked and saw the hills full of horses and chariots of fire all around Elisha" (2 Kings 6:15-17). The army of Aram was then temporarily struck blind.

3. *Angels assist God in things related to eschatology.* The word *eschatology* refers to the doctrine of the "last things," or teachings on death, the afterlife, heaven and hell, and the end times. The book of Revelation is filled with angels who are involved with the final affairs of the world. After the poor man named Lazarus died, he was carried away to Abraham's bosom (paradise) by angels (Lk 16:23).[20]

4. *Angels perform miraculous deeds.* Angels demonstrate the reality of the supernatural (Acts 5:19: 12:7-11; Ex 14:19). When Shadrach, Meshach and Abednego refused to bow down to king Nebuchadnezzar's golden image (Dan 3:8-29), they were thrown into a fiery furnace. But they were completely preserved from the flames when an angel of God appeared. Amazed at the sight, Nebuchadnezzar cried, "Look! I see four men walking around in the fire, unbound and unharmed, and the fourth looks like a son of the gods."(Dan 3:25)[21] An angel also came to Daniel's assistance in the lion's den (Dan 6:22).

Question 20: Do Angels or Demons Bring Calamity on the Wicked?

Are demons responsible for bringing calamities on the wicked, or is such a work reserved for God's angels? The Bible describes destructive angels that appear to be demonic. The angel of the abyss, whose name means destruction in both Hebrew and Greek, reigns over the fierce locust creatures that torment all who do not have the seal of God on their foreheads (Rev 9:1-11). This angel seems identical with the "beast that comes up from the Abyss" and kills the two witnesses of God (Rev 11:3-7).

After Saul rebelled against the Lord, "an evil spirit from the

LORD tormented him" (1 Sam 16:14; compare Judg 9:23). This spirit left Saul whenever David played the harp (1 Sam 16:23). Saul was under the influence of this spirit when he twice tried to kill David (18:10-11; 19:9-10). How could an evil angel be sent from God? It seems that God *permitted* a demonic spirit to torment Saul because of his backslidden state.

Micaiah the prophet described God enthroned with the heavenly host surrounding him. One spirit claimed that he could deceive wicked King Ahab: " 'I will go out and be a lying spirit in the mouths of all his prophets' he said. You will succeed in enticing him,' said the LORD. 'Go and do it' " (1 Kings 22:22). God permitted a lying spirit to deceive Ahab because the king had rebelled against God. The lying spirit influenced the false prophets to give the king a positive report that he would succeed in battle at Ramoth Gilead. Instead, Ahab died in battle, just as Micaiah had warned (2 Kings 22:6, 23-38).

In other cases, however, it seems that good angels bring calamity on the wicked. In Genesis 19:11 good angels struck the Sodomites with blindness; in Daniel 4:13-26 a good angel announced God's judgment on King Nebuchadnezzar because of his pride. In 2 Kings 19:35, the angel of the Lord struck down the army of the Assyrians after they challenged the God of Israel. The angel of the Lord brought a plague against Israel after David sinned by taking an illegitimate census of his army (2 Sam 24:16). An angel of God struck Herod with a stomach disease because he did not give the glory to God after the people shouted, "This is the voice of a god, not of a man" (Acts 12:21-23).

In other cases it is not clear if the angels are good or bad. The Lord sent a "band of destroying angels" against the Egyptians, for example (Ps 78:49). Much like the locusts in Revelation 9, a band of angels slays those not having a mark on their foreheads in Ezekiel 9:1-11.[22] First Corinthians 10:10 says that the Israelites who murmured against God were killed by "the destroying angel." Similarly, the Dead Sea Scrolls describe a class of angels known as angels of destruction who work for

Belial—another name for Satan (1QM 13:12; 14:10), but in other passages the angels of destruction work for the Lord (1QS 4.12; CD 2.6; compare *Testament of Naphtah* 8.6; Pseudo-Philo 15.5).

Thus we see that God seems to use both good and evil angels to send calamity on the wicked. Apparently, fallen angels desire to injure humankind, so God sometimes *allows* the evil angels to strike the unrighteous, but he *commands* the good angels to bring judgment on the wicked. As in the case of David's sin, God also brings judgment on the righteous when they commit grievous sins. God can also permit demons to attack the righteous in order to test their faith (Job 1—2). However, Scripture never seems to indicate that good angels bring calamity on righteous individuals who are faithfully doing God's will.

Question 21: How Were Angels Involved in the Life of Christ?

Angels intervened in the life of Christ throughout his ministry. They played four important roles: (1) making annunciations, (2) protecting God's children, (3) ministering to Christ and (4) assisting the Lord in end-time activities.[23]

First, angels announced special events in the life and ministry of Christ. Gabriel announced the birth of Christ to the Virgin Mary (Lk 1:26-38). An "angel of the Lord" charged Joseph to call the child "Jesus" (Mt 1:18-25; compare Lk 2:21). Angels announced the birth of the Messiah to the shepherds (Lk 2:8-13). The angel Gabriel announced to Zechariah the birth of John the Baptist, the forerunner of Christ (Lk 1:11-20). Angels also announced the resurrection of Christ in all the gospels (Mt 28:2-7; Mk 16:5; Lk 24:4-7; Jn 20:11-12).

Second, angels protected and guided those who were involved in the life of Christ. An angel warned Joseph in a dream to flee to Egypt before King Herod slaughtered every male child younger than two in the region (Mt 2:13). Angels also told Joseph that it was safe to return to Palestine (Mt 2:19-21). When Christ was arrested, he declared that twelve legions of angels from the Father were at his disposal to provide heavenly protection (Mt 26:53).

Third, angels ministered to Christ by strengthening and encouraging him. After Christ was tempted by Satan, having fasted in the wilderness for forty days, angels came and ministered to him (Mt 4:11; Mk 1:13). They may have provided him with food as the ravens fed Elijah in the wilderness after he had been persecuted by Queen Jezebel (1 Kings 19:5-8). God's angelic provision contrasts the devil's suggestion that Jesus jump off the pinnacle of the temple so that angels would protect him (Mt 4:5-6). An angel also ministered to Christ as he prayed in the Garden of Gethsemane (Lk 22:43).

Finally, angels will accompany Christ at his Second Coming (Mt 25:31; Mk 13:26; 14:62). They will gather the elect in Christ (Mt 24:31; Mk 13:27), separate the righteous from the unrighteous (Mk 13:36-42; compare Rev 14:14-20), execute judgment on the wicked (Mt 16:27; Mk 8:38), and sit in judgment with Christ (Mk 8:38; Lk 9:26; 12:8-9). The latter activity may indicate the special assignment of the heavenly "court" of "elect angels" mentioned in 1 Timothy 5:21.

The works of angels in the life and ministry of Christ mirror angelic activities in the Old Testament. For example, the angel of the Lord delivered birth annunciations (Gen 16:11; Judg 13:3-5). But no Old Testament angel, however, had the privilege of announcing a virgin birth or a resurrection from the dead. In the Gospels the function of angels centers on the person of Christ.[23] The primary role of angels in the New Testament is to advance the kingdom of God for the sake of Jesus Christ.

Question 22: Can Angels Reveal the Second Coming of Christ?

"Christ is coming back sooner than you think. In fact, Michael is getting ready to blow his trumpet any day now," were the last words said by an anonymous hitchhiker who disappeared from the back seat of a car driven by a Christian couple on a lonely stretch of highway in Arizona.[25] Can angels reveal the time of Christ's return?

Angels are definitely involved in revealing messages from God about the future (Gen 31:11-13; Zech 2:3-5; Dan 12:7-13; Rev 1:1). They know details about how Christ will return. For instance, the two angels who stood with the disciples after Christ ascended into heaven proclaimed, "This same Jesus, who has been taken from you into heaven, will come back in the same way you have seen him go into heaven" (Acts 1:11). However, Jesus specifically stated that God has hidden from the angels the time of Christ's return (Mt 24:36; Mk 13:32). No angel ever revealed to anyone the date of Christ's return.

Question 23: How Will Angels Assist God During the End Times?

Although angels do not know the time of Christ's return, they play a significant role in assisting God during the end times. In the book of Revelation they bring calamity on the wicked. Seven angels are in charge of the seven trumpets that bring seven different plagues on the wicked (Rev 8–9). After the sixth angel blows his trumpet, four angels are released "to kill a third of mankind" (Rev 9:15).[26] Seven angels are in charge of seven bowls that bring great calamities on humankind (Rev 16). These angels bring judgment on the wicked, not the righteous (Rev 19:14-21; 2 Thess 1:7; Jude 14-16; compare 1 En. 90.20-27; CD 2.5-7). In fact, an angel commands the four angels holding the four winds to refrain from further judgment until the righteous are marked on their foreheads with the seal of God (Rev 7).

The angels will also accompany Christ at his coming (Mt 16:27; Lk 12:8-9; Mk 13:26; 14:62; Dan 7:9-10; compare 1QH 3.35-36; 10.34-35; 1QM 15:14); they will separate the righteous from the wicked (Mt 13:39-42; 49-50; Rev 14:14-20); they will gather the elect in Christ (Mt 24:31; Rev 14:14-16; compare *1 Enoch* 100.4); and they are apparently in charge of keeping the records of the deeds of humans that are opened on judgment day (Dan 7:10; compare *1 Enoch* 89.61-77; 90.14-20; *2 Enoch* 19.5; *Apocalypse of Zephaniah* 3.7; Tertullian *De spectaculus* 27). Finally, one angel is assigned the task of binding Satan with a great chain and casting him into the abyss for a thousand years (Rev 20:1-3).[27]

Question 24: Are There Any Contemporary Examples of Angels Visiting Humans?

If we serve a God who can bless us in extraordinary ways, and if we believe that God is able to do miracles in this present age, then we can believe that God may occasionally bless humans with angelic visitations. Many contemporary Christians describe personal encounters with angels. The testimonies of two such encounters follow. I personally know the couple in the first testimony. It is always possible to explain away such accounts. But we should not simply try to rationalize everything out of an unwillingness to believe that anything supernatural can happen. Ironically, some Christians seem ready to believe that any contemporary supernatural encounter must be demonic rather than angelic, even though the Bible shows saints encountering angels much more often than demons. On the other hand, some occultists seem to consider their supernatural encounters uniformly angelic rather than demonic. In the end, you must decide for yourself whether or not you believe that the two encounters described below are genuine angelic visitations.

A few years ago, Benjamin and Jacquie Cortez of La Puente, California, had been praying to the Lord about adopting a child. While visiting a Christian rehabilitation home in Tijuana, Mexico, they met a young boy with an unusual zeal for God. He prayed and worshiped just like the men who also lived there. The rehabilitation director let him live inside the house because the boy had no home of his own. His mother was a prostitute, and he didn't know his father. Benji and Jacquie came to believe that it was God's will for them to adopt the boy. They still needed to get consent, however, from the mother. Jacquie searched through the streets of Tijuana asking people if they knew where the mother of the boy lived. No one seemed to know.

Then seemingly out of nowhere, a tall, handsome young man said he knew where Jacquie could find the mother. He led her to a dirty shack. Inside was the boy's mother. When Jacquie wished to thank the man, he was gone. The mother signed the adoption consent papers. Later Benji and Jacquie asked if anyone knew the man who had led Jacquie to the mother. No one had ever seen the young man, let alone knew who he was. Benjamin and Jacquie believe that the man who led them to the mother was an angel.

In January 1996 Doug McCleary, a pastor involved in the Toronto renewal, wrote on an e-mail list called "Awakening":

[At] our bi-weekly renewal meeting tonight, several of us heard (and a couple "sensed") the heavenly choir. It was the final song of our set . . . (I was at the piano . . .). Suddenly I heard what sounded like a group of very rich and well intoned voices echoing, "Holy, Holy, Holy" on a single note in rhythm with the music. . . . I couldn't figure out who was singing it. So I joined in at the microphone, singing what I was hearing. I said quietly into the mic., "Who's singing that part? It's really neat." No one answered. . . . Throughout this time (perhaps two minutes?), the atmosphere in the sanctuary became charged. People began dancing and celebrating and cheering, and I could still hear the voices . . . echoing, over and over, "Holy, Holy, Holy." When we were done . . . I asked the gathered congregation, "Did anyone else hear that?" Several raised their hands including our electric guitarist who said he had heard the singing, had looked out over the congregation, and realized no one was singing—it had to be angels.

Question 25: What Is a Good Way to Remember the Activities of Angels?

Ever wonder what angels do all day? Thomas Aquinas believed that higher-status angels enlighten lower-status angels. Since the higher angels are closer to God, they receive knowledge that they then pass on to the lower angels (*Summa Contra Gentiles* 106.1-3). More important for our purposes, William Hendrickson created a mnemonic device that can help us remember a few of the angels' biblical activities:[28]

Attendants of Christ (2 Thess 1:7), their exalted Head (Eph 1:21-22; Col 2:10)

Bringers of good tidings concerning salvation (Lk 2:14; 24:4; Acts 1:11; 1 Tim 3:16)

Choristers of heaven (Lk 15:10; 1 Cor 13:1; Rev 5:11-12)

Defenders of God's children (Ps 34:8; 91:11; Dan 6:22; 10:10, 13, 20; Mt 18:10; Acts 5:19; 2 Thess 1:7-10; Rev 12:7)

Examples in obedience (Mt 6:10; 1 Cor 11:10)

4

QUESTIONS
ABOUT FALLEN
ANGELS

D o you enjoy horror movies such as *The Exorcist, Friday the 13th, Night of the Living Dead?* Well, now at local Christian bookstores, you can pick up a copy of such bestselling books as Frank and Ida Hammond's *Pigs in the Parlor,* Rebecca Brown's *He Came to Set the Captives Free* and Bob Larson's *Dead Air.* Readers of such "Christian books" can enjoy the same eerie shivers they get from watching a scary movie.

Have we been gulled into believing that the forces of evil are more powerful than the Bible says they are? Goodness always prevails over evil in these Christian books, but isn't this true of many horror movies? Don't such books overemphasize the power of the devil? Both secular and Christian cultures have been inundated with an unhealthy fascination with evil. I think it's about time we put demons in their proper place by discerning what the Holy Scriptures really says about them. Let's put away the Christian horror novels as we look into the subject of demonology.

Question 26: Do Demons Actually Exist?

The subject of demons makes many people uncomfortable. Some modern thinkers deny the existence of demons, while others try to explain them away. The late biblical scholar Rudolf Bultmann consigned demons to myth. He claimed that "it is impossible to use electric light and the wireless and to avail ourselves of modern medical and surgical discoveries, and at the same time to believe in the New Testament world of daemons and spirits."[1]

Nineteenth- and twentieth-century occultism, however, suggests otherwise. Why are so many people intrigued by Satanism, witchcraft, spiritism and a host of other occultic activities? The fact is that many occultic practitioners today are finding real power through their practices—they are experiencing something genuine. This power comes from what Scripture would define as demonic.

Throughout history there have been documented reports of poltergeist or "haunting" activities (see also answer 34). Some reports turn out to be fraudulent, but not all. I myself once had such an experience. I felt as though I were being attacked by an unseen, hostile force—what the Bible calls a demon.[2]

And what about Christ's confrontations with demons? Was he merely putting on a show? The demon possessed knew that Jesus Christ was the Son of God (Mt 8:28-29; Mk 1:24, 34; 3:11-12). This suggests that higher spiritual intelligences, who recognized Jesus, possessed such individuals. S. E. McClelland explains that according to certain theologians, with a bias against the supernatural, Jesus' confrontations with demons "amounted only to his accommodation to the contemporary beliefs of the Palestinian peasant and in no way reflected his own opinion as to the cause of individual afflictions."[3] In other words, for the sake of the superstitious crowds who believed in demons, Jesus pretended to believe in them too and acted accordingly.

To deny demons is to discredit the gospel message, for

Jesus claimed that his power over demons was the sign that the kingdom of God had arrived (Mt 12:28; Lk 11:20).[4] Even Jesus' enemies affirmed that he cast out devils; they claimed, however, that he did it by the power of a demon (Mk 3:22; Mt 12:24). Ancient Jewish and Greco-Roman sources confirm that Jesus and his followers were known as sorcerer-exorcists.[5] Some of the early Jewish traditions, for instance, claimed that "Jesus the Nazarene . . . practiced sorcery and enticed and led Israel astray" (*b. Sanhedrin* 43a; compare 107b). Origen writes concerning one anti-Christian: "Celsus asserts that it is by the names of certain demons, and by the use of incantations, that the Christians appear to be possessed of [miraculous] power; hinting, I suppose, at the practice of those who expel evil spirits by incantations" (*Contra Celsus* 1.6). Jesus had such a powerful reputation as an exorcist that even non-Christians attempted exorcisms in his name (*Testament of Solomon* 6.8; 22.20; *Papyrus Graece Magicae* 4.1234; *Contra Celsus* 1.6; 2.49; compare Lk 9:49; Acts 19:13).[6]

It would be nice to believe that demons don't exist and can never bother or influence us, just as it would be nice to believe that no evil exists in the world. However, the reality of human atrocities bears witness to the reality of wickedness. The epitome of wickedness lies in demonic powers. Even psychologist C. G. Jung, himself a dabbler in the occult, admits the following regarding demons:

> The daemonism of nature, which man had apparently triumphed over, he has unwittingly swallowed into himself and so become the devil's marionette . . . when these products [demonic factors in the psyche] were dubbed unreal and illusory, their sources were in no way blocked up or rendered inoperative. On the contrary, after it became impossible for the daemons to inhabit the rocks, woods, mountains, and rivers, they used human beings as much more dangerous dwelling places.[7]

Question 27: What Concepts Are Used to Describe Demons in Scripture?

The Greek word for demons is *daimonion* (Mt 7:22; 9:34; Mk 1:34; Rev 9:20). The Greek term is used for concepts such as devil, unclean spirit or evil spirit, depending on what New Testament version is used. Several biblical concepts occur in association with the word *demon*.

1. Demons as daimon. The Greeks originally understood the word *daimōn* as referring to supernatural powers that mediated between gods and humans and supervised the cosmos (Plato *Symposion* 202e; Hesiod *Opera et Dies* 122).[8] These forces could be good or evil and were often associated with fate or protection. The Greeks often considered these to be spirits of the dead that were endowed with supernatural power.[9] In the New Testament and in the Septuagint (LXX; the Greek version of the Old Testament) demons are called *daimonion* or *daimonia* instead of the classical Greek word *daimōn*.[10] The biblical writers apparently transformed the word to emphasize the idea that the demons were entirely wicked; they are not the benign creatures or shades found in Greek literature. Nevertheless, Matthew uses the word *daimōn* to refer to the demon(s) called Legion that Jesus confronted (Mt 8:31).

2. Demons as the gods of the idolaters. The Bible portrays demons as the "gods" that idolaters worship (Deut 32:17; Ps 106: 37;1 Cor 10:20-21; compare Ps 91:6; 96:5 LXX; Is 13:21; 34:12; 65:3, 11). Nevertheless, demons were not literally gods. Paul claims there is only one God by nature (Gal 4:8), and those who commit idolatry are having fellowship with demons (1 Cor 8:1-5; compare 10:20-21).

The Hebrew word for these demons is *šēdîm* (Deut 32:17; Ps 106:37).[11] In Babylonian literature the *šēdîm* are sometimes hostile, sometimes protective. Perhaps during periods when Israel fell into idolatry, they exalted the *šēdîm* as gods, but then they acknowledged them as wicked spirits when they repented of their idolatry.[12]

3. Demons as the kingdom of darkness. It should come as no surprise that demons are related to "the kingdom of darkness" (Lk 22:53; 2 Cor 6:14; Eph 6:12; Col 1:12-13). In such contexts darkness signifies falsehood, sin and impurity, whereas light signifies truth, holiness and purity (compare Jn 3:19-21; Rom 13:12; 1 Thess 5:4-5; 1 Jn 1:5-7). In the Dead Sea Scrolls two forces fight against each other. The sons of light battle against the wicked sons of darkness (1QM 1.1-16; 3.6-9; 13.10-16; 14.17; 15.14; 1QS 3.18).

4. Demons as śeʿîrîm. The śeʿîrîm (from the root word śeʿîr, "he-goat") were sometimes called "hairy ones." In the Old Testament, the New International Version (NIV) translates this term as "goat idols" (Lev 17:7). They were often associated with the mythological satyrs that look like the Greek god Pan (2 Chron 11:15 KJV). Scripture depicts them as wild animals in abandoned desert ruins (Is 13:21; 34:14; compare Jer 50:39; Rev 18:2).[13] King Jeroboam created an idolatrous trend in the Northern Kingdom when he appointed priests to lead worship of the śeʿîrîm (2 Chron 11:15).

5. Demons as lîlît. In one passage of the Old Testament, the lîlît demon is referred to as the "night hag" (Is 34:14 RSV). We do not know if Isaiah understood the lîlît as a demon, or whether he simply understood it as a desert animal. The word lîlît may have come from Babylon, where it referred to a storm demon associated with the wind.[14] She is sometimes depicted as a "female night phantom."[15] In ancient Near Eastern tradition the lîlît attacked women in childbirth. The lîlît was said to consume the child much as Satan attempted to eat the newborn male child in Revelation 12:1-3 (compare Testament of Solomon 4.1-2; 13.1-3). Jewish tradition visualized lîlît as a satyr with long hair and wings that bore demonic children and sought to seize men in their sleep.[16]

Since we have only limited understanding of how the Old Testament authors understood some of the terms we have just examined, we should refrain from dogmatism. While it is true that ancient cultures and later Jewish traditions associated the šēdîm, śᵉʿîrîm and lîlît with demons, we can only guess that the authors of Scripture understood the terms the same way. It is clear that the demons are called *daimonion* in the New Testament, and they are clearly the source behind various evil practices.

Question 28: What Are Demons?

Scripture affirms that demons are wicked fallen angels who work alongside Satan (Rev 12:7; Jude 6; compare Mt 25:41).[17] By nature, then, demons are supernatural beings like angels, so we would expect them to have the same attributes as other angels. The primary difference between demons and angels lies in their character: demons are wicked and angels are good. In other words, demons work for the kingdom of Satan, who functions as a disrupter of God's people. Now we will examine their nature and attributes more closely.

1. Demons are spirits. Like angels, demons are immaterial beings.[18] Scripture declares that Christians do not wrestle against flesh and blood but against spiritual wickedness (Eph 6:11-12). Christ said when a demon is driven out of a person, it seeks another dwelling place, implying that demons may be disembodied spirits (Lk 11:24-26). They are called spirits *(pneuma)* in a number of passages (for example, 1 Sam 16:14; Mt 8:16; Mk 1:23; Mk 9:17-25; 1 Jn 4:1; compare *1 Enoch* 15.10-12; *Jubilees* 10.5-8; 11.5; *Testament of Dan* 6.1). But we must not attribute a demon to every biblical reference to the word *spirit*. Apart from the Holy Spirit, the human spirit, and wicked or unclean spirits, there are a number of passages that mention the word *spirit* in reference to attitude, influence, mind or disposition (Mt 5:3; 2 Tim 1:7 KJV).

2. Demons are personal beings. Demons are not impersonal forces. Whenever natural catastrophes such as tornadoes or floods destroy life and property, we do not characterize these impersonal forces as demons. Demons are personal beings that have intellect, emotion and will. First, demons have *intellect*. They know that Jesus is the Son of God (Mk 1:24, 34; 5:6). Demons can influence people to receive deceptive doctrines that will lead them astray (1 Tim 4:1-6; Jn 4:1-4). One slave girl had a "Python spirit," probably indicating her owners' claim that her prophecies were as good as Pytho's, or the god Apollo's (Delphi).[19] A demon that possessed her endowed her with a limited capability of telepathy and prediction (Acts 16:16-18).[20]

Second, demons possess *emotion*. Scripture often attributes fear to demons. They are said to tremble at God's presence (Jas 2:19) and fear Jesus. The demon-possessed man who saw Christ "cried out" and begged not to be tormented (Lk 8:28). Satan is depicted as becoming furiously angry at being cast out of heaven (Rev 12:12).

Third, demons possess *self-determination*. When Christ confronted the legion of demons, they preferred to enter into swine rather than be cast into the abyss (Lk 8:31-32). Angels fell because they chose to be disobedient to God (Jude 6).

3. *Demons are evil*. Demons are sometimes called "evil spirits" (1 Sam 16:14; Mt 12:43; Acts 19:12-13; compare Jub. 10.3-13; 11.4). They behave in sinful ways, such as lying (1 Tim 4:1-5; Jn 8:44), but primarily they are considered evil because they eschew all that is good and aim to thwart God's order and holiness in the creation. Demons are violators of holiness and are the spiritual antithesis of the Holy Spirit.[21] They are known as "unclean spirits" (Mk 1:24-27; 5:2-3; 7:26; 9:25; Acts 5:16; 8:7; compare 1 En. 99.7). The Gerasene demoniac dwelled in the tombs, which the Jews considered unclean (Mk 5:1-20; compare Num 19:11-16). Sometimes they are associated with unclean animals (Mk 5:13; Rev 16:13; 18:2).

4. *Demons have superhuman but limited power.* Demons have superhuman power that is manifested through the people they possess. The Gerasene demoniac was able to break apart chains, and no one in that region could physically subdue him

(Mk 5:1-4). One demon-possessed man overpowered seven brothers, causing them to run "out of the house naked and bleeding" (Acts 19:16). Demons also have the power to perform lying signs and wonders (Rev 16:13). But their power is limited, and they can only go as far as God allows them (Job 1—2).

Question 29: What Is the Origin of Demons?

Scripture does not clearly state the origin of evil spirits. Perhaps the authors of Scripture believed the subject had little to contribute to their readers' spirituality, or perhaps they assumed their readers already knew about demonic origins. Nevertheless, the question is worth considering. There are three major theories about the origins of demons.

Theory 1: The demons were created as demons by God. This view emphasizes God's sovereignty over all creation (Is 45:7; Ps 135:5). In the Old Testament even evil spirits are sent by God (Judg 9:23; 1 Sam 16:14). God is so sovereign that he can orchestrate good results out of the evil intentions of Satan in the book of Job. Biblical scholar David Aune observes, "According to a late mishnaic [Jewish] tradition God created the evil spirits [*mazzikim*] on Friday of the creation week" (*'Abot* v. 6).[22]

But if God created the demons *as demons,* this would make God the author of evil and call into question our grounds for saying that God is entirely good. Genesis demonstrates that after creating all things, God saw that it was all "very good" (Gen 1:31). It seems unlikely that all of creation was "very good" if God had created certain evil angels. Moreover, Paul asserts that all things were originally created with their goal in Christ (Col 1:15-16).[23] Yet we find that Christ needed to reconcile all things to himself through his death, including the principalities and powers (angelic powers, Col 1:20; compare 2:15; Eph 6:11-12). This implies that somewhere between the original design of creation and Christ's death, something went wrong. The things in the creation, including invisible angelic powers, had gone astray. Finally, the demons' ultimate destiny in hell argues that they are in some sense culpable for their actions (Mt 25:46). Evidently certain spirits went astray from God's original intent for them.

Theory 2: The demons fell with Satan during the early days of creation. If the first theory seems unpalatable, here's another one: God originally created all the angels good, but God cast a group of them out of heaven because they rebelled against him. They now ravage the earth, attempting to destroy the crown of God's creation—humanity. This view usually assumes that the demons fell with Satan. Although several theories are set forth regarding the exact nature of Satan's sin, few attempts have been made to understand why certain angels decided to follow him.

In ancient Jewish literature, the devil and his angels exalted themselves (*2 Enoch* 29.4) and refused to worship Adam when God charged them to do so (*Apocalypse of Sedrach* 5; *Life of Adam and Eve* 12.1–16.4). On the second day of creation, "Sataniel," apparently an archangel, fell from the heights with the angels under his command (2 En. 29, 69). Similarly, some in the early church taught that since angels do not have a sinful nature composed of flesh, the sin of fallen angels was spiritual, involving pride and envy against God. Demons sinned willfully at the moment of their creation or when Satan fell. The devil seduced many angels below his rank (Thomas Aquinas *Summa Contra Gentiles* 63.1-9; compare Justin Martyr *Dialogue with Trypho the Jew* 141).

The only biblical passage suggesting that angels fell in this manner is Revelation 12:9: Satan fell after battling Michael the archangel, and his angels fell with him. Some suggest that this event alludes to the demons' original fall, but others claim Revelation 12 will be fulfilled at some future date (compare Rev 4:1; 12:12).[24] In any event, the passage does not tell us *why* the angels decided to rebel. Both interpretations are possible, but in my view neither is adequate. In the context of Revelation 12 the fall of these angels signifies Christ's victory over the forces of darkness through his life, death, resurrection and ascension (Rev 12:5-12; compare Lk 10:17-18). Christ's first coming initiated the establishment of God's kingdom on earth and thus ushers us into the new eschatological era (or last days, Mt 12:28; Acts 2:17-23). In Revelation 12 the angelic expulsion portrays a heavenly event pointing to Christ's victory on the cross, and it has both contemporary and future ramifications.[25]

The idea of angels choosing to fall with Satan sounds appealing because it confirms that God is good and originally created all things good. To be consistent with the Genesis record, this approach implies that somewhere between the sixth day of creation (Gen 1:31) and the deception of Eve (Gen 3) the angels fell because they freely chose to sin against God. But all the Bible allows us to conclude is that there was one fallen angel during the time of Adam and Eve—the Serpent, who is commonly understood as Satan.

Theory 3: The demons are either the spirits of the "sons of God" who fell into sin in Genesis 6 or the spirits of their offspring the "giants," or both. Much evidence supports the idea that the "sons of God" were fallen angels. In the book of Job, when the sons of God present themselves before God, Satan is among these celestial beings (Job 1:6; 2:1; 38:7). We noted earlier that the phrase "sons of God" most likely refers to angels in Deuteronomy 32:8 (LXX). Moreover, the "son of God" or the "son of the gods" is understood as referring to angels, even by non-Israelites (Dan 3:25). This theory asserts that the sons of God manifested themselves in the physical world and sinned by having sexual relationships with human women. Consequently, they were wiped out by the flood. They, or their children the "giants," are now wicked, disembodied spirits who roam the world looking for bodies to inhabit (*1 Enoch* 15.8; 16.1; 19.1; Justin Martyr *Second Apology* 5, 10). (We will return to this subject in the next few answers.)

But it is not clear that the angels referred to in Genesis 6 make up the entire species of what we now call demons. If they do, it would seem that some of these demons were bound and banished to Tartarus (the term that the Greeks used for hell) until the day of judgment, while others remain free to wreak havoc (2 Pet 2:4; Jude 6; compare Lk 8:31; Rev 9:1; 1 Pet 3:19-21).[26] Alternatively, the angels that sinned in Genesis 6 were a separate class of fallen angels that are now all bound and judged. We would then have a set of angels who probably fell with Satan on the sixth day of creation, who are still free, and a second set of angels who fell in Genesis 6, who have already been punished and imprisoned in Tartarus.

Question 30: Who Are the "Sons of God" in Genesis 6?

Three views compete for the most popular interpretation of Genesis 6:1-4: "When men began to increase in number on the earth and daughters were born to them, the sons of God saw that the daughters of men were beautiful, and they married any of them they chose. Then the LORD said, 'My Spirit will not contend with man forever, for he is mortal; his days will be a hundred and twenty years.' The Nephilim ['giants' KJV; *gigantes* LXX] were on the earth in those days—and also afterward—when the sons of God went to the daughters of men and had children by them. They were the heroes [*gibbôrîm* MT; *gigantes* LXX] of old, men of renown."

View 1: The term 'sons of God' refers to the godly line of Seth. This view claims that the "sons of God" were the sons of Seth, the third son of Adam (Gen 5:3-4). "Daughters of men" refers to the line of Cain, the one who slew his brother Abel (Gen 4). In other words, the passage relates the mixing of the godly line of Seth with the wicked lineage of Cain. These marital relationships produced exceedingly wicked men; therefore, God sent the flood to wipe out everyone except Noah and his family (Gen 6:5-22).

Those who propose this view have a hard time finding any

corroborating evidence for their position. There is no good reason why we should think that "the daughters of men" refers to Cain's offspring. In Scripture, certain men are sometimes considered the sons of God (Deut 14:1; compare Ex 4:22; Hos 1:10), but such passages do not refer to the sons of Seth; they refer to the elect sons of Israel.[27] We find no supporting biblical evidence that the sons of Seth were considered the sons of God. This interpretation presupposes "that what Gen 6 really meant was that 'the sons of some men' married 'the daughters of other men.' . . . It is made the more implausible by 6:1 where 'man' refers to all mankind."[28] The interpretation that the sons of God are the sons of Seth appears to be an argument of special pleading contrived to avoid the unsavory conclusion that the sons of God were in fact angels.

View 2: "Sons of God" refers to royal rulers. This view assumes that the phrase "sons of God" is essentially another way of expressing the word *rulers.* Scripture in some places refers to kings as sons of God (Ps 2:7; 89:19; 2 Sam 7:14; 1 Chron 17:13; 22:10). Ancient Near Eastern cultures often referred to gods' "begetting" royalty, especially in Egypt.[29] Thus Genesis 6:2 means that the rulers of the earth apparently added to their harem any women they desired from the "daughters of men."

But there are problems with this view. The text emphasizes that the relationships in Genesis 6:2 and 6:4 are wicked (compare 6:3, 5). It is not clear, however, why God would abhor polygamy enough to destroy the entire earth by the flood. Long after the flood, the Israelites engaged in polygamy without incurring God's displeasure. Israel himself (Jacob) was a polygamist, as was King David. Thus this royal polygamy view seems contrived from later Jewish history. Gordon Wenham notes, "The royal interpretation [of Genesis 6:2] was introduced into Jewish exegesis about the middle of the second century A.D., partly, it seems, out of conviction that angels could not indulge in sexual intercourse and partly to suppress speculation about them."[30]

View 3: "Sons of God" refers to fallen angels. As strange as it may seem, this view has the most evidence going for it. First, the Bible supports the notion of angels as the "sons of God" or "sons of the gods" in other passages (Job 1:6; 2:1; 38:7; Deut 32:8 LXX; Dan 3:25). In the book of Jude these are the fallen angels who "did not keep their positions of authority but abandoned their own home" and are kept bound by chains and darkness until judgment day (Jude 6; compare 2 Pet 2:4). Jude cites a passage from *1 Enoch* (Jude 11), confirming that one of his sources was this particular Jewish tradition. In *1 Enoch* angels called the Watchers lusted after the beautiful women of the earth. Semyaz was the leader, and two hundred angels came with him to earth. They taught humans magical incantations, among other things, and had sex with the women to reproduce themselves in a race of giants (*1 Enoch* 6.1–16.4; 54.6; compare *2 Enoch* 18). This view is strengthened by the fact that many ancient sources support this angelic-human sexual relationship. First, many other Jewish traditions confirm the same story (Philo *De Gigantibus* 6-7, 16, 60; *Josephus Antiquities of the Jews* 3.1; *Jubilees* 5.1ff.; 7.21-22; 10.3-5; 2 *Apocalypse of Baruch* 56.11; 16; *2 Enoch* 7.1ff.; *Testament of Reuben* 5.6-7), as well as early Christian traditions (Tertullian *On the Veiling of Virgins* 1; *Against Marcion* 5.8; *On Prayer* 22; Clement of Alexandria *Paedagogus* 3; Paulinus of Nola *Letters* 23).

The Dead Sea Scrolls also interpret the "sons of God" as angels, who are described as the "Sons of Heaven," "Holy Ones" and the "Heavenly Watchers," who fell from their heavenly state.[31] Moreover, ancient Near Eastern culture, such as that described in Ugaritic texts, referred to the "sons of God" as members of the divine pantheon similar to the ancient Hebrew concept of angels standing before the council of God (Job 1–2).[32]

Second, understanding the sons of God as angels helps explain why the Israelites would have considered the marriages in Genesis 6 wicked. Sexual relations between angels and humans would have been similar to the sexual unions between gods and humans common in Greco-Roman myths. Such a mixed union would no doubt have violated the Israelite notion that holiness requires separation, order and wholeness. The mixing of two unrelated substances was forbidden by the law of Moses (Lev 19:19; 20:16; Deut 7:3; 22:9-11).

Third, identifying the sons of God as angels also fits well with the Jewish tradition that the angels' sin had to do with lust. Regarding Genesis 6:2, Gordon Wenham writes:

> The sequence of "saw . . . good . . . took" [in Genesis 6:2] parallels most closely the terminology in 3:6 [Eve's temptation in the garden] and suggests the sinfulness of the action of the sons of God. When the woman [Eve] saw and took [the fruit], she transgressed a boundary set by the LORD. The essence of Adam's sin was to acquiesce in his wife's transgression by eating the fruit she gave him. Here the fault of the daughters of man lies presumably in their consenting to intercourse with "the sons of the gods." It ought also to be borne in mind that the girls' fathers would also have been implicated, since, if there was no rape or seduction, their approval to these matches would have been required.[33]

Given the popular opinions and theories of the time, it seems that the original readers of Scripture, along with the apostles, probably understood the "sons of God" in Genesis 6 as fallen angels. Of course, this view opens up a fresh can of worms. How do we explain Christ's declaration in Matthew 22:30, which states that the angels do not marry, implying they are sexless? But what does this actually mean? Does it mean that the angels *cannot* marry because by nature it is impossible for them to do so? Or does it mean that they *do not* marry because they do not wish to violate God's proper boundaries for them? If the latter case is true, then it fits nicely with Jude 6. In Jude's allusion to Genesis 6, the angels seem to have violated God's standard by abandoning their proper disposition not to marry. And even if the angels could not marry during the time of Christ, this would not necessarily mean that all classes of angels, whether good or bad, *never* had been able to do so any time in the past.

There is a second problem with the sons-of-God-as-angels view: If we accept that the account in Genesis 6 actually happened in our history, how can we believe that angels really had sex with women and produced offspring? Should we forever consign Genesis 6 to science fiction? The idea that the gods had sex with humans pervaded many ancient cultures.[34] Greek mythology abounds with such legends. If all these legends were merely fictional, why do they seem so pervasive? If we believe that legends about a great flood from various cultures lend credibility to Noah's flood, could we not say the same about the "sons of God" legends? Maybe such notions about angels intermingling with humans violate the rationality of our modern minds. But then how is it that many still believe that angels are spirits or that angels ate with Abraham in Genesis 18:2-22? Or, for that matter, how is it that many Christians still believe in the virgin birth? The real issue, then, is whether we are willing to accept Genesis 6:1-5 as an inexplicable supernatural event.

If angels really did manifest themselves in human form, how is it that they were able to duplicate the human DNA structure necessary to produce offspring? (if indeed our current understandings of human structuring are correct)? Even if angels are supernatural and were intelligent enough to do so, creating human life seems to be a work that is reserved only for God.[35]

Perhaps the best ancient explanation of this sexual union comes from a Jewish and early church tradition that suggests the sons of God saw the wickedness of humans and asked God to clothe them with bodies so that they could come to earth to

teach men laws and morals. This happened during the time of
Jared, the son of Mahalalel (Gen 5:17-18). That is why Mahalalel named his son Jared, meaning "descension." It was at this
time that angels descended from heaven to earth. After they
were clothed with human flesh, however, they fell to the same
passions as do all humans, and so they gave themselves over
to the lusts of the flesh, desiring earthly women. Their offspring were mighty men of abnormal power. When God sent
the flood, the mighty men drowned and are now disembodied
spirits or demons (*Jubilees* 4.15; Pseudo Clement *Homilies* 8-9).
Alternatively, we could plead ignorance on this issue. We may
not have the capability of uncovering an adequate historical
explanation for this passage at this time.

Question 31: Why Are the Offspring of the Sons of God Called "Giants"?

Genesis 6 records that "giants" were the offspring of the "sons
of God." In Hebrew they are called the Nephilim (Gen 6:4-5).
If the sons of God are fallen angels, then the giants must be
partially demonic. But the King James Version and the Septuagint (LXX) call them "giants" after the Greek word *gigantes*.
Several possibilities have been advanced regarding their identity. Most likely, the Hebrew term *Nephilim* comes from the
word *nāpal* meaning "to fall." This implies several possible
explanations of the "Nephilim":

Type of Fall	Explanation
Moral fall	They fell away morally (committed apostasy). But this refers more to their fathers, unless we understand this as simply meaning that the Nephilim were immoral (Gen 6:5; compare Sirach 16.7).
Bastards	*Nepel* means abortion or miscarriage, perhaps identifying their birth as originating from the immoral relationship between their fathers and earth women (compare Num 5:11-31).

Murderers	They "fall" on others in the sense that they murder others. This fits their character in Jewish literature and Genesis 9:6.
Killed	They are the ones who "fall" or are killed. This assumes that either God completely wiped them out in the Flood (Gen 6:17; compare *Jubilees* 10.3-5; Wisdom of Solomon 14.6) or they were predecessors of the giants who were later destroyed by the Hebrews (Deut 2:10-12; 3:11; 2 Sam 21:16; compare Baruch 3.26-28).

Perhaps a combination of some of these meanings best captures the character of the Nephilim. The last definition leads to further implications if compared to Ezekiel 32:20-28. This passage may be alluding to Genesis 6:1-4, as it depicts the defeat of great warriors (compare Gen 10:8-9).[36] The Nephilim's status as great warriors may have something to do with their designation as giants. Beyond this, the meaning of the word *Nephilim* gives us little regarding their stature.

Genesis 6 aside, we find only one other biblical reference to the Nephilim. When Moses sent the twelve tribal leaders to spy out the land of Canaan, they brought back a discouraging report: "The land we explored devours those living in it. All the people we saw there are of great size. We saw the Nephilim there (the descendants of Anak come from the Nephilim).[37] We seemed like grasshoppers in our own eyes, and we looked the same to them" (Num 13:32-33).

This passage connects the Nephilim with the Anakim ("people of the necklace") and the Rephaim (Deut 2:10-11, 20-21). These people were of great size. The gigantic Philistine warriors, of whom Goliath was one, were descendants of the Rephaim (2 Sam 21:16-22; 1 Chron 20:4-8; compare 2 *Apocalypse of Baruch* 3.26). Og, king of Bashan, was a Rephaite whose bed or sarcophagus measured thirteen feet long and six feet wide (Deut 3:11)![38]

Apparently an ancient oral tradition originating in Mesopotamia affirmed that the Nephilim were men of great stature. We do not know their actual size, but we may guess that some of them were perhaps the size of Goliath (1 Sam 17:4). As Numbers 13:34 implies, the Hebrews already seemed to know about the great size of the Nephilim prior to the spies' report. Their status as giants is always assumed.

Question 32: Do Descendants of the Giants Exist Today?

We have already established that the Nephilim, or giants, in Genesis 6 existed before the flood. They were the offspring of the sons of God and human women. In Numbers 13:33-34, however, their name appears again. In the Israelites' tradition-history, this occurs hundreds of years after the flood. If the Israelites saw the Nephilim in the land of Canaan, are we to assume that the offspring of demons survived the flood of Noah? If we understand this as actual history, wouldn't this mean that some people living today are literally descendants of demons?

Some assume that the flood of Noah was local, affecting the region of Mesopotamia but not the entire earth. Thus some of the Nephilim escaped the flood by running to mountainous regions or by traveling by boat to distant places.[39] This approach is hard to reconcile with Genesis (6:17; 7:17-24), which emphasizes the universality of the flood in which "all the high mountains under the entire heavens were covered" (Gen 7:19). Since the purpose of the flood was to obliterate wickedness, why would God let some of the Nephilim escape (compare Gen 6:5-7)?[40]

Since Numbers 13:34 is the only other mention of the Nephilim in Scripture, we must examine it more carefully (see also answer 31). Joshua and Caleb reported that a strong race called the Anakites (Anakim) lived there, but they did not associate this tribe with the Nephilim (Num 13:26-30; compare

14:6-9). The other ten spies gave a negative report, mentioning the Nephilim and saying that they "seemed like grasshoppers" compared to them (13:32-33). Clearly, the bad report included exaggerations regarding the size of their opponents. If their report implies false information, they may have lied when they claimed that the Anakim were descendants of the Nephilim. Granted, they may have appeared to be similar to the Nephilim of old because of their great size, but the Anakim and Rephaim may not have been the *literal* descendants of the Nephilim. Similarly, Old Testament scholar Timothy Ashley writes, "As the text stands [Num 13:31-33] it is clear that the majority report [of the spies] is condemned as false and faithless."[41]

Since the mention of the Nephilim in Numbers 13:32-24 seems to represent false information made up by the Israelite spies, we can safely assume that the Nephilim were wiped out by the flood, leaving no descendants.

Question 33: Are Demons Ghosts?

A ghost is the "soul or spectre of a dead person, usually appearing as a living being or as a nebulous likeness of the deceased and, occasionally, in other forms."[42] Demons, on the other hand, are not the souls of the dead, unless we associate them with the souls of the Nephilim in Genesis 6. Sometimes in ancient literature, however, demons were thought to be the spirits of the dead (for example, Josephus *War* 1.599, 607; 6.47; Pliny *Nat. Hist.* 18.118). The Bible understands shades *(rᵉpaʾim)* as the spirits of the dead, or what we commonly think of today as ghosts (Job 26:5; Ps 88:10-11; Prov 2:18; Is 14:9; 26:14). When the disciples saw Jesus walking on the water, and again when he rose from the dead (Lk 24:39), they mistook him for a ghost *(phantasma,* Mt 14:26; Mk 6:49; compare Job 20:8 LXX; Wisd. 17.14; Josephus *Ant.* 1.331-33).

Can ghosts come back from the dead to visit or haunt us? A few passages support the idea of visitations from the dead.

Moses and Elijah appear to Christ on the Mount of Transfiguration (Mk 9:1-10; Lk 9:28-33), and it may have actually been the dead prophet Samuel who appeared to Saul when he consulted a medium (1 Sam 28:8-16).[43] Such cases are the rare exception, however, not the rule. And these visitations are not the same as hauntings. Consequently, Saul's consulting the witch of Endor was an act of rebellion in God's eyes and grounds for his death in battle (compare 1 Chron 10:13-14).

The dead rich man described in Lk 16:19-31 was not permitted to warn his brothers about the torments of Hades, which leads many to assume that the spirits of unbelievers are held "without bail" until the judgment day. The spirits of believers seem to go to the very presence of God as soon as they die (2 Cor 5:4-8; Phil 1:21-24). It is not a normative biblical teaching that the spirits of saints can come back to visit us; on the other hand, there is no explicit biblical evidence that they *cannot* visit us.[44] Still, the Bible regards consulting the dead (necromancy) as a serious sin (Deut 18:9-12; compare 1 Chron 10:13-14).

Many people claim that a dead relative has visited them, whether in a dream, in a vision, or in actual appearance. How do we discern visitations that are *not initiated* by the person who is visited? These incidents must be evaluated on a case-by-case basis to determine their source. It may be an intense dream triggered by grief or permitted by God to assuage the sorrow of losing a loved one (Acts 16:9). It could also be a hallucination, a demon, an angel or possibly the actual spirit of the person. Ultimately, if the ghost teaches secret or false doctrines, or if it encourages a person to dabble in the occult, we can conclude that it was not sent from God.

Question 34: What Is the Difference Between Gargoyles, Goblins, Poltergeists and Demons?

Gargoyles are simply architectural waterspouts sculpted on

the sides of buildings in ancient and medieval cultures. In ancient Rome many gargoyles were carved lions, but in Gothic art they became grotesque figures with horns and wings. Although they were considered protectors of the building, they are not thought to be real creatures. (In the Old Testament the two cherubim angels that protected the ark of the covenant seem to have had a similar function—Ex 25:17-22.) Far from being demons, gargoyles were meant to ward off evil spirits.

In Western folklore a goblin is a wandering spirit that is looking for trouble. Goblins were said to bang on pots and pans, rap on doors, move furniture and steal people's nightclothes.[45] The ancient Assyrians and Babylonians believed that the goblin was a kind of semihuman demon. Goblins were called the *lilu, lilitu* and *ardat lili;* hence they were associated with the Old Testament *lilit* demon (Is 34:14).[46]

Poltergeists (German for "noisy spirits") may be synonymous with the goblins of old. They move furniture, rattle pots, throw objects and shred clothes. Most often they are reported as throwing stones (often at slow speed) or setting clothes or humans on fire (spontaneous human combustion). John and Charles Wesley reported a poltergeist that often disturbed the Epworth parsonage during prayer time. They called it "Old Jeffrey."[47] Poltergeist activity can cause such damage and misery that people who experience it sometimes move from their homes, sustain injuries or even commit suicide.[48] People involved in occult activities and young adolescents are often the poltergeist's focal point.

Some claim that poltergeists are not spirits but an extreme form of psychokinesis—an explosive release of personal psychic energy. But since the phenomena are always destructive, never good, and are associated with the occult, poltergeists are more likely demons. J. Stafford Wright suggests that "since one person is commonly the storm-center, it is possible that the spirits make use of some vital force, frequently connected with sex development, which they can materialize sufficiently to move material objects. It would be a kind of physical sublimation of the sex instinct."[49]

Question 35: Are There Different Ranks Within the Kingdom of Darkness?

The kingdom of darkness must have some sense of order and rank, for the demonic forces have Satan as their leader and appear unified in their opposition to the work of God. Jesus said, "If a kingdom is divided against itself, that kingdom cannot stand. . . . And if Satan opposes himself and is divided, he cannot stand; his end has come" (Mk 3:24, 26). We do not know the demons' precise order and rank, nor do we have a list of all the demonic classes. But we do know that there are several types of wicked spiritual powers, although there may be some overlap between them[50] (1 Cor 15:24; Eph 1:21; 6:10-12; compare 2 Maccabees 3.24; *1 Enoch* 61.10; *2 Enoch* 20-22; *Testament of Levi* 3).

The principalities (archai). Biblical literature sometimes views "principalities" or "rulers" as something more than mere human rulers. Their high status is evident. Paul categorizes them as potential threats, but they cannot separate the saints (Christians) from the love of Christ (Rom 8:38; compare Col 2:10). These forces are heavenly beings who war against the saints (Eph 3:10; 6:12; Col 2:15).

The powers (exousia). Closely related to the "principalities" are the "powers." The term is used for worldly powers (Rom 13:1-3), and in some passages it takes on a spiritual dimension in opposition to Christ's kingdom (1 Cor 15:24; Eph 1:21; 3:10; 6:12; Col 1:16; 2:15; compare *Testatmet of Levi* 3.8; *2 Enoch* 20.1). Another closely related Greek term that sometimes refers to spiritual powers is *dynameis* (Rom 8:38; Eph 1:21; compare Dan 8:10 LXX; *1 Enoch* 61.10).[51]

The princes (śārîm). The Hebrew word *śārîm* refers to the "prince" of the kingdom of Persia and the "prince" of Greece, who are spiritual rulers (Dan 10:13, 20-21). They have great power because they seem to watch over entire nations. The prince of Persia fought Michael the archangel but lost. It is possible that the term "rulers of this age" *(archontes)* is Paul's New Testament equivalent for these beings.[52] If so, these "rulers" influenced human authorities to put Christ to death (1 Cor 2:6, 8). Paul says in the same passage that if these "rulers" had known the positive consequences resulting from Christ's death, they never would have crucified him.

The Watchers or sons of God. In 2 Peter 2:4 and Jude 6 the Bible refers to a set of angels who are now bound by chains in darkness because of their sin. Although their sin is not specified, it is evident that these passages refer to the "sons of God" who cohabited with the women of the earth in Genesis 6. These angels were known as the "Watchers" in Jewish tradition (see answers 29-30).

Demons. Scripture refers to demons, unclean or evil spirits, far more than many of the other classifications of wicked forces (for example, Mt 7:22; 8:31; 12:24; Mk 1:34; Lk 8:30; Rom 8:38; Jas 2:19). These are the spirits that are portrayed as attacking or possessing humans.

The various classes of demons that work against the kingdom of God are limited in power. The power of Christ far exceeds that of the forces of darkness (Eph 1:21; Col 2:9-10). Christ is supreme over all the forces of darkness because he created all spiritual powers, including the ones that later went astray (Col 1:16). He defeated them through his death and resurrection (Col 2:15; Mt 28:18; Phil 2:10-11),[53] and he will completely subdue them at the Second Coming (1 Cor 15:24-25). The love of Christ is so powerful that "neither height nor depth" can separate the saints from him (Rom 8:39). Daniel Reid notes that this passage in Romans "may refer to the zenith and nadir of the heavenly bodies and thus encompass[es] the full sweep of celestial powers (compare 1 En. 18.3, 11)."[54]

Question 36: How Many Demons Are There?

Some claim that the angels who fell with Satan referred to in Revelation 12:9 are the third of the "stars" that the dragon cast down from heaven in Revelation 12:3. They surmise that demons make up one-third of the entire angelic kingdom. But this interpretation lacks credibility for a few reasons.

First, there is insufficient evidence to affirm that the events in Revelation 12 depict the fall of Satan and his angels at the beginning of creation. The fall of Satan and his minions in Revelation 12 seems to best fit the time frame of the first coming of Christ, having future implications (Rev 12:4-5, 10-12; compare Lk 10:18).

Second, if "stars" refers to angels who were cast down to the "earth" by Satan in Revelation 12:4, how did they end up in "heaven" again in Revelation 12:7? This interpretation seems inconsistent with the context.

Third, in Revelation 12:3 "stars" seems to refer to the saints, not angels. The saints are compared to the "stars of heaven" (Dan 12:3; Mt 13:43; compare Phil 2:15) who inhabit "heavenly places" in Christ (Eph 1:3; 2:6; compare 1:20). In a prophetic passage similar to Revelation 12, the people of God are depicted as "stars" who were cast down by the Seleucid ruler Antiochus Epiphanes, a type of antichrist (Dan 8:10, 13, 24). Since Scripture depicts a great persecution and a falling away of God's people, the stars of heaven that are cast down in Revelation 12:3 may depict this (2 Thess 2:3; 1 Tim 4:1; compare Mt 24:9-13; Jude 13; Rev 9:1).

Scripture never gives us the number of demons that exist. Jesus cast out an entire legion of demons, presumably thousands, from the Gerasene demoniac (Mk 5:1-13). Paul asserts that Gentile idolaters are actually worshiping demons when they worship their idols (1 Cor 10:20-21). So if we assume that demons are behind just a fraction of all the idol worship in the world, we are still talking about a large number of demons. But there is no reason to believe that demons are numerous enough to spy on every human being on earth and attempt to continually harass them. Contrary to at least one Jewish tradition (*Berakot* 3a, 6a), we should not think they inhabit the trees, plants or rocks. We have no reason to believe that the billions of non-Christian peoples in the world are all demon possessed. Whatever the number of angels that fell, they are not numerous enough to defeat the good angels (Rev 12:7-8).

Question 37: Can Demons Materialize?

If good angels appeared as humans, can demons do likewise? In her book *He Came to Set the Captives Free* Rebecca Brown affirms that demons can manifest themselves as werewolves or other hideous creatures. According to one Jewish tradition, although demons are spirits, they need food and water, and they can manifest themselves as humans.[55] But there is no biblical reference to demons' manifesting themselves physically.

Yes, the "sons of God" in Genesis 6 may have manifested themselves, but the interpretation of this passage seems to suggest that they were not demons prior to their physical manifestation on earth (see answers 29-30). If demons could manifest themselves physically, why would they attempt to possess humans (Mt 12:43; Lk 11:46-48)? Nevertheless, they are able to accomplish harm through possessing a person's body (Acts 19:16).[56]

Question 38: What Does Christ's Power over Demons Signify?

Jesus confronts the forces of darkness in a number of Gospel passages, regularly casting out demons (Mk 1:34, 39; 3:11-12). Once in the synagogue he cast out a demon that revealed Christ's identity as "the Holy One of God" (Mk 1:23-24; Lk 4:33-36). In the land of Gerasa Jesus healed a violent demoniac who lived among the tombs by casting a legion of devils out of him. The demons took possession of a herd of swine, which then fell off a cliff and drowned (Mk 5:1-20; Lk 8:26-33). Christ also healed a young man from a destructive demon of epilepsy (Mt 17:14-21; Mk 9:14-29; Lk 9:37-43). He cast seven demons out of Mary Magdalene (Mk 16:9; Lk 8:2) and healed a woman who was apparently crippled by a spirit that deformed her back (Lk 13:10-17). Without being physically present with a Syro-Phoenician girl who was possessed, Jesus nonetheless expelled the demon from a distance (Mk 7:24-30; Mt 15:21-28).

The crowds were amazed at the authority that Jesus possessed over the forces of darkness (Mt 9:32-34). Some spread the message of Jesus' power (Mk 1:25-28), while others—who were once afraid of demoniacs—became afraid of Jesus instead (Lk 8:34-37). Rather than admit that he operated through the Spirit of God, some religious leaders chose to blaspheme the Holy Spirit by claiming that Jesus cast out demons by the power of Beelzebub, the prince of devils (Mt 12:22-32).

Christ proclaimed that his authority to drive out demons was a sign that the kingdom of God was now breaking forth on earth (Mt 12:28; Lk 11:20; compare Acts 8:5-12; 10:38; Heb 6:5).[57] David Aune suggests that the Old Testament has only one exorcist, David, who played the harp to cast an evil spirit from Saul's presence (1 Sam 16:14-23; compare Pseudo Philo 60). Jewish tradition claims that David's son Solomon was an expert exorcist (Josephus *Antiquities of the Jews* 8.2.5; *Pesiqta Rabbati* 69a; compare *Testament of Solomon*). The Jews therefore anticipated a future era when demons would be driven out by a Davidic figure (Zech 13:2; compare 1QS 4.19-21; 1QM 14.10). Thus Jesus, the new "son of David," fulfilled this expectation by casting out devils and proclaiming the beginning of the era of the last days (Mt 12:22-23; 15:21-28; compare Mk 7:29-30; Acts 1—2).[58]

Christ's divine authority, as well as his claim that the old age influenced by the kingdom of darkness was drawing to a close, distinguished him from other Jewish exorcists of that era (Lk 10:18; Jn 12:31). New Testament theologian James Dunn states:

He [Jesus] did *not* imply that the Jewish exorcisms likewise

demonstrated the presentness of the kingdom. On the contrary, he distinguished himself from them; *his* exorcisms were preformed by the *Spirit/finger of God.* This is so too in the following saying about the binding of the strong man (Mt 12:29/Mk 3:27/Lk 11:21f.). Jesus saw his exorcisms not merely as the healing of demented people, not merely as the casting out of demons, not merely as a victory over Satan, but as that binding of the powers of evil which was looked for at the end of the age. The final battle was already joined and Satan was already being routed (cf. Lk 10:18). These claims imply a *clear sense of the eschatological distinctiveness of his power:* Jesus' mighty acts were in his own eyes as epochal as the miracles of the Exodus and likewise heralded a new age."[59]
To advance the kingdom of God here on earth, believers of the new era should exemplify Christ's authority over demons by operating in the power of the Spirit. For, as Dunn notes, "Where the *Spirit* is there is the kingdom."[60]

Question 39: What Are the "Doctrines of Demons"?

"The Spirit clearly says that in later times some will abandon the faith and follow deceiving spirits and things taught by demons" (1 Tim 4:1). Scripture declares that some teachings come from demons. What are these doctrines? Paul states that anyone who teaches any gospel other than the true gospel, even if he received the teaching from an angel of heaven, is accursed (Gal 1:8-9; compare 1 Cor 15:1-3). Paul warned the Ephesian church that false teachers would arise after he departed (Acts 20:29-30). Jesus also warns about false prophets (Mt 7:15-20; 24:4-5, 23-27). Any doctrine that leads people away from Christ is of the "spirit of antichrist" (1 Jn 4:1-6).

Why does Scripture stand so severely against false doctrine? First Timothy 4:1-5 relates the doctrines of devils to hypocrites and liars who forbid people to partake of God's natural blessings, such as certain foods and marital sex. The forces of darkness attempt to lead believers astray through false teachings in order to get them to abandon the Christian faith for another spirit, another gospel, and another Christ (2 Cor 11:1-14). Likewise, people's lives are destroyed when the meaning of biblical scriptures is twisted (2 Pet 3:16). One present-day example of this is the Jehovah's Witness sect. Their Watchtower organization prohibits them from receiving blood transfusions, based on their misreading of Scripture, and many Jehovah's Witnesses have died needlessly.

It is essential that we know *why* we believe *what* we believe, and we should stand clear of any cult leader. We need to test all doctrines (Acts 17:11; 1 Thess 5:21). Do they really conform to biblical scripture? Do they glorify Christ as the only savior who died on the cross to save humankind from sin (Jn 3:16)? Do they teach Jesus as God the Son, second person of the Trinity, who is the Creator and not a creation (Jn 1:1-3; Mt 28:19; Tit 2:13; Heb 1:8)? Do they teach that salvation is completely by grace through faith (Eph 2:8-9)?

Demons lead many astray morally, especially into idolatry (1 Cor 10:1-22; Lev 17:7; Deut 32:17; 2 Chron 11:15; Ps 106:37; Acts 17:18; compare *1 Enoch* 99.7; *Jubilees* 1.11; 22.17; Justin Martyr *First Apology* 1.5; Athenagoras *Supplicatio* 26.1; Origen *Contra Celsum* 7.69).[61] Idolatry distorts the true image of God and draws people's attention away from worshiping God alone, leaving them open to further temptations. Ultimately, idolatry gets people to worship the demons who may impersonate the gods, idols or images that are venerated (1 Cor 10:20; Rev 9:20).

In summary, the doctrines of demons consist of teachings or influences that lead people away from the true God into false teachings, moral deradation and the influence of deceptive spirits.

Question 40: Are Demons the Cause of Sickness and Disease?

The New Testament contains many examples of demons causing sickness. Jesus cast out a demon of epilepsy from one lad (Mt 17:14-21; Mk 9:14-29, 33; Lk 9:37-43). He cast out devils from those who were blind and mute (Mt 9:32-34; 12:22; Lk 11:14-15), and expelled devils from those who suffered from insanity (Mt 8:28-34; Mk 5:1-20; Lk 8:26-39). But we must not think that every case of blindness, epilepsy or other diseases arises from demonic activity. Healing sicknesses and casting out devils are not always the same thing (Mk 1:34; Mt 8:16; Lk 7:21; Acts 5:16; 8:7).[62]

When praying for the sick, Christians should avoid what many faith healers do. Unless they have special evidence that they are dealing with the demonic, they should not speak directly to epilepsy, cancer or any other sickness as though it were an intelligent demon that can heed their rebuke. An impersonal sickness cannot hear us! If we presumptuously assert that a sickness is demonic and the person we pray for is not healed, the devil appears to have prevailed. There's a better way to pray for the sick. Let us take the attention off the sickness itself, off our own personal power, and let us ask God through Christ to heal such individuals.

Probing into the world of the demonic is no light matter. Some may already feel a sense of uneasiness as they read through this book. We are trying to understand the demonic forces so that we ourselves will not be deceived by them. Ignorance is not bliss when it comes to such a serious subject. (Chapter six discusses a number of other questions related to the human struggle with demons.) The Christians have nothing to fear in regard to demons (1 Jn 4:4). Christ said the one we should revere is God, who has the authority to cast the wicked into to hell (Mt 10:28). Werner Foerster writes, "In the great reduction of fear of demons, however, we are to see an effect of the NT [New Testament] faith in God as the Guardian of His people. In the light of this faith all fear of demons necessarily yields to steadfast assurance."[63]

5

QUESTIONS ABOUT SATAN

Old Red," "Old Horny," "Old Hairy," "the bogeyman," "Jack Flash," "Dickens," "Old Nick" and "Old Scratch" are nicknames that the devil has been called throughout the centuries. Such names transform the devil into a mischievous sprite, fairy, gnome, gremlin, or leprechaun. J. B. Russell notes:

Hundreds of such names exist, such as Terrytop, Charlot, Federwisch, Hinkebein, Heinekin, Rumpelstiltskin . . . Robin Hood, Robin Goodfellow, and Knecht Ruprecht. Such nicknames were popular not only because of their association with the "little people" but also because to give the Devil an absurd name is to offer an antidote to the fear he engendered.[1]

We must never underestimate the devil as an adversary. Though portrayed as a comical, red-horned satyr with a pitchfork, in biblical scripture he is Satan, leader of the fallen angels. In this chapter we will look at who Satan is, how he fell and what he does. We will also separate the mythical aspects of Satan from the biblical Satan.

Question 41: Was Satan Once a Beautiful Angel Named Lucifer?

The most popular belief about Satan's fall is based on Isaiah 14:12 (KJV): "How art thou fallen from heaven, O Lucifer son of the morning!" The passage goes on to say that Lucifer tried to raise his throne above the stars and become like the Most High, but God cast him down to the depths of the pit (Is 14:13-15).

This passage is often compared with Ezekiel 28:11-19, which allegedly speaks of Lucifer as the king of Tyre living in the Garden of Eden. He was a beautiful cherub angel, but God said to him, "Your heart became proud on account of your beauty, and you corrupted your wisdom because of your splendor. So I threw you to the earth; I made a spectacle of you before kings" (28:17). Some even claim that Lucifer was the choir director of heaven based on the names of instruments listed in the King James translation of Ezekiel 28:13. Hence popular theory has it that Satan, as Lucifer, fell sometime at the beginning of creation. The Bible, however, never directly affirms anywhere that Satan is Lucifer. A contextual reading of Isaiah 14 and Ezekiel 28 raises serious doubts about the reliability of the popular "Lucifer is Satan" theory.

The king of Tyre is a man who acts like a god (Ezek 28). There is no good reason to equate Ezekiel's king of Tyre with either Satan or Lucifer. In fact, it makes no sense at all when we read that the Lord (through Ezekiel) denounces the king of Tyre: "You are a man and not a god" (Ezek 28:2). Satan is neither a man nor a god, but the leader of fallen angels (Mt 25:41; Rev 12:7-9). Furthermore, if this passage depicts the original fall, when did Satan get thrown to earth and turned to ashes before the kings (28:17-18)?

Ezekiel 28 obviously depicts what it claims to depict—the

king of Tyre. Ezekiel (25—32) denounces various ancient nations and their kings, including Ammon, Moab, Edom, Philistia and Egypt. Tyre is but one of the nations on which Ezekiel prophesies judgment. Ezekiel (26—28) seems to employ hyperbolic and sarcastic language against the king, who represents his city of Tyre (28:4-5,13, 15, 18; compare with the hyperbole in Ezek 31, esp. vv. 8-9). The king, as a metonymy for the city, is portrayed with great beauty and glory due to the city's wealth, trade and accumulation of precious stones. Ezekiel thus sarcastically alludes to the king as living in the best of circumstances and beauty: as a cherub angel living in God's presence and as Adam in the delightful Garden of Eden (28:13-15). This makes his downfall even more vivid—his city is reduced to a heap of ashes (v. 18). God faults the king not only for pride but also for dishonest trade (v. 18). This would hardly be true of Lucifer or Satan.

Some recognize that this passage refers to a human king while maintaining that in a deeper sense it depicts the origin of Satan because of the Garden of Eden imagery and the idea of a glorious angel gone bad.[2] However, the king's blamelessness prior to his sin (Ezek 28:15) might not be an allusion to the cherub's original state of purity but, as many scholars note, to Adam's (Ezek 28:15; 28:13; compare Gen 2).[3] Yet even if we concede the possibility that this passage implies the fall of Satan, how would we determine what verses and words suggest the fall of Satan without becoming arbitrary in our selection? In any case, the text does not clearly indicate anywhere that Satan was once an angel named Lucifer.

Lucifer is the king of Babylon (Is 14). The word *Lucifer* appears in the King James Version. The word in Hebrew is *hêlēl*, coming from the verb "to shine" and meaning "bright one" or "daystar." The word *Lucifer* is the Latin translation of this word. It was introduced into the text of Isaiah 14:12 by the texts of church fathers such as Origen's *Hexapla* and Jerome's Vulgate.

The Vulgate Bible (which was widely used in the Western church from about 600 C.E. also uses the word *Lucifer* for the light of the morning in Job 11:17 and Psalm 109:3 (110:3 MT) and for the zodiac signs in Job 38:32. I am not aware of anyone deriving Satan from Lucifer in those passages!

The context of Isaiah 14 explicitly states that this passage is a "taunt against the king of Babylon" (Is 14:3). The king is metaphorically portrayed as a Babylonian god named *hêlēl*, who attempts to reach the heavens. Instead of becoming like the Most High, however, the king is cast down to the pits as a mere man (compare Nebuchadnezzar's pride and subsequent humiliation by God in Dan 4; also see Obad 4). Isaiah might be utilizing a popular Babylonian myth, but he gives the myth a startling twist. He replaces the fallen-god *hêlēl* motif with the king of Babylon.[4] This technique is like starting with the "Humpty Dumpty" rhyme and then substituting the name of a national leader for Humpty Dumpty.

The king of Babylon, not Satan, is in view because he subdues "the nations" (Is 14:12). It is difficult to see how Satan could subdue entire nations in his original fall when none yet existed. The one who claims to be like the Most High in Isaiah 14:14 is also the one who is brought down to the grave and is twice declared to be a man (14:15-17). Satan may have assumed the form of a serpent, but he was never a man. We should also note that *hêlēl* was cast down to the "pit" (Is 14:15; compare 14:12, 19-20). In the Old Testament the word *pit* frequently denotes a place of burial or a prison (Ps 28:1; 30:3; Is 24:22; 38:18; Jer 37:16; Ezek 31:14; Zech 9:11; compare Rev 9:1). The context in Isaiah 14 likewise demonstrates this usage. If this passage depicts Satan's original fall, how is it that he was brought down to the pit when he is later found accusing Job before God *in heaven* (Job 1—2; compare Zech 3:1-4; Eph 2:2; 6:12)?

As with Ezekiel 28, some might think that while Isaiah 14:12 portrays the king of Babylon, it also alludes to Satan's original fall

as Lucifer.[5] But if we read this passage *without* being precondi-
tioned to think that Satan is Lucifer, we probably would not come
to the conclusion that Isaiah 14 alludes to Satan's original fall.
How then did we arrive at the dogmatic assertion that Satan was
once a good angel named Lucifer?

There is no assertion in the New Testament or in the
apostolic fathers that Satan was once a beautiful angel named
Lucifer. The Jewish traditions do not even make a clear
connection between Satan and Isaiah 14 prior to about 100 C.E.[6]
And as we have already seen, Jewish traditions speculated
freely about angels and demons.

Origen, the third-century church father, seems to be responsible for promulgating the Lucifer-as-Satan theory in the Christian church (Origen *De Principiis* 1.4-5; compare Preface 6;
Hexapla Is 14:12). Many resisted Origen's theory. As late as the
fourth century, for instance, a Christian bishop could still be
called St. Lucifer, and his followers the Luciferians![7] Later church
fathers who popularized the notion that Satan was once a good
angel named Lucifer include Augustine, Peter Lombard and
Thomas Aquinas (for example, Augustine *De Genesi ad literem*
3.10; Peter Lombard *Sentences* 2.6).[8] According to Old Testament
scholar John Oswalt, the early Reformation expositors did not
seem to make a connection between Satan and Lucifer in Isaiah
14:12. In his masterpiece *Paradise Lost* (1667) John Milton connects Satan to the fall of Lucifer (1.80; 5.743). Nowadays the
Satan-as-Lucifer theory has become "gospel truth" without a
single shred of compelling biblical evidence. This is not to deny
that Satan may be a fallen angel, but we need to question our
basis for calling him Lucifer.

Question 42: How Did Satan Fall?

In the absence of compelling evidence identifying Lucifer as
Satan, what do we know about the original fall of Satan? Several
passages of Scripture have been used to describe the fall of
Satan, but on close examination, none clearly refer to his

original fall. Genesis 3 describes a serpent that deceives Adam and Eve (compare Rev 12:9; 20:2; *Apocalypse of Moses* 17.4). The serpent was punished by God, who cursed it to grovel on its belly in the dust and to be set at enmity with humans (Gen 3:14-15). If this passage refers to the original fall of Satan, we are not told why he chose to deceive Eve in the first place; the text presupposes Satan's deceptive character. Nevertheless, biblically speaking, this is about as close as we can get to Satan's original moral failure.

Christ's presence on earth marked the beginning of Satan's defeat. Jesus said, "I saw Satan fall like lightning from heaven" (Lk 10:18) and "now the prince of this world will be driven out" (Jn 12:31; compare 16:10). But these passages do not refer to Satan's original fall. The dragon and his minions are cast down, after fighting against Michael and his angels, at the culmination of Christ's earthly ministry (Rev 12:9-11; compare *Testament of Asher* 7.3; *Odes of Solomon* 22.5; *Testament of Solomon* 14; *2 Apocalypse of Baruch* 29.4; *Psalms of Solomon* 2.25; *Sibylline Oracles* 8.85; *Ladder of Jacob* 12-13).

The dragon stands for the creation chaos monster of ancient Near Eastern literature. Some thus suggest that by applying the principle of *Urzeit wird Endzeit* (primeval time becomes end time) found in apocalyptic literature (for example, allusions to Genesis in Revelation 21—22), Revelation 12 may allude to the original moral fall of Satan. But Revelation 12 is a *positional* fall that already presupposes Satan's wicked character. It does not explain why he originally fell away *morally*.[9]

As the "accuser of the brethren," Satan had access to God's council in heaven and requested permission to test individuals (Job 1—2; Zech 3:1-4; Lk 22:31-32; compare *1 Enoch* 40.7; *Jubilees* 1.20; 48.15-18; *Apocalypse of Zephaniah* 4.2).[10] Revelation 12:10 indicates that he was "fired" from this position when Christ died and rose again.[11] Satan's consignment to the bottomless pit for a thousand years and his later banishment in the lake of fire appear to be different judgments (Rev 20). Thus

Scripture records several "falls" that are better understood as
various judgments against Satan's power:

Judgments on Satan	Scripture
Original moral fall?	Genesis 1—3?
Judgment in the Garden of Eden	Genesis 3
Judgment at the inception of Christ's kingdom of God here on earth—and the beginning of the new era	Luke 10:18; compare 10:17, 19-20; 11:20-22
Judgment through the atoning work of Christ in the new era	John 12:31-32; 16:5-10; Hebrews 2:14-17; Colossians 2:14-15; compare Revelation 12:9-11
Judgment and binding during the last days	Revelation 20:1-4
Final destination in the lake of fire	Revelation 20:10

Since Satan's fall can be viewed in stages, some may think
that his sin was progressive. His role as the heavenly accuser
in the Old Testament may lead us to conclude that he did not
act against the will of God. His turning point would have been
his tempting of Christ in the wilderness (Mt 4). But Jesus states
that the devil was a liar and a murderer "from the beginning"
(Jn 8:44; compare 1 Jn 3:8). The NIV translates the Greek
phrase *ouk estaken* in John 8:44 as "not holding" to the truth.
The imperfect Greek tense here may imply that Satan lived in
a *continual* state of falsehood and murdering. The word *beginning* is associated with Satan's role as a murderer. Since Satan
cannot murder angels (as spirits, they can never die), his role
as a murderer is in relation to humans. The devil is a murderer
because he instigated Adam's fall, which spread death to all
humankind (Heb 2:13-14). As the instigator of wrongful hatred, he caused Cain to slay Abel (1 Jn 3:8, 11-15). Hence John
8:44 affirms that the devil has been sinning since the beginning of Israel's history, but it does not address what happened
before then.[12]
Some claim that 1 Timothy 3:6 implies the original fall of

Satan. The verse states that a bishop must not be a novice, "lest being lifted up with pride he fall into the condemnation of the devil" (KJV). Does this mean that Satan originally fell because of pride and conceit? The "condemnation of the devil" in this verse should not be understood as God's judgment on Satan but the devil's judgment on any bishop who becomes prideful. The devil, who brings "reproach" and a "snare" in 1 Timothy 3:7, is the same one who brings "condemnation" in 1 Timothy 3:6 (compare 2 Tim 2:26; 1 Tim 5:14). The Greek word for condemnation, *krima,* has no definite article in front of it. This suggests that the devil is allowed to bring an unspecified judgment on sinful church leaders. If this verse referred to the fall of Satan, we would expect the Greek article *to* before *krima (to krima): the* judgment God put on the devil.[13]

Since Scripture says little about this issue, we may find a reasonable conjecture regarding the original fall of Satan in the writings of the church fathers. Origen believed the devil fell due to his pride and God created the physical universe to compensate for the sin of the devil and his angels. While not affirming all that Origen taught, the church fathers Athanasius, Basil and Augustine also believed that pride caused Satan's downfall. The Dominican monks, such as Albert the Great and Thomas Aquinas, believed the devil sinned in the first instant of creation due to pride.[14] But it seems unlikely that he fell prior to the sixth day of creation, since everything in God's creation was very good until the sixth day (Gen 1:31). This leaves us with several alternatives regarding the origin of Satan's fall.

1. God created Satan as Satan. We could appeal to the sovereignty of God and claim that he created Satan as Satan for God's own good purposes. This view, of course, opens up another can of worms regarding the goodness of God and the problem of evil (see answer 28). It does not explain why Satan is morally corrupt and judged by God (Lk 10:18; Rev 12). Are God and Satan merely putting on a big show of "good guy versus bad guy" for our sakes? This line of reasoning leads to an apparent contradiction of all we know about the goodness and truthfulness of God.

2. *Satan fell because of pride.* The most popular theory is that Satan fell because of pride. But since this theory is usually based on identifying Satan with Lucifer in Isaiah 14 and Ezekiel 28, it lacks contextual support. Nevertheless, the antichrist—who is the embodiment of all that is evil, hence Satanlike—has the characteristic of pride, boasting of great things and speaking arrogant words against God. He also seeks to obtain self-worship (2 Thess 2:3-4; Rev 13; compare Dan 7:8, 20; 8:10-11).

3. *Satan fell due to envy.* According to certain Jewish traditions, out of envy Satan refused God's request to worship Adam (see answer 28). But why would God have his angels worship Adam when worship is reserved for God alone? An ancient Jewish document, *Life of Adam and Eve* (12–16), attempts to mitigate the problem by claiming it was the image of God *in* Adam that Satan refused to worship.[15]

The veneration of Adam's image aside, if Satan's original fall was somehow connected with envy, the object of his envy might well have been Adam.[16] Satan might have envied an earthly creature made in God's own image, especially when that creature received special attention and privileges denied to Satan (Gen 1:26-30; 2:9-16, 22-25). This line of reasoning fits with God's creating everything "very good" up to the sixth day of creation (Gen 1:31). It suggests that Satan's first judgment was the curse that God pronounced on him as the serpent in Genesis 3:14-15 (see answer 44). His actual first sin would have been harboring envy in his heart and planning to deceive the primal human couple.

Of course, Satan's first sin could have been a combination of envy and pride (or almost anything else for that matter). If Satan's fall took place in the Garden of Eden, pride might be connected with the idea of envying because there seems to be a prideful aspect about the serpent in the garden (see answer 44).

4. *How Satan fell remains a mystery.* Maybe we should swallow our pride and admit that Satan's fall remains a mystery (Deut 29:29). We should avoid trying to force biblical passages to answer questions that they perhaps never intended to answer.

Question 43: Why Did God Allow Satan to Fall If He Foreknew the Evil and Suffering That Would Follow?

If Satan did fall at the beginning of creation, why did God allow him to fall? A God who knows the future must have known that creating angels with the freedom to rebel could eventually bring chaos, suffering and evil into his creation. So why did he allow it all to happen by creating an angel he foreknew would rebel against him? Related to this question is the whole problem of evil. If God was a good God, why does he allow evil to persist in his creation?

But what are we really saying here? Would we want God to create a world without according free will to his subjects? What glory would God receive if angels and all humans were pre-programmed to worship him? What genuine love relationship could God share with his creatures if they were forced to love him? Both angels and humans can choose what is evil instead of what is good, yet having freedom of choice itself *is* a good thing. There could be no love for God and no godly character development without the real potential to choose against God.

I believe God did foreknow the evil that would arise out of giving Satan free will. Apparently God thought it a greater good to share a mutual love relationship with some of his creatures than to have all his creatures love and worship him involuntarily. We ourselves make similar decisions when we choose to marry, raise children, become friends, and so on, even though we know the potential pain and suffering these actions may cause us. If a woman falls in love with an older man, will she choose against marrying him because he will die years before she does? If she loves him, she will probably marry him, even though she knows that she will experience great suffering when he dies. Why? Because she judges that the love they share is worth possible future suffering.[17] This analogy perhaps explains why God created Satan, angels and humans as free moral agents. Jim Stafford Wright writes:

> If you are a parent, would you choose to have a ventriloquist's doll, or a child who may break your heart? The question why God created beings who would ultimately fall may well be a foolish question, if it means that we are demanding that God would do two contradictory things at the same time: namely, create free beings who are not free.[18]

Question 44: Was Satan Literally the Serpent in the Garden of Eden?

We all know the story of the Fall. The serpent, the most crafty animal in the Garden of Eden, tempted Eve to eat the fruit of the tree of the knowledge of good and evil, bringing sin on the human race. Although the Old Testament never states that the serpent was Satan, in the New Testament John calls the dragon "that ancient serpent called the devil or Satan" (Rev 12:9; 20:2). After Adam and Eve sinned by eating the forbidden fruit, God pronounced curses on Adam, Eve and the serpent. Beginning with the serpent, God declares, "Cursed are you above all the livestock and all the wild animals! You will crawl on your belly and you will eat dust all the days of your life" (Gen 3:14). He goes on to set future enmity between the serpent and humans.

Was Satan literally a snake? Are all snakes descendants of Satan? Does this mean that Satan has offspring? Although Genesis 3 describes the primitive characteristics of an actual snake, this particular snake had some unique features. It was able to talk, and it was cognizant of the consequences that eating the fruit of the tree would entail (Gen 3:5). Clearly snakes are not the present-day offspring of Satan, nor was Satan literally a snake.

Snakes are associated with the creation of the world in many religious traditions. Such stories are found around the world, including the Middle East, India, Africa, South America, the South Pacific and so on.[19] Various mythologies include a world tree that is the key to the center of the universe and provides a pillar to reach the heavens. A serpent symbolizing evil is sometimes found at the bottom of the tree, while an eagle perches on the top.[20] Serpents are often villains in these myths. Hydra and Typho would be two such characters in classical mythology. In the Babylonian Gilgamesh Epic the hero Gilgamesh finds a plant that gives eternal life. But a snake swimming in a pond swallows it.

If we take the account of Adam and Eve as a historical event, as did the New Testament writers (Mt 19:4-6; Jn 8:44; compare Heb 2:14; Rom 5:12-19; 1 Cor 15:20-26, 45-56), we can suggest that these world myths point to the reality of a very ancient event described in Genesis 3. To rule out the historical value of Genesis 3 is to rule out the New Testament explanation for sin and death. So we had better think twice before throwing away the account of the serpent in the Garden as mere fiction!

Assuming that the serpent/Satan in the Garden of Eden was real, how can we explain Satan's assuming the guise of a serpent? There are three possible explanations: (1) Satan disguised himself as a serpent; (2) Satan possessed the body of a real serpent; (3) by means of ventriloquism or thought suggestion, Satan tricked Adam and Eve into believing that a serpent was communicating with them. Ancient Jewish tradition describes Satan as a master of disguises.[21] In some sense the devil "covered himself" with the serpent (compare 3 *Apocalypse of Baruch* 9.7). Paul claims that Satan masquerades as an angel of light (2 Cor 11:14).

Why then does God curse the snake itself, making it travel on its belly and eat dust, if it is only an instrument used by

Satan? Why does God curse the serpent for something Satan is responsible for? One explanation is that an object used for sinful purposes was often destroyed or cursed. If a human had sex with an animal, for instance, both the human and animal were to be killed (Lev 20:15; compare Ex 21:28; Heb 12:20).[22] Another explanation some suggest is that the snake once stood upright. Jewish tradition claims the snake once had legs (Josephus *Antiquities of the Jews* 1.1.50; *Genesis Rabbah* 20.5). This might imply that the serpent lost its original genetic makeup in the Fall. The snake's lowly status became an object lesson for all time. A third explanation is this: if the serpent had always traveled on its belly, then the curse applied to Satan himself, symbolically predicting his ultimate subjugation by attributing to him the lowly qualities that snakes have always had.

Alternatively, the curse may apply to both Satan and the serpent. Some might infer from Genesis 3:1 that the "craftiness" of the serpent "above all the beasts of the field" implies the stately nature and high status the serpent had before it groveled in the dust. Thus Satan chose this creature as his instrument because he believed the serpent's original qualities complemented his own character![23] But contrary to the devil's assumed high status, God placed him in a humiliating and subjugated position of lowliness, depicted by the snake's crawling on his belly and eating dust after the Fall (Gen 3:14-15; compare Ps 72:9; Is 49:23; Mic 7:17). God may be saying to Satan, "You wanted to impersonate a snake? So be it! I will now change the character of the proud snake to a lowly animal, so that you yourself will eventually be considered a lowly, subjugated creature, and the descendants of Eve will crush your head!"

Question 45: Why Is Satan Called a Leviathan Dragon?

The myth of sea serpents or dragons seems as old as humanity itself. Why is Satan called a dragon? We must first distinguish between Satan as a person and the dragon as a symbol that represents Satan. The seven heads of the dragon in Revelation 12 allude to a leviathan dragon. In the ancient Near East the leviathan ("twisting one") dragon was the personification of chaos. An Ugaritic text calls him "Lotan," or "Litan": "Because you [Baal] smote *Ltn* the twisting serpent, [and] made an end of the crooked serpent, the tyrant with seven heads, the skies will become hot [and] will shine."[24] Leviathan is sometimes called Rahab (Hebrew for "boisterous one"; compare Ps 89:10; Job 3:8; 26:13; Is 27:1). But the Leviathan does not always appear to be a chaotic sea/cloud monster in creation stories. In Job 40—41 God refers to Leviathan as an animal without any necessarily evil connotations (Ps 104:26; compare *tannîn,* "sea monster," Gen 1:21).[25] In other places Leviathan seems to represent Egypt or another world power (Ps 87:4; Is 30:7; 51:9-10; possibly Ps 74:14; compare Ezek 29:3-5; 32:2-10). These passages show that Old Testament writers did not normally think that Leviathan was literally Satan.

The leviathan dragon was sometimes used as a symbol for Satan (Rev 12:3; compare Is 27:1). Perhaps the Jews eventually connected the snake in the Garden of Eden with the ancient Near Eastern notion of Leviathan because both were animals in creation narratives.[26] God defeats the leviathan monster at the beginning of creation, perhaps symbolizing God's power over the threatening forces of nature (Ps 74:14; 89:10: Job 3:8; 9:13; 26:12). Similarly, the defeat of the leviathan dragon in Revelation 12 emphasizes Christ's power over Satan, the most threatening force of all. God has dominion over everything connected with Leviathan, whether Satan, the fearsome natural forces, worldly powers or a serpentlike creature (Ps 29, 65, 74, 93).

Question 46: What Are the Devil's Titles?

The devil has many titles in Scripture. As we have already noted, he is called the "dragon" and the "serpent," and he is

associated with the terms *leviathan* and *rahab*. Other designations include Belial, Beelzebul and Azazel. Below are common
designations for Satan.

1. *Satan as the adversary*. The most popular name for the
devil is Satan, a Hebrew term meaning accuser or adversary.
It can apply to humans as well as celestial beings (Num 22:22,
32; 1 Sam 29:4; 2 Sam 9:23; 1 Kings 5:18; Ps 38:21; 71:13; 109:6;
1 Enoch 40:7). This word draws our attention to the devil's Old
Testament role as the accuser of the brethren (Job 1—2; Zech
13:1-4; 1 Chron 21:1; compare *Testament of Job* 3.6; 6-8; 1QH4.6;
45.32).[27] The word *śaṭān* emphasizes accuser but can also
mean slanderer, depending on the context.[28]

According to Jewish tradition he was called "Satanael" before
he fell (*3 Apocalypse of Baruch* 4.8; *2 Enoch* 18; 29; 31). The
Hebrew word *'ēl* at the end of his name means God, implying
his cooperative relationship with the Almighty. After he fell, he
lost the privilege of bearing the *'ēl* at the end of his name and
became "Satan" (compare *3 Apocalypse of Baruch* 4.7-9).[29]

In the New Testament the name Satan is used in contexts
that emphasize the devil's role as schemer, tempter and
seducer (Acts 5:3; 1 Cor 7:5; 2 Cor 2:11; 1 Tim 5:15). He
seduced Judas into betraying Christ, so much so that "Satan
entered Judas" (Lk 22:3; compare Jn 13:27). Paul refers to
Satan as one who brings judgment on apostates (1 Cor 5:5; 1
Tim 1:20). Scripture also calls the devil "Satan" in passages that
refer to Christ's authority over him (Mt 4:10; Lk 10:18; Acts
26:17; compare Rev 12:9; 20:2). Paul claims that God will crush
Satan under the saints' feet (Rom 16:20).

2. *Satan as the devil*. The word *devil* comes from the Greek
word *diabolos*, which may have come from the word *diaballō*,
"to separate." Hence, it is possible that the word *diabolos*
implies the idea of one who separates God and humans.[30] The
term *devil* is used in the sense of calumniator or slanderer. The
word *devil* emphasizes his role as prosecutor in the Septuagint,
the Greek version of the Old Testament (Job 1—2; Zech 3:1-2

LXX; compare *Testament of Job* 3.3).

New Testament writers use the word *devil* in contexts where he is seen as an incarcerator who captures or imprisons his victims (Acts 10:38; Eph 4:27; 2 Tim 2:26; Rev 2:10). He is also a fierce destroyer who leads men to discord and violence (1 Pet 5:8; Lk 8:12; Jn 8:44; 1 Jn 3:8, 12; compare *Testament of Gad* 4.7; *Testament of Benjamin* 7.1). During early persecutions by Rome (70-200 C.E.), the apostolic church fathers used the term *devil* far more frequently than the word *Satan*. It appears thirty-two times in standard second-century church literature.[31] The term also highlights the motifs of temptation, sin and death (Mt 4:1; Acts 13:10; Heb 2:14;1 Jn 3:8; Wisdom of Solomon 2.24; *2 Enoch* 11.74; *Testament of Reuben* 4.7; *Testament of Joseph* 7.4).

3. *Satan as the evil one.* Referring to the devil as "the evil one" focuses on his wicked character as the father of all evil. John the apostle often uses this title in his writings. The Lord's Prayer refers to the devil as the evil one (Mt 6:13). When Jesus interceded for the church, he prayed that God the Father would protect his followers from the evil one (Jn 17:15; compare 2 Thess 3:3). The evil one is said to be in charge of the fallen world (1 Jn 5:19). He snatches the word of God from people's hearts (Mt 13:19). Cain, who slew his brother Abel, belonged to the evil one (1 Jn 3:12). The Christians' shield of faith quenches the flaming arrows that the evil one throws their way (Eph 6:16). John writes that those who are strong and have the word of God living in them have overcome the evil one (1 Jn 2:13-14; compare 4:4; 5:18).

4. *Satan as the prince of this world.* Satan is called the prince of this fallen world, or the "god of this world" (2 Cor 4:4; Jn 12:31; 14:30; Eph 2:2; compare *Martyrdom and Ascension of Isaiah* 10.11-12; Ignatius *Letter ot the Ephesians* 17.1; 19.1; *Letter to the Magnesians* 1.2; *Letter to the Philadelphians* 6.2). This title emphasizes his authority over the fallen world system (Lk 4:5-7; 1 Jn 5:19; compare *3 Enoch* 30; 26.12). Why would Paul,

who believed in the existence of one God (Gal 4:8), designate Satan as "the god of this world"? G. Vos writes:

The point of this bold comparison seems to lie in this, that as the true God by His Spirit illumines the minds of believers, enabling them to behold the glory of Christ in the Gospel, so the false god of the present age has a counter-spirit at work (or is a counter-spirit) which blinds the mind of the unbelieving that the light of the glory of Christ should not dawn upon them.[32]

5. *Other titles for Satan.* Satan has many titles that focus on a particular attribute of his character or work. They include the "strong man" whom Jesus bound when he established the kingdom of God on earth (Lk 11:21); the "tempter" (Mt 4:3; 1 Thess 3:5; *Barnabas* 2.10; 21.3); the "enemy" or "adversary" proper (Mt 13:25; 1 Pet 5:8; compare *Testament of Job* 47.10), the "murderer," "father of lies" (Jn 8:44) and possibly the "king of terror" (Job 18:14).

Jewish literature includes even more designations for Satan. In Tobit, for instance, Satan is sometimes associated with the destroying demon called Asmodeus (Tobit 3.8). In the Dead Sea Scrolls he may be identified as the prince or angel of darkness (1QS 3.20-24). In other Jewish traditions he may be associated with the spirit "Mastema," meaning hatred or enmity (*Jubilees* 10.8; 11.5; 17.16; 19.28; compare 1QM 13.4; Hos 9:7-8).

Question 47: Did the Biblical Concept of Satan Come from Zoroastrianism?

The Jews went into captivity when the Babylonians destroyed Jerusalem about 587 B.C.E. The Babylonians were later conquered by the Persians (2 Chron 36; Dan 1—6). We read about the Jews under Persian rule in the books of Esther, Nehemiah and Ezra. Since the only three references to Satan in the Old Testament were written around the time of the Persian dominion over Israel (Job 1—2; 1 Chron 21:1; Zech 3:1), some claim that the Jewish idea of the devil came from the Persian religion of Zoroastrianism. In the Zend-Avesta (the Zoroastrian scriptures) Angra Mainyu, or Ahriman, the evil spirit, opposes the good god, Ahura Mazda.

The role of the Persian devil is similar to the role of the prince of darkness in the Dead Sea Scrolls (1QS 3.11–4.26).[33] In the Apocrypha the name *Asmodeus,* coined for the devil that pursues Tobit, might be identified with term *Aesma Daeva,* or *evil demon,* found in Persian literature. Like Satan, the Persian devil is the father of lies who brings death into the world, leads demonic forces and afflicts with disease. He will be conquered by the good forces in the last days.[34]

Significant differences exist, however, between the Jewish and Persian devils. First, Satan is subordinate to God (Job 1–2). We find no equally powerful or equally eternal forces of good and evil (dualism) in the Old Testament, as we do in Persian literature. Second, Satan's primary role as a courtroom accuser is unique to the Old Testament. Third, the book of Job may have been written around 700 B.C.E., preceding both the Babylonian and the Persian exiles.[35] The oral tradition of Job could also have been circulating much earlier than that. Thus in Job 1–2 we see Satan as an accuser figure that could antedate any Persian influence.

Nevertheless, angels play a more prominent role in Jewish literature after the Babylonian captivity. This emphasis on angels may have been influenced by Persian literature. The Persian captivity seemed to sharpen the Jewish perception of good versus evil; we find this influence in some postexilic Jewish literature, such as the Dead Sea Scrolls. Moreover, the harm the Jews experienced at the hands of their captors may have demonstrated to them that evil and spiritual wickedness were all too real. Thus we see that although the Jewish idea of Satan may have been influenced by the Persian religion of Zoroastrianism, it did not originate there.[36]

Question 48: Was the Biblical Idea of Satan as Belial Influenced by the Dead Sea Scrolls?

The apostle Paul contrasts Christ and Belial (2 Cor 6:14-15): "For what do righteousness and wickedness have in common? Or what fellowship can light have with darkness? What harmony is there between Christ and Belial?" Rebellious and impious Israelites were sometimes called "sons of Belial" (Judg 19:22 KJV; 1 Sam 2:12; 2 Sam 22:5; 1 Kings 21:10-13; compare Nahum 1:15). Scholars have attributed various meanings to the Hebrew word *belial,* including yokeless or lawless, worthless, unsuccessful and "the local hell raisers"! The sons of Belial often have a part in causing chaos in their communities (Judg 19:22; 20:13; 1 Sam 2:12; 10:27; 2 Sam 20:1). The sons of Belial lead Israel astray by influencing them to worship other gods (Deut 13:13).[37]

But the sons of Belial are always human. Paul is the only one who connects Satan with Belial. He seems to have derived this connection from Jewish literature—possibly the Dead Sea Scrolls, which frequently recognize Belial as the leader of demons (1QS 1.9-11; 3.24; 4.18; 1QM 13.11; 1QH 4.29; compare Pseudepigrapha Martyrdom of Isaiah 1-5). In the War Scroll Belial heads the army of the sons of darkness against the sons of light. He raised up Jannes and Jambres, the Egyptian magicians who opposed Moses (CD 5.18; compare Ex 7:11). But his forces will be wiped out by God in the last days (1QM 1.4-16; 18.1-3).

We can see how Jewish literature associated Satan with the term *Belial,* given the infamous character of the sons of Belial in the Old Testament. Since first-century Jews understood Belial as another name for Satan, Paul apparently adopts this usage. When he uses Belial for Satan, he stresses the contrast between light and darkness (2 Cor 6:14), as did the Dead Sea Scrolls.[38]

Question 49: What Is the Connection Between Satan and Azazel, the Scapegoat?

Each year on the Day of Atonement, before the feast of

tabernacles, the high priest presented two goats before the Lord at the entrance of the tabernacle. He cast lots to determine which goat would be presented before the Lord and which one would be the scapegoat. The high priest then sacrificed as a sin offering the goat that was presented before the Lord, but the scapegoat (Hebrew *ʿăzāʾzel*) performed a different function. The high priest laid his hands on the head of the scapegoat while he confessed all the sins of Israel. This goat was then led into the desert (Lev 16:6-22). The goat that was slain represented the covering or atonement for the sins of the people, while the scapegoat represented the removal of sin from the community.

What is the meaning behind the word Azazel? Scholars claim it could mean rugged cliff, destruction, entire removal or angry god.[39] Is Azazel Satan? Jewish literature portrays Azazel as the chief of demons who dwells on the earth, having been banished to the desert (*1 Enoch* 8.1; 10.4; *Apocalypse of Abraham* 13.17—14.6). He is considered the leader of the fallen angels who headed the rebellion of the Watchers in Genesis 6 (1 En. 6; 10.4; Apoc. Abrah. 13.16; 14.4-6).

In the Bible, demons (sometimes portrayed as *śeʿîrîm*, or he-goats, Lev 17:7) were said to inhabit the desert, as did the Azazel goat (Is 13:21; 34:14; Mt 12:43; Rev 18:2; compare Tobit 8.3). If Satan plays the role of a court accuser in the Old Testament (Job 1—2), we have some difficulty accepting that the early Hebrews associated Satan with the banishment of Azazel. The two goats in Leviticus 16:8 might be understood as types of Christ and Satan.[40] Christ (the first goat) was sacrificed for the sins of the entire community, while Satan (the azazel goat) was banished from God's presence (the tabernacle and the desert).

Question 50: What Does the Word *Beelzebub* Mean?

Irritated at the irrefutable evidence of Christ's power to cast out demons, the religious leaders who opposed him claimed, "It is only by Beelzebub, the prince of demons, that this fellow drives out demons" (Mt 12:24). How did Satan get this name?

The Vulgate, the Latin version of the New Testament, apparently equates Beelzebub with the Philistine god of Ekron, "Baalzebub" (1 Kings 1:2-3, 6, 16; compare Josephus *Antiquities of the Jews* 19.9). *Baal* means lord in Hebrew, and *zebub* refers to a fly. Hence, Baalzebub meant "lord of the flies." The Philistines believed that this god averted swarms of harmful insects. The Greek word in Matthew, however, is *beelzeboul,* not Beelzebub. The Canaanite Ras Shamra texts use this word to mean "Lord of the high place." Jewish literature often portrayed Satan as the evil one who made his dwelling in the "high places," or the air (*Targum of Job* 28.7; compare Eph 2:2; 6:12). Beelzebul came to be understood as a defecator, or "lord of the dung." Thus *Beelzebul* was a title of opprobrium used by the rabbis to belittle Satan.[41] According to the *Testament of Solomon* (6.2), Beelzeboul was the only demon that survived of the fallen angels that were cast into Tartarus (2 Pet 2:4). So we are left with several possible explanations for the word *Beelzebub.* What is important to remember is that Jesus equates Beelzebub with Satan (Mt 12:25-27; Mk 3:22; Lk 11:15).

Question 51: Does Satan Know Our Thoughts?

There is no biblical evidence that Satan can read our thoughts. Only God is all-knowing (Is 46:9-10; Dan 2:27-28; compare Eph 3:10). He alone knows "the hearts of all men" (1 Kings 8:39). Augustine believed that their quick mobility and their numerous years of experience gave the demons knowledge surpassing that of humans so that they are able to make guesses on thoughts (*De divinatione daemonum.* 3.7; 5.9). Hence, Satan can "read" humans in a limited sense. He can observe human reactions to certain events, people and so forth, and thus can orchestrate scenarios that seem to show awareness of their thoughts.

Here is an example of how this could be done. A demon that observed me reading an article on 1960s fashions last night could speak through a psychic the next day to "reveal" to me that I am intrigued by 1960s fashions, and be correct. This would involve observation and educated guessing by a being of high intelligence, not reading my mind. Demons may also be able to plant or suggest thoughts into our minds. Perhaps the best counter to this is to fill our minds with thoughts that honor God (Phil 4:6-8).

Question 52: How Powerful Is Satan?

Satan has limited power. He is the prince of demons and of the fallen world system (Mt 4:8-9; 2 Cor 4:4; Eph 2:2). With the world at his disposal, he is able to persecute God's people. He afflicted Job by instigating the Sabeans and the Chaldeans to steal Job's possessions and kill his servants (Job 1:12, 15, 17), and he used natural catastrophes (such as fire and strong wind) to destroy Job's sheep, shepherds and children (Job 1:16, 18-19).[42] Then he afflicted Job's body with a horrible disease (Job 2:7-8).

Satan is no match for God, however (Rom 16:20; Rev 12, 20). He had to get God's permission to test Job (Job 1—2), and he asked for God's permission to attack Peter (Lk 22:31-32). His attacks reveal the limits of his power. He was not allowed to take Job's life (Job 2:6), and Jesus' intercession protected Peter. Graham Twelftree writes concerning Lk 22:31-32, "Satan is limited in contrast to the authority of Jesus' prayer for his followers. Satan is able to 'shake in a sieve' *(siniazō)* but not totally destroy Peter and the disciples."[43] Although Satan has control of the world system, God protects the believer from him (1 Jn 5:18-19). Christians are assured that the God who is in them is greater than the devil who is in the world (compare 1 Jn 4:4; Rev 12:11).

Although the devil is permitted a limited amount of power, he has been a defeated foe ever since Jesus overpowered him and established the kingdom of God (Lk 11:17-22; compare 10:18; Acts 10:38; 26:18; Heb 2:14; 1 Jn 3:8). Satan has been in retreat ever since. The tide of battle in World War II started to turn after the formation of the Allied forces in 1942. However, the final defeat of the Axis powers did not occur until 1945. Similarly, when Christ began his ministry, Satan and his minions went into retreat. Their final defeat will occur when Christ returns.

Question 53: Does Satan Live in Hell?

A popular misconception is that the devil lives in hell, making his abode somewhere in the earth's fiery core. But the Bible calls Satan the prince of the power of the air *(aeros)*, and his minions rule in the heavenly regions (Eph 2:2; 6:12). For the biblical writers, the air is apparently the region existing between heaven (the throne of God) and earth, and this is where Satan and his angels dwell.[44] Azazel, the chief of demons, lives in the ethereal regions of the earth, according to Jewish sources (*Apocalypse of Abraham* 13.7-14; *1 Enoch* 10; *Jubilees* 10.1; *Targum of Job* 28.7). This area appears to include the region of darkness (Philo *On Creation* 7). Satan's domain is the "first heaven," the atmosphere and clouds (*2 Enoch* 3). The limits of his territory are unknown, but rest assured, wherever humans boldly go on their journeys into outer space, they will find Satan there.

Satan is in the very courts of God in Job 1—2. If God cannot stand the presence of sin, how is it that Satan has access to heaven? Apparently God tolerated Satan's presence prior to Christ's death on the cross (Acts 17:30; 14:16; Lk 22:31-32). But once Christ's atonement was accomplished, the devil was judged and permanently cast out of the highest heaven (Rev 12:9; Jn 12:31; 16:30). In the church era we no longer see Satan accusing the brethren in the very presence of God.

Question 54: Why Is the Devil Portrayed with Red Skin, Horns and a Pitchfork?

In many cartoons the devil is a red, hooked-nosed, half-man, half-goat creature with a tail, horns and a pitchfork. The Bible never ascribes any specific appearance to him. So where does the cartoonish image of Satan come from? We can trace half-human, half-animal monster images back to ancient times. Such creatures are found depicted in art from the ancient Near East and Greece.[45] The devil's popular image resembles Pan, the Greek god of hunters and leader of the satyrs.[46] One of the names for demons is *śeʿîrîm*, which is sometimes translated "satyrs" (2 Chron 11:15 KJV; see answer 27). Medieval plays would sometimes portray him as a satyr.[47] This image gradually became standardized.

The dragon in Revelation 12 is red and has horns, but it is difficult to determine whether later artists derived their images of the devil from Revelation. The dragon has seven heads, but Satan is usually pictured with one. Older pictures color Satan black, emphasizing his character as the prince of darkness. The church council of Toledo (447) describes Satan as "a large, black, monstrous apparition with horns on his head, cloven hooves, ass's ears, claws, fiery eyes, gnashing teeth, huge phallus, and sulphurous smell."[48] Red then became the devil's predominant color, highlighting medieval misconceptions that he lived in the fiery underworld and that red-haired people were evil. This color may also have pointed to his role as a bloody murderer. He wields a trident or pitchfork to torture his victims in hell.[49]

Like any monster picture, the devil's image is ugly and distorted. In older art Satan often appears as an impish half-man/half-animal, sometimes with wings. He is misshapen and grotesque because he fell from heaven and also because these features represent his sinful inner defects. J. B. Russell suggests, "The symbolism was intended to show the devil as deprived of beauty, harmony, reality, and structure, shifting his shapes chaotically, and as a twisted, ugly distortion of what angelic or even human nature ought to be."[50]

Question 55: Why Doesn't Satan Repent?

Some may think that if pride caused the devil to fall in the first place, pride may be what prevents him from repenting. Biblically speaking, however, we do not know for a fact that pride caused his downfall (compare answers 41-42). Satan obviously knows the Bible and knows that it predicts his ultimate doom. If he is aware of his future destiny (Mt 8:29; Mk 1:23), why doesn't he swallow his pride and repent? Maybe unbelief is a better explanation than pride. Like many humans who know the Bible but refuse to repent of their wicked ways, Satan may not believe it really predicts his fate; he might think he can outsmart God's future plans. But this is all speculation.

A better explanation comes from Scripture. We read that "it is not angels he [Christ] helps, but Abraham's descendants" (Heb 2:16). This passage implies that angels have no provision for forgiveness. Thus the devil and his angels have no provision: Christ took on the nature of a human and died for humans, not angels. Colossians 1:20 states that God has reconciled "all things, whether things on earth or things in heaven, by making peace through his [Christ's] blood, shed on the cross." But this reconciliation does not mean that Satan and his minions will repent. It refers to the future result of Christ's death, reconciling heaven and earth to their proper order prior to the fall of humankind (Rom 8:19-23; 1 Cor 15:24-28; Eph 1:10).[51] When Christ returns and restores harmony to all the universe, that harmony will include Satan's judgment (Rev 20). Satan and his angels will be forced to submit whether they like it or not (Phil 2:10-11; compare *Ascension of Isaiah* 11.23)!

Why didn't God provide an atonement for Satan and his angels? The church fathers present differing views. Origen claimed that Satan and the demons would eventually repent (*Principiis* 1.6.3) because God is a loving, merciful God. Cyril of Jerusalem (c. 315-86) claimed that certain fallen angels did in fact repent (*Catechesis* 2.10).[52] Other church fathers, however, contested this view.[53] Anselm of Canterbury (1033-1109) suggested that fallen angels are no longer God's elect. When the angels fell, a gap in the heavenly abode needed to be restored. To restore cosmic order, God elected a corresponding number of humans to replace the fallen angels (*Cur Deus Homo* 1.16-18).

In my opinion sixth-century Primasius of Hadrumetum was on the right track when he suggested three reasons for Satan's lack of repentance: (1) humans are tempted by the devil, but the devil is tempted by no one, yet he still sinned; (2) humans yield to their natural fleshly appetites when they sin, but the devil sinned as a spirit, so this was inexcusable; (3) humans had not reached the presence of God as did Satan; once again, this was inexcusable.[54] William Gouge, a nineteenth-century biblical scholar, adds that demonic sin is more heinous than human sin because the former sinned with more light of understanding than did humans. Satan also tempted the first couple to sin, introducing death and sin to all succeeding generations. Above all this, he still tempts humans to this very day (compare Augustine *De correptione et gratia* 10.27; Gregory the Great *Moralia* 4.3.8).[55]

Thus no forgiveness is possible for angels, because the fallen angels have apparently committed unpardonable sins. This may be something similar to humans blaspheming the Holy Spirit (Mt 12:32; Mk 3:29). The one who has more understanding about the ways of God is more culpable for what he or she knows (Mk 12:38-40; Jas 3:1). To sin boldly in the face of God, after fully knowing and experiencing God, may constitute a reprobate conscience that cannot, or simply will not, repent (Heb 6:4-6; Rom 1:28; 1 Tim 4:2). In any case, if prophecy is true, we know from Scripture that Satan and his minions will not repent, for their ultimate destiny is in the lake of fire (Mt 25:46; Rev 20:10-15).

Question 56: Did Satan Cooperate with God in Having Christ Crucified?

God's plan included the crucifixion of his Son, Jesus Christ (Acts 2:23; 3:18; Rev 13:8). So why did Satan influence Judas to betray Christ to be crucified (Lk 22:3-5; Jn 13:2)? Doesn't this mean that Satan cooperated with God in crucifying Christ?

God is able to change a negative situation into a positive one. He can bring good results out of the most evil intentions of humans or Satan (Job 1—2; 42; Prov 16:9; 19:21; Rom 8:28; 2 Cor 12:7-10). Although Joseph's brothers sold him into slavery, God turned the situation around so that Joseph saved many lives when a famine struck Egypt and surrounding areas. After he was reconciled with his brothers, he said, "You intended to harm me, but God intended it for good to accomplish what is now being done, the saving of many lives" (Gen 50:20).

Even though Satan, out of his wicked intentions to destroy Jesus, influenced Judas to betray Christ, God sovereignly carried out his divine plan through the entire situation to save many lives. We may assume that as a finite creature limited in his knowledge, Satan did not fully comprehend the significance of the atoning work Christ accomplished on the cross. If he had known, he would have done his best to try to *prevent* Christ's crucifixion (1 Cor 2:6-8; Eph 3:10; 1 Pet 1:10-12).

Question 57: Why Did Satan Influence Peter to Discourage Christ from Being Crucified If He Later Influenced Judas to Betray Him?

In Matthew 16:21-23, after Jesus tells his disciples that he must die on the cross, Peter forbids him to do so. Jesus responds, "'Get behind me, Satan! You are a stumbling block to me; you do not have in mind the things of God, but the things of men." Yet in Lk 22:3-5 we read that "Satan entered Judas" to betray Christ, who was then crucified (compare Jn

13:2). Is this a contradiction?

Matthew 16 never claims that Satan actually influenced Peter. Jesus calls Peter "Satan" because Peter regarded human values above the intentions of God (Mt 16:23). Werner Foerster asserts, "Thus what is human is so much opposed to God that it can be called satanic, and this because it is set against the way of God for the salvation of men."[56] We should not assume that Satan literally influenced Peter to say what he said. Jesus did not rebuke Peter because Satan possessed or influenced him; rather, he rebuked Peter because, just like Satan, Peter was talking in a way that opposed the plan of God.

Even if we assume that Satan really did influence Peter's thoughts to discourage Christ from the cross, this would not necessarily contradict his later instigation of Judas. We must remember that Satan did not fully comprehend the significance of the cross. Throughout Christ's ministry, the devil may not have had either Christ's crucifixion or the prevention of his crucifixion as his consistently primary goal. As the wilderness temptation amply demonstrates, Satan wanted to get Christ to sin any way he could in order to break his fellowship with God (Mt 4). In Matthew 16 Satan may have tried to persuade Jesus to sin through feeling self-pity or a sense of injustice, that the Father was somehow unfair to Christ by sending him to the cross.

Question 58: Did Jesus Confront Satan Between His Death and His Resurrection?

People often ask what happened to Christ's spirit during the three days between his death and resurrection. Some faith preachers speculate wildly that Christ burned in the flames of hell to become born again! So what did Christ experience between the cross and the resurrection? Some claim that Ephesians 4:8, Colossians 2:15 and 1 Peter 3:19 describe what happened during this intermediate state.

1. Ephesians 4:8: He led captivity captive. Ephesians 4:8 states:

"When he [Christ] ascended up on high, he led captivity captive, and gave gifts unto men" (KJV). Some may claim that this passage refers to Christ's spirit as overcoming the forces of darkness (the "captivity") when he died and went to heaven prior to his resurrection (compare Lk 23:43, 46). If this interpretation is correct, a spiritual confrontation may have taken place—but it happened in the heavenly regions, not in hell. When Jesus died, he did not go to a spatial location, wrongly described as hell, existing deep down under the earth.[57] As noted earlier, Satan and his minions do not live in the center of the earth. Ephesians describes them as living in the air (Eph 2:2; 6:11-12).

On the other hand, Ephesians 4:8 more likely refers to Christ's bodily ascension into heaven *after* he was resurrected (Acts 1:9-11). Not many days after his ascension he distributed the Holy Spirit (Acts 2) and "gave [spiritual] gifts to men" (Eph 4:8; compare 4:7, 11-12). This interpretation may suggest that "captivity" is simply a general way of declaring Christ's victory over enemy forces achieved through his death, resurrection and ascension. A third perspective is that the phrase *he ascended* refers to Christ's postresurrection exaltation with no particular time frame in mind (Eph 1:20-22).

2. Colossians 2:15: He made a public spectacle of the principalities. Colossians 2:15 claims that when Christ "disarmed the powers and authorities, he made a public spectacle of them, triumphing over them by the cross." When did Christ make a "public spectacle" of the forces of darkness, disarming their power? Some claim this happened after he died but before he rose again. Christ unarmed Satan by snatching away his power over death (Heb 2:14; Rev 1:17; compare Rev 12:9-11). Christ indeed triumphed over various powers,[58] but Colossians 2:14-15 only indicates that this was a *result* of Christ's death on the cross. This passage does not necessarily claim that a *literal* confrontation between Christ and Satan took place between his death and resurrection.

3. 1 Peter 3:19: He preached to the spirits in prison. Another puzzling Scripture speaks of Christ preaching to "the spirits in prison" after he died (1 Pet 3:18-19; compare "seen of angels" in 1 Tim 3:16). Some believe that this passage pictures what happened to Christ between his death and resurrection: he proclaimed to the spirits who are now bound in Tartarus their coming condemnation and his power over death (2 Pet 2:4; 2 Cor 2:14; Col 2:15; Rev 12:7-11; Is 61:1 LXX; Jon 3:2-4).[59] Many early church fathers also believed that Christ confronted these demons in between his death and resurrection.[60]

Biblical scholar J. Ramsey Michaels, however, suggests another alternative.[61] In 1 Peter 3:18, "he was put to death in the body" contrasts "but made alive by the Spirit." This suggests Christ's death and bodily resurrection (compare Rom 1:3-4; 1 Tim 3:16; 1 Pet 3:22). The Greek word for "made alive" *(zōopoieō)* often refers to the resurrection of the body (Jn 5:21; Rom 4:1; 8:11; 1 Cor 15:22). It was *after* Christ's resurrection, not between his death and resurrection, that he confronted the demons, announcing that they must now submit to his authority even in their places of refuge:[62] "The point is simply that Christ went and announced his sovereignty to these spirits *wherever they might be,* in every place they thought they were secure against their ancient divine Enemy [God]."[63]

Did Jesus literally confront Satan between his death and resurrection? None of us knows for sure. The Scriptures cited to support this confrontation are not conclusive. Christ probably did proclaim judgment on Satan and his demons, but we have noted that this may have happened during his ascension in Acts 1:9-11, *after* he rose from the dead. Christ may have gone to Paradise immediately after he died (Lk 23:43, 46), but we do not know any other details.

The Jews believed that a person's spirit remained near the body for a few days (compare Jn 11:1-6, 14, 17). Maybe the three days of Christ's death suggest nothing more than that he *really* died. His real death makes for a real resurrection! Maybe

God never intended us to know what happened during those three days because it might remove our attention from the most important aspects of the Christian: Christ's death and resurrection. What happened *between* Christ's death and resurrection is of minute importance compared to the fact of Christ's death and resurrection.

Question 59: What Was Paul's Thorn in the Flesh Given by Satan?

After Paul had his "third heaven" experience, he writes: "To keep me from becoming conceited because of these surpassingly great revelations, there was given me a thorn in my flesh, a messenger of Satan, to torment me" (2 Cor 12:7). What was this thorn in the flesh? Scholars have proposed a number of options throughout the centuries.[64] One option is that the "thorn" had to do with some kind of temptation. Medieval Catholics, after the Latin Vulgate *(stimulus carnis),* believed Paul's thorn referred to sexual lust.[65] But Paul does not seem to have a problem in this area (1 Cor 7:7). Luther and Calvin suggested broadly that it was some spiritual temptation.

A second option comes from Tertullian, who believed the thorn was a headache or an earache *(On Modesty* 13). Along these lines many have proposed various illnesses, including a speech impediment (1 Cor 2:1; 2 Cor 10:1), epilepsy (Acts 9:3-8; 22:17) or a relapsing malaria that Paul apparently caught in Pamphylia (Acts 13:13). The most popular suggestion is that Paul was afflicted with an eye disease that resulted in poor vision (Gal 4:13-14; 6:11; Acts 23:5).[66] Satan is definitely able to afflict with physical illness (Job 2).

A third option, presented by John Chrysostom (347-407), was that the thorn referred to Paul's enemies. Augustine believed it referred to Paul's general sufferings (2 Cor 11:16-33). Paul had opponents in Corinth whom he considered false apostles influenced by Satan (2 Cor 11:1-15). Moreover, "thorn in the flesh" is also used of physical harassment in the Old

Testament (Num 33:55; Ezek 23:24). Paul claims he was "buf-feted" *(kolaphizō)* by the enemy. The word is often used for physical beatings (1 Cor 4:11; compare Mk 14:65; Mt 26:67). Paul's mention of his third heaven vision as happening four-teen years earlier (2 Cor 12:2) suggests this affliction happened early in his ministry. Perhaps the thorn came from a physical ailment he received when he was physically attacked under persecution (compare Acts 14:19).[67]

Each option has its strengths and weaknesses. Two impor-tant points are worth remembering: First, Paul's thorn in the flesh was ultimately "given" by God to prevent Paul from becoming conceited by his third heaven experience (2 Cor 12:7). Paul must have understood this because he seeks the Lord, instead of rebuking the devil, about this situation (2 Cor 12:8). Though Satan may harass us, God is ultimately in control. Second, God said no to Paul (2 Cor 12:9). God's decisions for our lives, at times painful, are always best (Rom 8:28). God's power was perfected in Paul's weakness, and his grace for Paul was sufficient. God's grace upon Paul resulted in Paul's spiritual power in ministering to people (12:9, 12; 13:3; 1 Cor 2:4-5).

Question 60: What Is the Relation Between Satan and the Antichrist?

If Jesus is the incarnation of God, shouldn't we consider the antichrist as the incarnation of Satan? Jewish traditions some-times identify the antichrist as Satan or Belial (for example, *Martyrdom and Ascension of Isaiah* 4). But we should refrain from trying to draw too close a juxtaposition of Christ and the antichrist. Nowhere in Scripture are we told that Satan is literally the antichrist. Instead, Satan is the one who gives the beast (who is understood by many to be the antichrist) "his power and his throne and great authority" (Rev 13:2).

Satan and the beast are distinguished as separate persons in Revelation. When Christ returns, the beast gets thrown into the lake of fire while Satan is bound for a thousand years in the bottomless pit (Rev 19:19—20:2). Only when Satan is released from his prison after a thousand years and attempts to attack the saints is he cast into the lake of fire. The beast (along with the false prophet) were there for a thousand years *before* Satan was also cast in (Rev 20:10). Together "they [third person plural] will be tormented day and night forever and ever." Thus it is biblically incorrect to equate Satan with the antichrist.[68]

Question 61: What Works Will Satan Do Before Christ Returns?

Satan definitely lost authority when Christ came on the scene, (Mk 3:25-27). Yet, since we live in the paradoxical era of "now and not yet," we can experience the blessing of salvation, but we will not see its final results until Christ returns (Rom 8:18-23; Heb 6:4-5). Similarly, we should consider Satan bound in terms of "now and not yet." We recognize his defeat on the cross, but we will not see his final defeat until Christ returns. The harm the world has experienced in the last two thousand years, the wars, murders, rapes, and other forms of havoc, argue forcibly that we live in an era when Satan is "filled with fury, because he knows that his time is short" (Rev 12:12; compare Rom 16:20).

According to Scripture, some demons have already been bound in the abyss (2 Pet 2:4; Jude 6; compare Lk 8:31). In Revelation we see the angel of destruction, called "Apollyon" or "Abaddon," releasing locustlike creatures from the abyss that are commanded to torment humans like creatures who do not have the "seal" of God upon them. (Rev 9:1-11). We also see Satan behind a great falling away of the saints in 2 Thessalonians 2. If we compare this with Revelation 13, we can assume that after this falling away takes place, the antichrist or beast is revealed and rules the entire world, persecuting the saints and pressuring humans to follow him. This man of lawlessness receives his authority from Satan himself (Rev 13:1-4).

But at the Second Coming, Christ will defeat the beast and his armies, casting the beast and the false prophet into the lake of fire (Rev 16:13-16; 19:11-21; Is 24:21; compare 1QM 18.1-2; *Hymn Fragments* 4.6, 5.3; *1 Enoch* 54.6; *Testament of Levi* 18.12. *Testament of Judah* 25.3; *Testament of Moses* 10.1). The world system, which Satan ruled, is destroyed in Revelation 17—18. In Revelation 20, after Satan is bound in the abyss for a thousand years, he is released to lead the nations against the camp of the saints. At this time he gets thrown into the lake of fire (compare Mt 25:41).

These images impart several teachings to those who have put their faith in Christ. First, we find that Satan's defeat is certain. The saints will see the devil's defeat and will stand as judges against the forces of darkness (1 Cor 6:3). No matter how bad things may look in the world or in our personal lives, we have the hope of knowing that Christ will completely subdue Satan at his Second Coming. Second, since the devil has little time left in the plan of God, we should never drop our guard. We must always be alert, for the devil "prowls around like a roaring lion looking for someone to devour" (1 Pet 5:8). Third, we know that through Christ we have the victory over any situation Satan might throw our way (1 Jn 4:4). Finally, from Matthew 25:41 we learn that punishment in hell (Gehenna or the lake of fire) was intended for the devil and his angels, not for humans. In New Testament theology, the people who end up in hell get there as a result of decisions they make on earth (compare 2 Pet 3:9).

6

QUESTIONS ABOUT SPIRITUAL WARFARE

D o angels and demons ever do battle? The Bible pictures warfare that is waged on a heavenly scale, but it does not supply many details other than to say that Michael and his angels fought against Satan and his angels (Rev 12:7-9; compare Dan 10:13, 20). More important for our purposes is the spiritual struggle between humans and demons (Eph 6:11-12). If we stand for the kingdom of God, we will be drawn into the war that exists between the two camps. Nevertheless, as we delve into the topic of spiritual warfare, let's strive to maintain a balanced perspective.

Question 62: What Is Spiritual Warfare?

Spiritual warfare is sometimes defined as the invisible confrontation between the forces of God and the forces of the devil, the kingdom of God versus the kingdom of darkness. Unlike earthly warfare, spiritual warfare involves fighting an invisible enemy (2 Kings 6:15-18). Donald Grey Barnhouse calls this the "invisible war." Sometimes this battle brings about circumstances that can hurt people physically, emotionally, mentally or spiritually. In the New Testament, the forces of darkness knew that Paul was God's servant, and they attacked him (Acts 19:15; 2 Cor 11:23—12:9).

Although the New Testament does not speak directly to the experience, a number of people claim that demons have pestered them at night or have attacked them in the manner of a poltergeist (see answer 34). But focusing on such accounts can easily lead to sensationalizing spiritual warfare. It is not the devil's primary objective to cause us physical discomfort or to attack us at night. Instead, we can assue that he primarily desires to keep unbelievers from placing their faith in Christ and to render believers powerless or completely undermine their faith, hoping that Christians will follow his example and turn away from God.

Too often we abuse the subject of spiritual warfare. Some look for demons in every struggle they experience. They spend their time rebuking demons in prayer, imagining themselves on the frontlines of demonic attack. But it is important to remember that apart from the devil and his demons, we also have conflicts with our weak, sinful nature and the influence of fallen people in a fallen world, which is cause enough for the majority of our problems!

If we feel that we are struggling against an opponent that we cannot see, we must trust in the God of the Bible—not our own spirituality, cleverness or war strategies—for the victory (2 Cor 5:7). We should keep our minds focused on the things of God instead of speculating about the devil's next move (Phil 4:8).

Question 63: What Are Some of the Strategies of the Devil?

Satan's ultimate mission in the New Testament seems to be to obstruct the purposes God desires to accomplish through

Christ and his saints (Lk 22:31-32; 1 Pet 5:8; Acts 13:10; 1 Thess 2:18; Rev 2:10; 12:13-17). He can attack the saints with physical sickness, as he did Job and the apostle Paul (Job 2:7; 2 Cor 12:7; compare Lk 13:16). He attempts to devour the messianic male child, pursues the child's mother and then makes war on the rest of her children (Rev 12). He persecutes Christians through the decisions of unbelievers in high places (Rev 16:12-15, 17), and he influences some to commit murder (1 Jn 3:10, 12). He himself is a murderer and a persecutor of the saints (Jn 8:44; Rev 12:5, 12). He was behind Judas's betrayal of Jesus (Jn 13:2; compare 14:30).

The biblical Satan takes pleasure in causing hatred and strife among people (1 Jn 3:8-12; Eph 4:25-27) and in taking advantage of divisions and unforgiveness among Christians (2 Cor 2:11). In the Old Testament he accused the saints (Job 1—2; Zech 13:1-4; compare Rev 12:10), and in the New Testament he uses unbelievers to slander believers (1 Tim 3:6-7;1 Jn 5:19). He is able to influence unbelievers to fulfil his purposes because he has blinded their minds to the truth of the gospel (2 Cor 4:4; compare Mk 4:15; Mt 13:38-41). He is a master of deception, for he himself is the father of lies (Jn 8:44; Acts 13:10; 2 Cor 11:2-14; 2 Thess 2:9; 1 Tim 5:15; Jas 3:14; Rev 12:9; compare Rev 2:9; 3:9; 1 *Enoch* 69:6).

Satan tempted David the king to sin by numbering the people of Israel, (1 Chron 21:1).[1] He tempted Christ by trying to persuade him to act on his own will and power instead of depending on God (Mt 4:1-11). Satan tempts married couples with sexual infidelity (1 Cor 7:5).

When Satan persuades God's people to sin, disaster naturally follows. When Ananias and Sapphira lied to the Holy Spirit regarding their giving, as Satan influenced them to do, they died instantly (Acts 5). He is allowed to attack apostates, as with the sexual offender in 1 Corinthians 5:1-5. Paul delivers the offender over to Satan "so that the sinful nature may be destroyed and his spirit saved on the day of the Lord" (1 Cor

5:5). Paul hands over Hymenaeus and Alexander, two apostates, "to Satan to be taught not to blaspheme" (1 Tim 1:20). Paul might understand Satan as "the destroyer" in 1 Corinthians 10:10 (compare Rev 9:1, 11; *Testament of Benjamin* 3.3; *Jubilees* 11.11; 49.2; *Assumption of Moses* 10.1). One of Satan's ultimate goals is to cause the saints to fall away from the faith (1 Thess 3:5; 2 Thess 2:1-12).

Question 64: How Do the Demons Undermine the Work of Christians?

In C. S. Lewis's book *The Screwtape Letters* a senior demon named Screwtape instructs a junior demon named Wormwood on undermining the faith of a Christian. Similarly, demons appear to take their orders from Satan. In biblical Scripture, one of their objectives is to destroy human life by inflicting diseases on people (Job 2:7; Mt 17:14; Lk 13:10-17; compare Jub. 10:10-13) and by causing mental torment (1 Sam 16—23; Mk 5:2-5, 15; compare Jn 7:20; 8:48-52; 10:20-21; *Jubilees* 15:31). Through possession, deception and false religion, demons influence their victims to perform human sacrifices or injure themselves (Ps 106:36-38; Mk 5:3-4; compare 1 Kings 18:28). They can also destroy life through instigating murder, violence and war (1 Sam 18:10-11; Rev 16:13-14).

Like Satan, demons wish to lead the saints astray (Rom 8:38; 1 Tim 4:1-5). Essentially, demons will resort to any venue that can disrupt our peace and fellowship with God. Spiritual disciplines such as prayer and faith constitute an essential resource in our struggle against the forces of darkness (Eph 6:10-18). The Bible warns God's people not to give the devil a foothold in their lives (Eph 4:27).

Question 65: Do Christians Have Authority to Rebuke Satan and His Demons?

Have you ever watched a televangelist lead an entire congregation in a prayer that goes something like this: "Satan, I bind and rebuke you! Take your hands off my rightful possessions"? Is this biblical? Scripture teaches that Christians do have authority over demons (Lk 9:1;10:17, 20; Mt 10:20; Mk 16:17), but this does not mean that they can go around rebuking Satan under every rock. Nowhere in Scripture do we see the disciples directly chewing out Satan and his minions. They confronted demons through demonically influenced *people* (Acts 13:6-12; 16:16-18). This is a far cry from what goes on in some pulpits.

Too often in church prayer meetings charismatic Christians start rebuking Satan out loud when they pray. Sometimes their prayers seem more focused on the devil than on God! Some may rebuke Satan in their minds, not realizing that the devil cannot read their thoughts (see answer 51). Let's not overestimate Satan's power. He is not all-knowing. He may not even know that an entire congregation is praying against him unless he is present. I doubt that demonic forces hear all the rebukes that Christians make against them.

What are some wise ways to rebuke Satan and his demons? First of all, make sure that they are present to hear your rebuke! When we confront demon-possessed persons, we know that we are in the presence of demons. But at a Christian prayer meeting demons may be nowhere present.

Second, if you pray against a demonic force oppressing another person who is *not* present with you, address your prayer to *God,* not Satan or demons. A demon who is oppressing someone miles away cannot hear you. But if you pray for God to rebuke the devil, God can hear your prayer no matter where you are. "Long-distance" deliverance is certainly possible in such cases (Mk 7:24-30; compare Acts 19:11-12).

Third, if you have good grounds for believing that the forces of darkness are present, a biblical way of rebuking them is by saying, "The Lord rebuke you!" Jude 9 states that Michael the archangel did not dare to blaspheme the devil, but said to him, "The Lord rebuke you!" (compare Zech 3:1-2; 2 *Apocalypse of Baruch* 21:23; *Life of Adam and Eve* 39). The Bible denounces those who take it upon themselves to speak presumptuously against higher powers (2 Pet 2:10-12; Jude 8-10).

The authority that Christians have to rebuke demons comes through the name of the Lord Jesus Christ; this authority over the forces of darkness rests in his authority, not in human power (Mk 1:34; 3:11-12; Lk 4:35-36; Acts 4:7; Phil 2:9-11; 2 Thess 2:8;1 Jn 4:4; Rev 19:11). Christ's death and resurrection established forever his authority over all creation, including Satan and his minions. Thus Christians have power through the name of Jesus and through his precious blood (which represents the atoning, sacrificial death of Christ and, by inference, the benefits this entails: Rev 12:11; Eph 1:7; Col 2:15; Heb 2:14; Mt 28:18).

The Hebrew word translated "rebuke" (*gā'ar*) suggests reproof. As the creative word of God gives life (Is 55:10-11), so the rebuking word of God calls God to bring destruction on the objects of his displeasure (Job 26:11; Ps 18:15; 103:7; 105:9; 2 Kings 22:16; compare 1QapGen 20.28-29; 1QM 14.9-10).[2] In the New Testament the word *to rebuke* (Greek *epitimaō*) is normally a prerogative reserved to Jesus Christ, declaring his position as Lord (Lk 4:31-37; compare Mk 8:32-33; Mt 16:22; Lk 9:55).[3] Christ alone rebukes the forces of nature, for he created them (Mk 4:39-41; 11:23; compare Jn 1:1-3, 14; Col 1:15-18).

Question 66: What Is "Binding and Loosing"?

"I bind the works of Satan in the name of Jesus and loose the blessings of God!" Televelangelists often make statements like this. Where did they get this concept of binding and loosing? When Peter confessed Jesus as the Son of God, Jesus blessed him and declared, "I will give you the keys of the kingdom of heaven; whatever you bind on earth will have been bound in heaven, and whatever you loose on earth will be loosed in heaven" (Mt 16:19).[4] The power of binding and loosing was given to all the disciples (Mt 18:18).

Some think that Jesus was giving power over demons to Peter. In Jewish literature "binding" and "loosing" were sometimes used in reference to exorcisms (*Testament of Levi* 18:12; *Testament of Solomon* Sol. 1:14). Matthew 16:18 states that the gates of hell will not overcome the church. But the phrase *gates of hell* does not refer to demonic forces.[5] We have already noted that the devil and his minions do not live in hell (see question 53). In Matthew 16:18 Christ is claiming that *death itself* (hell [Hades]) will not prevail against the church as a result of Christ's resurrection power (compare Rev 1:18; Rom 8:38-39; 1 Cor 15:51-57). The Revised Standard Version correctly translates this phrase as "the powers of death shall not prevail against it [the church]" (Mt 16:18).

Moreover, if Christ is bestowing power over demons to the disciples in Matthew 16:19 and 18:18, in what sense are they receiving a power they did not already have? After all, Christ had already given them power over the demons when he sent them out to preach (Mt 10:1; Lk 9:1). If these passages denote "binding" Satan, wouldn't it follow that the "loosing" also refers to Satan? How does one "loose" Satan? Biblical "binding and loosing" has little to do with spiritual warfare as such or with directly "binding and loosing" Satan.

More applicable to spiritual warfare is the binding of the "strong man" in Mark 3:27. This verse depicts Jesus binding the strong man, a term that refers to Satan in Mark 3:24. Through his ministry Christ established the kingdom of God on earth and defeated the powers of darkness by conquering death itself (Heb 2:14; Col 2:15; Gal 4:9).

Peter is able to "bind" and "loose" because he has the "keys." What does "the keys" refer to? Isaiah prophesied a blessing on Eliakim, the porter of the king's palace (Is 22:22). He would be given a key, and no one would be able to get into the royal house without the key of Eliakim. In a similar way Jesus was making Peter and the other disciples the porters of the kingdom of God. Thus the terms *keys, binding* and *loosing* are figurative expressions better understood in terms of Jesus bestowing the disciples with the authority (key) of forbidding (closing/binding) and permitting (opening/loosing) people access to the kingdom of heaven (Rev 3:7; compare Rev 1:18; Lk 11:52; *2 Enoch* 40.9-11; *3 Apocalypse of Baruch* 11.2; *b. Sanhedrin* 113a).[6]

This all makes sense once we understand the context of binding and loosing in Matthew 18:15-20. The topic of this passage focuses on forgiving ("loosing") or excommunicating ("binding") an unrepentant sinner from the church. Jesus gave the disciples the authority to make decisions that would affect the welfare of the church. Likewise, he gave them teaching authority to declare the true gospel, which is exemplified by the forgiveness of sins (Jn 20:22-23; Acts 2:37-42, 47; 3:19; 4:11-12; 8:20-24; compare Job 42:9-10 LXX; *Targum Noefiti I of Genesis* 4.7).

So should Christians "bind" the devil? If they are calling the forces of darkness to recollect their defeat (their "binding"), which Jesus accomplished through his ministry and death on the cross, then binding the devil in this sense is perfectly legitimate. More often than not, however, I suspect that many Christians use the word *bind* in reference to the binding and loosing in Matthew 16:19 and 18:18. Binding and loosing the devil is not the meaning behind these Scriptures. It is not necessarily wrong to use the word *bind* when rebuking demonic forces; one needs to realize, though, that it is not asociated with these passages.

Question 67: How Do We Resist Satan and His Demons?

St. James exhorts, "Submit yourselves, then, to God. Resist the devil, and he will flee from you" (Jas 4:7). There are many ways to resist Satan. Perhaps the most explicit passage on spiritual warfare is Ephesians 6:10-18. Here Scripture elaborates on fighting the devil by using imagery associated with a

Roman foot soldier. Our struggle "is not against flesh and blood, but against the rulers *[archas]*, and the authorities *[exousias]*, against the powers *[kosmokratoras]* of this dark world and against the spiritual forces of evil *[pneumatika tēs ponērias]* in the heavenly realms" (Eph 6:12; 2 Cor 10:4-5).

We must take our stand against "the wiles" of the devil (Eph 6:11 KJV). Discernment, wisdom and common sense go a long way in this war, for the devil seldom shows his true colors in any attack. As Andrew Lincoln claims, "The devil does not always attack through obvious head-on assaults but employs cunning and wily stratagems designed to catch believers unawares."[7] Our strength, however, does not rest in ourselves, but in God's mighty power (Eph 6:10). This passage borrows from Jewish sources that depict the Lord as the ultimate warrior (Is 11:1-5; 59:14-19; compare Wisdom of Solomon 5.15-20; 1 Maccabees 2.42-3:5). Nevertheless we who are the Lord's servants must also put on the entire armor of God. Ephesians 6:14-17 mentions several pieces.

1. The belt of truth. As God is true because he declares things as they really are and does not lie (1 Sam 15:29; Ps 31:5; Heb 6:18), so we should be truthful in our words and conduct (Eph 4:25; 5:9). Thus the first piece of our armor refers to a moral virtue (compare Is 11:5). Our manner of conduct testifies to who we are and what we believe. When James exhorts his readers to resist the devil, he also exhorts the double-minded ones to purify their hearts (Jas 4:8). The moral life of God's soldier has no room for a divided allegiance. Hence Scripture declares that a soldier must avoid worldly entanglements (2 Tim 2:4). Soldiers must be strong, alert and persevering (1 Thess 5:6; 2 Tim 2:1, 3; 1 Cor 16:13; Eph 6:10-13).

2. The breastplate of righteousness. Christians are made righteous through the righteousness of Christ that is imputed to them by faith. Yet as one theologian notes, "One who by faith is declared righteous also by faith seeks to do the deeds of righteousness and to grow in righteousness by God's grace

(Rom 6:12-18; Eph 4:24; 5:9; Phil 1:11; Heb 11; Jas 2:17-26; 1
Pet 2:24; 1 Jn 2:29)."[8] If we are to do righteous deeds, all of our
conduct must be just (Mic 5:8; 2 Cor 6:7). Although we can
never achieve perfection in this life (compare 1 Jn 1:8, 10) we
can seek righteousness through self-surrender and through
placing Christ first in our lives. When we do sin, we must
confess, and he will forgive us (1 Jn 1:9; 2:1-2). Unconfessed
sin opens a door of opportunity for the enemy.

3. *Feet shod with the preparation of the gospel of peace.* The
Bible portrays the feet of the righteous as bringing good news
or the gospel of peace (Is 52:7; Nah 1:15; Rom 10:15). In
Ephesians the gospel of Christ (the message of the good news
of Christ's death, burial and resurrection, as well as the benefits it gives, 1 Cor 15:1-8) restores cosmic harmony to the
universe (Eph 1:10; 3:10)[9] and brings peace between humans
and God and between Jew and Gentile (Eph 2:14-18). Those
who stand firm in the gospel and advance it into enemy
territory are in the process of restoring harmony in a universe
that is confused and damaged by Satan. They are preaching
the gospel to "all creation" (Mk 16:15).

4. *The shield of faith.* Faith in Christ is absolutely essential
for salvation (Eph 2:8-9; Acts 16:31; Rom 10:9-10; Jn 3:16; 1 Jn
5:4-5), but the shield of faith seems to refer to a continuing
trust in the Lord amid adverse circumstances. Through faith
we are able withstand the flaming arrows (the temptations and
attacks) of Satan. Although Roman shields were often made of
wood, they were sometimes covered by leather that was
soaked in water. This shield protected the soldiers from flaming arrows shot their way (Thucydides *History of the Pelopon-
nesian War* 2.75.5). The one who has faith overcomes the
world, or *kosmos,* the hostile territory ruled by the enemy (1
Jn 5:4-5, 18-19; 4:4; compare Jn 16:33).

Through self-control, alertness, trusting and depending on
God, we can successfully resist Satan the "roaring lion," knowing that others throughout the world face the trials we face (1

Pet 5:8-9). Daniel P. Fuller, former dean of Fuller Theological Seminary, points out that misfortunes should not deprive us of our future hope (1 Thess 3:2-5), for God makes all things work for good (Rom 8:28; Jer 29:11).[10] We must therefore fight the good fight of faith amidst adverse circumstances, as the early saints did (1 Tim 6:12; 2 Tim 4:7). We should also recognize that the decisive point in this war already turned in our favor when Jesus died and rose again.

5. *The helmet of salvation.* Christians are not subject to the alienation from God that comes from sin and death (Eph 2:1-9; Rom 3:23-26; 6:23). Salvation, however, has a paradoxical aspect of "now and not yet." Christians are saved, but their ultimate redemption awaits them in the future (Eph 1:13-14; 4:30; 1 Cor 1:18). They must therefore stand fast in the assurance of faith, enduring to the end (Heb 3:12-14; Mt 24:13). Christians who face severe persecution overcome Satan by loving God more than their own lives (Rev 12:11). No matter how Satan tries, he cannot snatch us away from God if we continue in the faith. We have assurance that God will never leave us nor forsake us (Heb 13:5; Jn 10:28-30; 1 Jn 5:13).

6. *Sword of the Spirit—the Word of God.* In Ephesians the phrase "word of God" seems to refer to the gospel of salvation (Eph 1:13; 5:26; compare 1 Pet 1:25). By proclaiming reconciliation between God and humans, we are enabled to overcome the wicked one.[11] Every time a person testifies about Christ, he or she is reminding the devil and the forces of darkness about their defeat through the cross!

The sword of the Spirit supplies the word's effectiveness or "cutting edge."[12] The Holy Spirit provides power and penetration whenever one proclaims the gospel message (1 Thess 1:5). Hence, in order to effectively wield the "sword," we should seek to be filled with the Spirit (Eph 5:18). Being filled with the Spirit also enables a person to excel in nurturing and protecting the church through their spiritual gifts.[13]

Naturally, to proclaim the gospel message of salvation effectively, we must first understand it ourselves and appropriate it to our own lives. We come to understand that message through continuing the study of biblical scripture. When Jesus was tempted by Satan, he quoted the Word of God (Scripture) to him (Mt 4; compare 1 Jn 2:14). We too can overcome the evil one that way.

7. Prayer. Although prayer is not one of the pieces of armor, it is nevertheless mentioned in the context of resisting the devil (Eph 6:18). Prayer should be done "in the Spirit" (Jude 20). The Spirit-filled life includes praise, worship and singing (Eph 5:18-20; 1 Cor 14:15). When David played the harp (perhaps singing spiritual songs), the evil spirit departed from Saul (1 Sam 16:14, 23). Spirit-led prayer, petitions and intercession for others are a vital part of spiritual discipline (1 Tim 2:1-3). Paul tells the Thessalonian church to pray ceaselessly (1 Thess 5:17). Christians must develop the habit of prayer (Lk 21:36; Col 4:2-4; Phil 4:6; 1 Thess 5:17). Jesus says stubborn demonic powers can be broken by prayer (Mk 9:29; Mt 17:21). We resist Satan when we draw near to God by turning away from sin (Jas 4:7-8; Zech 1:3; Mal 3:7; compare 2 Chron 15:2; *Testament of Dan* 6.2).

Those who put their faith in Christ overcome Satan through ethical, righteous living, advancing God's kingdom, trusting in God's provision for and preservation of our lives, knowing and acting on the gospel message and maintaining a consistent, Spirit-led prayer life. Daniel Fuller lists five more practical counter-strategies against the devil:

1. We must keep ourselves occupied, for idleness leads to sin (1 Tim 5:13-15).

2. Discipline should never be so severe that it implies perpetual unforgiveness (2 Cor 2:6-11).

3. Appointed church leaders must have a good reputation (1 Tim 3:2-7).

4. Married couples should not abstain from sexual relations

so long as to allow temptation through a lack of self-control (1 Cor 7:5).

5. New religious converts should not be put in positions of leadership, no matter how gifted or talented they might be, for "Satan works to incite the inbred human tendency to self-exaltation (1 Tim 3:6)."[14]

Question 68: Do Territorial Spirits Exist?

They gathered together for a prayer meeting in San Francisco. The purpose of the meeting was to rid the city of the territorial "spirit of lust" that influenced its inhabitants. What does the Bible say regarding territorial spirits? Deuteronomy 32:8-9 states that "when the Most High gave the nations their inheritance, when he divided all mankind, he set up boundaries for the peoples according to the number of the sons of God. For the LORD's portion is his people, Jacob his allotted inheritance."[15] As was mentioned under answer 16, the "sons of God" are probably angels who watch over the nations. In Daniel 10 we find angels watching over Persia and Greece (Dan 10:13, 20; compare Job 1:5-6; 2 Kings 18:35; Is 24:21-22; 2 *Maccabees* 5; *Jubilees* 15.30-32; 1 *Enoch* 20:5; 89-90; *Sirach* 17:17; 1QM 17:5-18). Deuteronomy 32:8-9 may suggest that while other nations are under the influence of other powers, Israel belongs to God.[16] In the New Testament, the saints are contrasted with the fallen world (Eph 2:2-4; 2 Cor 4:4; 1 Jn 5:19). Thus "territorial spirits" may exist, but this does not justify the common misconceptions certain people have about them.

First, these angels seem to play the role of guardians. They do not necessarily specialize in a particular sin. The city of San Francisco may include residents who are wicked and lustful, but this does not necessarily mean that a gigantic demon of lust lurks behind it all. Second, nowhere in Scripture is anyone specifically commanded to either identify or pray against territorial spirits. If this were the case, then we might expect God to have charged Daniel to rebuke the prince of Persia instead of directing his prayer to God (Dan 10:1-13). Finally, we should never address demonic spirits in prayer unless they are actually present, confronting us. If we feel burdened to pray about the influence of lust in San Francisco or the influence of oppression in a particular country, we should talk to God about the problem, not a demon.

Wayne Grudem adds four more misconceptions regarding territorial spirits. "In no instance does anyone in the New Testament 1) *summon a 'territorial spirit'* . . . 2) *demand information from demons about a local demonic hierarchy* . . . 3) *say that we should believe or teach information derived from demons* . . . 4) teach by word or example that certain *'demonic strongholds' over a city have to be broken* before the gospel can be proclaimed with effectiveness."[17]

Question 69: Was Jesus an Exorcist?

The office of an exorcist is first mentioned in the church in the middle of the third century by Cornelius, bishop of Rome. During the early church era the duties of an exorcist involved laying hands on the demonized and mentally disturbed *(energumens)* and exorcising those preparing for baptism *(catechumens)*.[18] The convert renounced Satan and his ways before being baptized. The water of baptism was said to expel demons,[19] and the sign of the cross repelled them *(apotropaic)*. The office of an exorcist still remains in the Roman Catholic Church. In the apocryphal book of Tobit, Tobias seizes a fish out of the water at the request of the angel Raphael. The heart and liver of the fish was used as a fumigant against attacks from demonic spirits (Tobit 6:1-9). The exorcism rituals practiced by pagans were even more extraordinary and magical.[20]

Jesus was not an exorcist who used magical objects or performed "hocus-pocus" incantations. But he did cast out demons, famously. Unlike many pagans and Jews of his day, Jesus cast out devils by his own authority, using a few brief words such as "be quiet and come out" (Mk 1:25), "never enter him again" (Mk 9:25), and "go" (Mt 8:32). Jesus even drove out devils from a distance (Mt 15:21; Mk 7:24-30; compare Acts 19:12). And he gave the disciples similar power over demons (Lk 9:1; 10:17; Mk 3:14; 16:8; Acts 5:16; 8:7; 16:18). His power was so extraordinary that the people cried, "Nothing like this has ever been seen in Israel" (Mt 9:33; compare Lk 4:36). Jesus considered his casting out of demons an operative token that the kingdom of God had arrived. Satan was now being bound and defeated (Mk 3:22-27).

Question 70: Do Generational Spirits Exist?

Some claim that demon possession or occult powers are inherited from parents or ancestors, calling it a generational spirit or curse. People can inherit the bad characteristics of their parents, and God declares that the sins of the parents are visited on their children "to the third and fourth generation" (Ex 20:5). Some understand the term "familiar" spirit in the King James Version to mean a family spirit (compare Lev 19:31 KJV; Deut 18:10-12).

The one possessing a familiar spirit, however, is better understood as a spiritist or a necromancer, as more updated Scripture translations indicate. One scholar writes that the subject of familiar spirits "was introduced at a time when belief in the existence of evil spirits became deeply rooted, and when it was supposed that it was in the power of man to conquer and subdue such spirits and force them to serve their master in any office to which he might choose to appoint them."[21]

While it is true that we often inherit some of our parents' characteristics, the subject of demon transference is a completely different issue. The phrase "third and fourth generation" likely refers to an extended family household in which the grandparents, parents and children, and sometimes great-grandparents, all lived together under one roof (Num 16:31-34; Josh 7:24; Ps 103:17; 109:12). Since the elders of the household were responsible to instruct the children in the ways of God, it is evident that sinful parents who refused to do so incurred God's disfavor or "curse" upon their family (Deut 4:10; Deut 28–30). But God's disfavor was broken once a household member turned from "hating" to "loving" God (Ex 20:5-6). Hence this passage does not refer to demonic transferences.

Nevertheless, when children follow in the footsteps of parents or grandparents who are involved in the occult, demon possession or oppression is always possible. This seems especially true of children whose parents have dedicated them to demonic or occult powers. Possession can occur through occult practices, idolatry, spells and psychic healing.[22] Perhaps possession is also possible through mind-altering drugs or through any state that leaves the mind emptied and open to external influences (compare Mt 12:43-45; Lk 11:24-26).[23]

Question 71: What Are the Indications of Demon Possession?

Demon possession is not always easy to discern. Some who suppose that demons do not exist attribute genuine cases of demon possession to mental, emotional or physical illnesses.[24] Others go to the opposite extreme by attributing any mental, physical or spiritual infirmity to demonization. What complicates the issue is that the categories of mental, physical, spiritual and emotional often overlap in cases of genuine demon possession. In the Bible demons sometimes cause physical and mental infirmity (Mt 8:28-34; 9:32-34; 17:14-21; Lk 13:10-17), but sometimes they do not (Mk 1:34; Mt 8:16; Lk 7:21).

Nevertheless, there are physical, psychological and spiritual characteristics that can help us discern possible cases of demon possession. But these traits do not constitute all of the symptoms, nor does a person who is possessed necessarily exemplify all of the traits. Moreover, if a person manifests only one of these traits, this does not necessarily confirm that he or she is demon possessed. This paradigm is merely descriptive, providing general characteristics of possession. It is not meant to be exhaustive.[25]

Physical Symptoms	Psychological Symptoms	Spiritual Symptoms
Superhuman strength (sometimes violent or self-destructive)	Clairvoyance ("crystal ball" ability to see things that lie beyond normal abilities)	Immoral character (for example, profanity, nudity, foul language, blasphemy)
Altered facial expression (a look of hatefulness or maliciousness)	Telepathy (communication beyond the five senses)	Verbally or physically threatening anything representing Christ or Christianity
A change in the voice (harshness, derisiveness)	Ability to predict the future	Falling into a trance when someone prays
Symptoms resembling epilepsy (convulsions, prostration)	Ability to speak foreign languages unknown to the person possessed	Inability to confess Jesus Christ in a reverent manner (often blaspheming Christ)
Insensitivity to pain	Trance state (often unable to remember activities in the trance)	Poltergeist phenomena (for example, inexplicable noises, objects overturned, foul odors)
Mt 8:28; Acts 19:16; Lk 4:33-34; Mk 9:18-22; 5:1-5	Acts 16:16-18; Mk 1:21-24, 34; Lk 4:33; 1 Sam 18:10; Mk 9:18-22	Acts 13:4-11; Mk 5:1-5; Lk 9:41-42; 1 Jn 4:1-6; 1 Cor 12:3; 1 Sam 18:10

Question 72: How Do We Distinguish Between Demon Possession and Mental Illness?

"Don't confuse a mental disorder with a demon. Too many zealous-but-untrained people have done more harm than good by identifying demons that were not present," says Basil Jackson, director of the Jackson Psychiatric Center in Milwaukee. Jackson has encountered many ministers who in ignorance misdiagnosed a mental disorder, such as schizophrenia or depression, as demon possession. A false diagnosis of demon possession can have a catastrophic effect on someone who is mentally or emotionally ill, leading to intense feelings of guilt and a sense of being abandoned by God. This outcome can be

avoided with referral to appropriate psychiatric treatment.[26]
Schizophrenics may resemble demon-possessed persons in
certain respects, such as altered personality, unaccustomed physical strength, altered voice and facial expressions, and so forth. As
we noted earlier, demon possession and mental illness may
overlap. At times the symptoms may point to mental illness only.
Or a person may be succumbing to role enactment. That is, their
mental illness makes them think they are possessed, and they
behave accordingly.[27] Naive ministers might unwittingly reinforce
this behavior by affirming that the person is indeed possessed.

According to Henry A. Virkler, there are several differences
between undifferentiated schizophrenia and demon possession. First, schizophrenics often speak incoherently, not with
the sophistication of a demon-possessed individual. Second,
schizophrenics believe they are someone they are not, and this
is usually discernible by others. Third, schizophrenics often
make claims that can be proven false in reference to clairvoyance and telepathy. The extrasensory capabilities of demon-
possessed individuals, on the other hand, are usually genuine.
Fourth, most schizophrenics do not react negatively toward
prayer, but the demon possessed do. Fifth, poltergeist activity
is usually absent in cases of mental illness. Sixth, schizophrenics often respond to proper medication, while demon-possessed people do not. Finally, exorcisms usually fail or are
short-lived when the affected person is merely schizophrenic.

The chart of demon-possessed characteristics under answer
71 provides help, and answer 75 is also helpful. A minister who
feels incompetent to handle a delicate case involving a mental
disorder should seek the advice of a competent psychiatrist
who is knowledgeable about demon possession.

Question 73: Can a Christian Be Demon Possessed?

A number of conservative evangelicals believe that Christians
can be demon possessed. Merrill Unger, author of *Biblical*

Demonology, once believed that Christians could not be possessed. But he has changed his mind after reading numerous letters from missionaries that seem to document cases of Christians being demon possessed.[28] Many claim to have witnessed Christian demon possession. But there is no biblical evidence directly supporting such a phenomenon. Here we have the problem of Scripture diverging from supposed personal experience.

Only unbelievers experience demon possession in Scripture. Satan did influence Ananias and Sapphira, who were believers in Christ, to lie to the Holy Spirit in Acts 5:3-4, but there is no evidence that he actually possessed them. He possessed Judas (Lk 22:3), but we must raise the question whether Judas was ever a true believer. If we believe that he was, it seems more plausible to say that he completely fell away from his faith than to present him as a case of Christian "demonization," especially since he lived at a time when the term *Christian* was still inoperative. Saul presents another case of demon possession or oppression in an era prior to Christianity. As with Judas, can we say that he was a "believer" after the Spirit of God departed from him (1 Sam 16:14)? He, like Judas, seems to be severely backslidden.

If Christians are baptized into the body of Christ and have the Holy Spirit living in them, it seems contradictory to say that those who faithfully abide "in Christ" can be demon possessed (Rom 8:9-11; 1 Cor 12:13; 6:19; 1:30; Jn 15:1-5; compare Mt 7:16-20; Jas 3:11-12; Num.23:23). Christ has delivered Christians from the kingdom of darkness, and the devil cannot harm them in any ultimate sense (Col 1:13;1 Jn 4:4; 5:18). *I do not believe that Spirit-filled Christians can be demon possessed.*

What then do we make of alleged cases of Christian demonization? Some cases may involve mental illness, while in others severe demonic attacks may be mistaken for demon possession. Still other cases may involve weak-willed, insecure individuals pretending to be possessed or psyching themselves into believing they are possessed in order to gain attention. Preachers or peers who have an unbalanced view of spiritual warfare and demonology may lead these individuals to react as though they are possessed when in reality they are not.

The question of identity lies at the heart of the issue. Is the person who is possessed really a Christian? A professing believer in Christ may not necessarily be a genuine Christian (1 Jn 2:19; Acts 8:9-24; Mt 7:21-23; Lk 6:46). Imagine Jesus calling the rich young ruler one of his followers simply because he kept the Ten Commandments. Instead of affirming the man as a true believer, Jesus addressed the vice that controlled this man's heart—the love of riches (Mk 10:17-23). I believe that converts who do not address and surrender sinful or occultic vices in their lives may not be genuine Christians. Saying "I believe in Jesus" is not enough if one remains willfully bound by sinful and occultic habits. Believing in Jesus means making him Lord of our lives (Lk 6:46; Rom 10:9-10; Phil 2:9-11); hence, we must repent of our sins (Lk 13:3; Acts 2:38; 3:19; Rev 2:5).

On the other hand, I believe that a backslidden Christian can be demon possessed. But was such a "Christian" ever really a Christian? Some would say that such a person was never really saved to begin with. Others would say that such a person is no longer saved. In either case, the person who is possessed is no longer considered a Christian. In Scripture only those who have committed apostasy or heinous sins are "delivered over to Satan" (1 Cor 5:5; 1 Tim 1:20; compare 1 Jn 5:16-18).

A number of problems are connected with the belief that Christians can be demonized. For instance, a Christian who indulges in a particular sin may resort to getting a "demon of lust" cast out of her instead of taking responsibility for her own actions. "The devil made me do it" is easier to confess than "I have sinned." Many sinful vices arise out of our own sinful nature, not demons (Jas 1:13-16; Gal 5:19-21). The Bible never tells Christians to have demons cast out of them whenever they sin. Instead, they are to confess their sins and turn away from them (1 Jn 1:9—2:6).

Question 74: What Is the Difference Between Demon Possession and Demon Oppression?

Demon oppression is popularly defined as a severe external attack caused by demons, while demon possession often refers to demons' actual entering in someone's body and bringing it under their control. But such definitions are problematic. Does demon possession entail the complete overriding of a person's own will? A partial overriding? An overriding of the body in opposition to the person's own will? Does demon oppression involve a partial or a temporary overriding of a person's body or will? Is an oppression sporadic, constant or occasional? There are no easy answers to these questions.

Those who reject the possibility of Christians' being possessed by demons sometimes understand demonic oppression as virtually any prolonged demonic attack, temptation or subjection of Christians (Lk 4:2; 13:11-16; 2 Cor 12:7).[29] Here again problems of definition present themselves. Theologian Wayne Grudem writes:

> We are simply asking how abnormal a Christian's life can become, especially if that person does not know about or make use of the weapons of spiritual warfare that are available to Christians, persists in some kinds of sin that give entrance to demonic activity, and is outside the reach of any ministry that is accustomed to giving spiritual help against demonic attack.
> . . . *It seems better simply to recognize that there can be varying degrees of demonic attack or influence on people, even on Christians, and to leave it at that* [emphasis mine].[30]

Question 75: How Is an Exorcism Performed?

In the New Testament, Christ gave his disciples the power to cast out demons (Lk 9:1; Mk 16:17), and some in the Christian church today may be gifted in the area of exorcism (1 Cor 12:4-11). Performing an exorcism is no light matter. I am by no means an expert on this subject. My practical advice comes more from study and discernment than personal experience. I do not recommend that everyone become an exorcist. Any who find themselves suddenly confronted with a demonic situation can be assured that God has given Christians authority through Christ over the demon(s) (1 Jn 4:4; compare Mk 16:17 KJV). So I would recommend that those who believe they are gifted by God for such a task, are confronted with the opportunity, and are mature enough to handle the situation should be involved in casting out demons. New converts generally should not be allowed to perform such a task, but of course, anyone can pray for the deliverance of an individual.

For the Christian, qualifications for performing an exorcism are much the same as the qualities listed in Ephesians 6:10-18 (see answer 67). Godly living, faith, knowledge of Scripture and persevering prayer are absolute musts. Prayer and fasting before the exorcism is advisable (Mk 9:29; Mt 17:21).[31] A team of church members should be present at the exorcism, including at least one mature believer who has already performed exorcisms. An intercessory prayer group should also be praying for the person who is demon possessed.

We can derive some insight from the exorcisms described in Scripture. First, Jesus did not spend a long time conversing with the demon-possessed individual, but cast out the demon quickly (Mk 1:25; 9:25). Second, the exorcisms in Scripture did not require the cooperation of the possessed, so we may assume that at least some exorcisms may be performed successfully in like manner today. The individual's consent is preferred, but not necessarily required.[32] Third, being present with the demon-possessed individual is not always mandatory either. Some demons were cast out from a distance (Mt 15:21; Mk 7:24-30; compare Acts 19:12). Fourth, Christians must stand in the name of Jesus Christ and cast out demons by his authority (Acts 4:8, 12; 16:18). Fifth, there should be a renunciation of all sin, including occultic activities, objects and beliefs (Acts 19:17-20; Deut 18:9-13). Finally, when demons were cast out in Scripture, there was tangible evidence to that effect (Mt 12:22; Mk 7:25-30; 9:25-26; Acts 19:11-12). The most important objective confirmation, of course, was the deliverance/healing itself.

Once the demon or demons have been exorcised from an individual, Christians need to help the person continue in daily prayer, Bible study and church attendance. The late occult specialist Kurt Koch used to recommend, among other things, that the one who has been delivered break off all contacts with occultism (including occultic friends) be filled with the Spirit, join a prayer group and seek a counselor.

Question 76: Are the Spirit of Fear, the Spirit of Cancer and Related Spirits Demonic Spirits?

We know about the Holy Spirit, the human soul/spirit and demonic spirits. The Bible also uses the word *spirit* to refer to other concepts such as mind, attitude, influence, and state or disposition, depending on the context. These concepts are especially mixed in the King James Version. Naive Christians and faith preachers often mistake "the spirit of fear," for instance, for a demon that specializes in bringing fear to its victims (2 Tim 1:7 KJV). But the "spirit of fear" is no more a demon than are the spirits of "power, love and a sound mind"! The word *spirit* in this passage more likely refers to an attitude or a disposition: God has not given us an *attitude* of fearfulness, but one of love, power and a sound mind.

The terms "spirit of poverty" (Mt 5:3) and "spirit of crushing"

(Ps 34:18) do not refer to demons any more than "spirit of steadfastness" (Ps 51:10) and "spirit of quietness" (1 Pet 3:4) refer to angels. Some of these spirits may refer to bad influences, but this still does not make them demons. Such are the "haughty spirit" (Prov 16:18), the "spirit of dizziness" (Is 19:14), the "spirit of despair" (Is 61:3), the "spirit of prostitution" (Hos 4:12) and the "spirit of stupor" (Rom 11:8).

Some spirits are not even found in Scripture, but we often hear the televangelists rebuke them anyway. Some of the most popular spirits of this sort are often related to sicknesses, sinful activities or undesirable habits, such as the "spirit of cancer," the "spirit of alcohol," the "spirit of smoking" and the "spirit of masturbation." Some of these spirits border on the ridiculous, such as the "spirit of forgetfulness," the "spirit of allergy" and the "spirit of fingernail biting."

Ministers who rebuke such "spirits" ought to realize that unbelievers are often watching them perform such theatrics. Their bizarre actions make Christians appear to be a bunch of superstitious morons without a shred of common sense. Natural explanations suffice for many of these "spirits." Someone who has allergies should take allergy medication and stay away from known allergens; someone who has a problem with bad breath should not eat so much garlic.

Some sicknesses and vices may indeed be caused by demons, but this is not true in every case. Too often people throw around the term *spirit* without any proof that a real demon is behind the problem. Not every "spirit" that the faith healers rebuke is a real demon.

Question 77: Can Satan Intercept Our Prayers?

In Daniel 10:13 we read that a being called the prince of Persia hindered God's answer to Daniel's prayers. Does this mean that Satan can intercept our prayers? We should note that Daniel 10 records a unique, mysterious event. The prince of

Persia hindered the angel Gabriel from entering his territory. We are not told that the prince of Persia *knew* he was deliberately hindering an answer to Daniel's prayer.[33] On the other hand, some Christians think that Satan cannot understand them when they speak in tongues (unknown dialects). Of course they themselves cannot understand what they are praying either (1 Cor 14:2, 14-15). In any case, Paul claims that praying in tongues is meant for worship, praise and self-edification, not as insurance that Satan will not be able intercept the prayer (1 Cor 14:4; Acts 2:4, 11).[34]

Many would affirm that demons can plant doubt or guilt in our minds, and they can tempt us to sin. In such ways their activities may result in the hindrance of our prayers (compare 1 Pet 3:7; Rom 14:23). Nevertheless, they cannot prevent God from hearing any prayer that is offered up by faith. The Bible never claims that Satan is omniscient. He does not hear every prayer, nor can he read our minds to hinder our silent prayers. Even if he could hinder us from receiving an *answer* to prayer, he could not permanently hinder us from receiving that answer. Sooner or later, every prayer in faith is answered, according to Scripture (Mt 7:7-10; Jn 14:13-14; 1 Jn 5:14-15).

Question 78: Are Phenomena like Speaking in Tongues, Getting "Slain in the Spirit" and Convulsing of the Devil?

There is no evidence that the gift of tongues (speaking in unknown languages) ever ceased in the church.[35] There is also no biblical evidence that tongues will ever cease during the church era. Tongues will cease only when Christ returns (compare 1 Cor 13:8-13). Christians who speak in tongues have every biblical reason to do so. Paul himself charged the Corinthian church, "Do not forbid speaking in tongues" (1 Cor 14:39).

A recent movement called the Toronto Blessing, or the Holy Laughter Renewal, reports people laughing in the

Spirit, getting "slain in the Spirit" (fainting), convulsing, roaring and behaving in unusual ways. Such activities find no direct support in Scripture. Are these bodily manifestations of the devil?

I have written an entire book discerning the various bodily manifestations associated with the Toronto Blessing.[36] These phenomena appeared quite frequently in the great revivals of the past. The First and Second Great Awakenings included participants who laughed, groaned, fainted, "jerked" and the like. The Azusa Street and Welsh revivals of the twentieth century also included similar phenomena. Jonathan Edwards, John Wesley, Charles Finney and others, however, were critical of *excessive* bodily phenomena, but they did not rule out every instance as coming from the devil. In fact, often they affirmed that people were experiencing a touch from God. In every true revival there will be manifestations coming from God, the flesh and the devil.

After examining both Scripture and previous revivals, I have concluded that most manifestations associated with this renewal are frail human reactions (and overreactions) to a sense of the Holy Spirit's presence.[37] Some Toronto Blessing and Pentecostal/charismatic services may become rather disorderly, but that does not mean they are of the devil. Paul exhorted the "charismatic" Corinthians to be more orderly (1 Cor 14:26-33, 40), but he still considered them Christians and believed the Spirit moved through their congregation *despite* the disorder (1 Cor 1:1-9, 3:16; 6:19-20; 12:13).

The devil is losing too many unbelievers and lukewarm Christians to these renewals to be the source of them. This is especially true now that the Toronto movement is making a serious turn to evangelize the lost and backing it up with prayer and fasting. Whatever revivals of the past have experienced, we see similar things now happening in the Toronto Blessing, including the good, the bad and the bizarre. In any case, this movement as a whole is not a counterfeit revival.

Question 79: How Do We Discern Whether a Supernatural Event Is of God or of the Devil?

Jesus and his followers are not the only ones who perform signs and wonders in the Bible. Jannes and Jambres, the Egyptian sorcerers, opposed the miracles God did through Moses by performing a few wonders of their own.[38] The Lord, however, proved more powerful than the magic of Egypt (Ex 7:11-12, 22; 8:7, 18-19; 2 Tim 3:8).

The Bible predicts that during the last days false prophets will perform incredible signs and wonders that will lead many astray (Rev 13:11; 16:13; Mt 24:20). The purpose of these demonic activities is to deceive people and lead them away from the kingdom of God (2 Thess 2:9-12). The question to ask in regard to whether a supernatural event is from the Lord or from Satan is, Does the event lead people to the kingdom of God or to the kingdom of darkness? If a genuine supernatural event draws a person into the occult, idolatry, sin or heretical doctrine,[39] then I believe that demons are behind the event (compare Deut 13:1-3). Conversely, if a miracle draws someone to accept the gospel of Christ or to desire godly things (such as prayer, Bible reading, fellowship, reaching hurting people, and other good works that glorify God), then I think God should get the glory for the miracle.

QUESTIONS
ABOUT
THE OCCULT

One unfortunate soul breaks a mirror, another walks under a ladder on Friday the thirteenth, still another sees a black cat cross his path. A 1990 Gallup poll on belief in the paranormal demonstrated that many people hold on to classic superstitions.[1] Despite the silliness of superstitions, they abound where fear and ignorance come together. Superstitions represent the silly side of the occult—a kingdom whose influence is not so silly. Spiritism, astrology, reincarnation, New Age, UFO sects, transcendental meditation, witchcraft and Satanism are but some occult influences. Real and fake forms of the occult provide avenues for the devil to draw people into his fold.

Question 80: What Is the Occult?

The word *occult* comes from a Latin word meaning "to conceal." Sociologist and cult specialist Ronald Enroth defines the occult as hidden wisdom that "is beyond the range of ordinary human knowledge . . . mysteries or concealed phenomena . . . inexplicable events."[2] "The occult" thus refers to concealed or hidden arts, practices and beliefs that bring "persons in contact with supernatural powers, paranormal energies, or demonic forces."[3] Occult practitioners harness occult powers in an effort to manipulate people or circumstances. Occultism is set in contrast to Christianity; the former is based on secret arts, the latter on the open, revealed word of God.

The occult is an empire in its own right with a wide range of occult beliefs, groups and activities:

General Occult Practices	Mediumship, palmistry, fortune-telling, etc.
Eastern Mysticism	Yoga, meditation, trance, Tibetan Buddhism, Hare Krishnas, TM, etc.
New Age	Theosophy, Silva Mind Control, Forum (est), Lifespring, etc.
Esoteric Groups	Freemasonry (the Masonic Lodge), Rosicrucianism, etc.
Animism/Folk Religions	Voodoo cults, Santeria, Yoruba, Macumba, Umbanda, etc.
Neopaganism	Witchcraft, Druids, veneration of Norse and Greek gods, etc.
Satanism	Anton LaVey (Church of Satan), Michael Aquino (Church of Set), etc.

Although some label any occult group a cult, there is a difference between cults and the occult. As understood by today's popular media culture,[4] a cult involves a religious sect (a splinter group from a major religion or denomination) that gives virtual blind allegiance to the revelations and/or interpretations of an allegedly specially endowed leader. The occult, on the other hand, primarily involves mystical/esoteric practice. Not all cultists practice the occult, and not all occultists belong to a cult. For instance, the Jehovah's Witnesses, who are commonly identified as a cult, condemn various forms of occultism. Richard Ramirez, the Satanic "night stalker" who committed serial murders in the 1980s, would be considered an occultist, but he did not belong to any cult. Some substitute the more vogue word *paranormal* for "the occult."

Question 81: What Are Some Occult Practices?

Occult practices seem to fall into four basic categories: (1) contacting a celestial being, spirit or ghost (for example, mediumship and channeling), (2) contacting or improving the "higher self" (for example, yoga and meditation), (3) manipulating persons or reality for a desired end (for example, magic and witchcraft), (4) pursuing hidden knowledge (for example, ESP, fortunetelling). These basic categories are not rigidly maintained, and an occult practice may combine two or more of them. The practices described below are only a sampling of what is out there.[5]

Spiritism. Spiritism flourished in the nineteenth century, popularized by the Fox sisters: Margaret and Katie Fox from Hydesville, New York. Spiritism is a practice that seeks communion with spirits, whether angels, demons, ghosts or other spirits. The deceased are contacted through a medium, usually at a séance. This practice is called necromancy in Scripture (Deut 18). The New Age movement has revived interest in mediumship with channeling—the practice in which an alleged alien from another planet, the spirit of a dead person or some other power speaks through a person who "channels" the entity. The danger with spiritism is obvious. Demons can disguise themselves as deceased humans, ETs or other entities. A medium or channeler is vulnerable to demon possession.

Extrasensory perception (ESP). ESP is the term used to refer to communication by means other than the five senses. Clairvoyance is the practice of being able to see physical objects that are out of sight, classically by using a crystal ball. A variant of clairvoyance is dowsing, using a V-shaped rod to find lost or hidden objects. Telepathy involves the alleged ability to read, communicate or induce thoughts.[6] Telekinesis (psychokinesis, or PK), popularized by the novel and horror movie *Carrie*, involves moving physical objects by psychic means. Psychic healing involves the use of secret arts to treat illnesses instead of using modern medical treatment. A client may meditate, drink a potion or use an object such as a crystal ball. Psychics employ prayer and any number of physical techniques to allegedly rid a client of disease. Psychic surgery is a popular form of psychic healing. The client lies awake as the psychic "surgically" removes a disease. The operation leaves no scar. This scam is usually done by sleight of hand, a gizzard and chicken blood. But not all forms of psychic healing are necessarily fraudulent. It is possible for demons to perform supernatural feats, and they could temporarily "heal" people of some ailments for the purpose of deceiving them. Psychic healing is the opposite of divine healing (a healing through faith in God). The latter draws a person to the kingdom of God, the former draws a victim closer to the kingdom of darkness.

Yoga and Eastern meditation. Yoga is a set of theories and practices that attempt to "yoke," or harness, the mind to concentrate (meditate) in order to achieve a desired benefit—so-called alpha tranquillity, or self-realization.[7] Some practice yoga as a means of exercise, but genuine yoga is steeped in mysticism. It generally involves deep meditation that can include visualization, guided imagery and a focus on alleged body centers called *chakras*. These centers are said to be concentrated psychic points that Hindus call gods. The mother goddess is called *kundalini*, a coiled serpent or electrical force that is said to reside near the base of the human spine. This force is said to open up the psychic centers of the body. One danger with yoga is that a deeply altered state of consciousness can be vulnerable to demonic influence or possession. The misuse of *kundalini* can result in death or insanity, as certain yogis warn. Some attribute the mysterious phenomenon of spontaneous human combustion—often associated with poltergeists—to the misuse of this practice.

Fortunetelling. This occult practice involves palm reading, horoscope reading, card reading and so forth. The fortuneteller "predicts" someone's future through adroit use of facial expressions, body language, good guessing and a good understanding of human nature and what most clients desire (money, sex, power, revenge). Often what the fortuneteller actually reads is human gestures, as does the psychic reader. Nevertheless, since demons have a limited knowledge of the future (Acts 16:16-19), they may be the source of some of the predictions made by fortunetellers.

Astral projection. Astral projection, "soul travel" or "shamanic journeying," asserts that a human spirit can leave its physical body and travel about on the earth or on different planes of existence, including the "astral" plane (often understood as the after-death plane). Some claim that Paul's third heaven experience and John the apostle's prophetic encounters "in the spirit" (2 Cor 12:2-4; Rev 4:1-3) support this phenomenon. However, the experiences that Paul and John had may have been visions like Peter's (Compare Acts 10:10-11). Even if such passages involve actual out-of-body experiences, the apostles made no attempt to travel through different astral planes. Their experiences were initiated by God, not themselves.[8] They did not attempt to meditate and concentrate on their spirit leaving their body. As with many occult practices, those who practice astral projection run the risk of opening themselves up to a deeply altered state of consciousness that invites demonic influence or possession.

Many occult practices involve frauds and scams, but this does not mean that demons cannot influence or deceive the people involved in these activities. For almost every supernatural spiritual gift we find in Scripture, the devil seems to have his counterfeit. Nevertheless, God's power is far greater than Satan's (Ex 7:11-13; 8:10; Mk 3:27; 1 Jn 3:8; 4:4).

Question 82: What Does the Bible Say About the Occult?

Various aspects of the occult are mentioned in biblical scripture. Deuteronomy 18:9-13 gives an extensive listing of occult practices. The Canaanites indulged in practices similar to or the same as the occult. These practices are identified as abominations or detestable things. God expelled the Canaanites from the land of Palestine because they practiced these early forms of occultism.[9]

Concept	Description
One who makes his son or daughter pass through the fire (ma^{a}bîr b^{e}nô-ûbittô ba'ēš, Deut 18:10; Lev 18:21; Gen 31:19; Judg 17:5; 2 Kings 23:10; Jer 7:31; 19:6; 32:35)	Sacrificing children to another god or idol (in this case, Molech). Apparently this was an ordeal by fire. An omen was determined by seeing if the child was scorched or unscathed when passing through fire.
One who practices divination (qosēm q^{e}samîm) (Deut 18:10; Num 23:23; 1 Sam 15:23; Zech 10:2; 2 Kings 17:17; Jer 14:14; Ezek 13:6-23; 21:21-26; Mic 3:6-11)	A practice suggesting the drawing of arrows until one fell out. The outcome was considered a decision made by a god. The Hebrews may have used teraphim, or household gods, for this purpose.
One who practices sorcery (m^e'ônēn) (Deut 18:10; Lev 19:26; Judg 9:37; 2 Kings 21:6; Is 2:6; 11:6; 47:13; 57:3)	Observing the times (prototype astrology) or clouds, using the "evil eye," conjuring up spirits, humming and soothsaying.
One who interprets omens (m^{e}nahēš) (Deut 18:10; Lev 19:26; 2 Kings 17:17; 21:6; Is 3:3-20; 26:16; Jer 8:17)	Divination based on looking for signs in actions, word choice, serpents, birds or changes in the forces of nature and the stars.
One who engages in witchcraft (m^{e}kaššēp) (Deut 18:10; Ex 7:11; 22:17; 2 Chron 33:6; Jer 27:9; Dan 2:2; Mic 5:11; Mal 3:5)	The use of drugs, herbs, spells or other such things for producing magic or enchantment.

One who casts spells *(hober haber)* (Deut 18:11; Ps 58:6; Is 47:9-12)	Making unintelligible clamor, serpent charming or using charms, perhaps tying magical knots or binding a spell (for example, sympathetic "voodoo" magic).
One who practices mediumship or spiritism *(šo' ēl 'ôḇ wᵉyidd ᵉ'onî)* (Deut 18:11; Lev 19:31; 1 Sam 28:3-11; Is 8:19; 29:4; 19:3; 2 Chron 33:6)	Necromancy or consulting a ghost, and perhaps employing ventriloquism as coming from the ground. The term can refer to a wide range of ideas from consulting ancestral spirits to demons.
One who consults the dead *(dorēš el-hammetîm)* (Deut 18:11; Is 8:19; 65:4)	Another form of necromancy, or perhaps any other divination such as sleeping in the tombs to inquire of spirits.

Biblical passages on the occult do not exhaust the wide range of occult practices. The Old Testament writers targeted only certain occult expressions because these forms were the ones Israel faced in the land of Canaan. Later on, they faced a new barrage of practices including hepatoscopy (consulting entrails), astrology and the use of amulets (for example, Ezek 13:18-20; 21:21; Dan 2:2, 10, 27; Is 8:20). As David Aune notes, "From Assyria and Babylonia came an interest in astrology. From Egypt came an emphasis on the power inherent in the spoken or written word, especially the secret name. From Persia came an emphasis on demons, both as causes of illness and human problems and also as agents that could be enlisted to carry out the wishes of the magical practitioner."[10] Many modern occultic practices are similar to the ancient ones. But the fact that Scripture does not mention an occultic practice does not mean that it is acceptable.

Some may notice similarities between occultic divination and biblical prophecy. Both claim supernatural insight from a higher power. Clairvoyance might be similar to the Charismatic understanding of the "word of knowledge," and seeking the decision of a god through casting arrows or consulting a liver is not much different from the biblical practice of casting lots (Acts 1:24-26). So why are occultic practices condemned when similar practices are performed in the name of God?

What radically distinguishes one set of practices from the other is not so much the form they take, but their source and motive. Christianity's source of power is the Holy Spirit. Occultic practices (that are not faked) draw their power from unknown forces or demons, manipulating reality without God's approval (Deut 13; 18:14; 32:16-17; Lev 17:7; 2 Chron 33:6; 1 Cor 10:20-21). Hence, when Paul encounters Elymus the sorcerer, he calls him "a child of the devil" (Acts 13:4-12; compare Gal 5:19-21). When he confronts a fortuneteller, he casts a demon from her (Acts 16:16-19).[11] The saints warned that those who practice witchcraft and manipulative magic will not inherit the kingdom of God (Gal 5:19-21; Rev 21:8; 22:14-15). And since the Bible exhorts us to be sober-minded, a deep altered state of consciousness obtained by trance, yoga, astral projection or another such means would be contrary to God's Word (1 Thess 5:6, 8; Tit 2:2, 4, 6; 1 Pet 1:13; 4:7; compare Prov 25:28; Gal 5:19-21).

Question 83: What Objects Are Used in Occult Practices?

Occultists use various objects. Generally speaking, occult objects supposedly help the occultist release subconscious powers by altering normal consciousness. Some objects are used to determine the future, while others are superstitiously applied to good and bad luck.

Tarot cards. Tarot cards are thought to have originated in Italy in the fourteenth century. The cards picture archetypal figures such as kings, princes, the grim reaper and so forth. Standard tarot combines fifty-two cards plus four knights and twenty-two additional cards called the *major arcana.* There seem to be few Christian images; two are the pope and the final judgment. Fortunetellers often use these cards to predict the future by interpreting what the pictures supposedly represent symbolically.

Crystal ball. Fortunetellers and psychics use the crystal ball for clairvoyance and other occult practices.

Rod and pendulum. The rod and pendulum are used for dowsing and for locating earth rays in order to protect people from the alleged radiation that comes from these rays.

The ouija board. The ouija board is available at many hobby and toy stores. The board contains the alphabet, numbers and a few words by which players ask questions. They receive answers by placing their fingers on or near a disk that moves over the symbols. It has introduced many to occultism.[12]

Sprays and repellents (apotropaics). Repellents allegedly prevent spiritual harm or bad luck from coming on an individual. A so-called gambling spray, for instance, supposedly prevents bad luck or incurs good luck in gambling.

Love potions. Occult shops often sell love potions, which are strange fragrances that are believed to attract the desired person. Sometimes they are potentiated by a charm with a prayer recited from a mystic or occultic book.

Good luck charms. A wide variety of objects are used as good luck pieces. A rabbit's foot or a lucky rubberband is not necessarily occultic. Superstitious individuals do not realize that such things have no intrinsic power whatsoever. The occult becomes involved when prayer is offered to the charm or to some other power, or if the object has been somehow blessed by a person in the occult. Objects devoted to the occult can attract demonic presences. A person who suspects that an object has been devoted to occult purposes may want to throw out the object (compare Acts 19:13-20).

Occult symbols. Various written symbols are connected with occult activities. The most popular include the number 666 (the mark of the beast), the pentagram (a five-angled star used in occult ceremonies) and the upside-down question mark with a cross (a Satanic symbol).[13]

We should avoid developing a phobia toward anything that

resembles an occult object. The fact that a New Ager wears a crystal ball does not mean that I cannot possess any crystal objects in my home. An occultic object is one that is meant to represent or symbolize an aspect of the occult, has been blessed by an occultist, draws a person into occultic activities, or attracts demonic powers. Biblical scripture teaches that the instruments used for occult or idolatrous beliefs and practices must be destroyed (Ex 34:13-14; 2 Kings 23:4; Hos 4:12-14; Jer 3:9; Acts 19:13-20).

Question 84: What Is Magic?

The word *magic* has multiple meanings (see answer 85). David Aune writes that "a religious deviance is magical only when the goals sought are considered virtually guaranteed through the management of supernatural powers."[14] The term *magic* in this sense seems to involve manipulating invisible or supernatural forces to achieve personal ends.[15] From most ancient times people have distinguished between white magic, which is used for good ends, and black magic, which is used for evil ends. Both forms, however, tap into psychic forces and demonic powers (see answer 86).

In biblical times ancient cultures commonly employed this form of magic. Words and invocations were believed to have power to force spirits to do the bidding of the one employing the spell or incantation.[16] Pagans used magic primarily for protection, altering fate, aphrodisiacs, curses, healings and special knowledge.[17] The book of Ephesians may be combating several of these assumptions.[18] The source behind such powers would naturally be demonic (cf. Eph 2:2-5; 4:27; 6:10-18). Many people in Ephesus, fearing the danger of the demonic, ended up burning their magical arts books (Acts 19:13-19). For the Ephesian church, Christ is supreme over all natural, demonic or magical powers (Eph 1:19-23; 4:8-10). Christ demonstrated his authority over all other powers by casting out demons and rising from the dead (Mt 12:28-29; 28:18; Acts 19:15).

The Bible condemns magic when it is understood as a means of manipulating or coercing supernatural forces. It is related to sorcery and witchcraft (Gk. *pharmakeia* [Heb. *mᵉkaššēp̄*] and related words, Deut 18:10 LXX; Ex 7:11; 2 Chron 33:6; Mal 3:5; Gal 5:20; Rev 9:21; 18:23; 21:8; 22:15; compare Ex 22:17 MT; Lev 19:26-31; 20:6, 27; 2 Kings 23:24; Gal 3:1). Simon Magus was a magician who thought he could manipulate the power of the Holy Spirit. Peter squarely rebuked him for trying to buy the power of the Spirit (Acts 8:19-24).[19]

Question 85: Are Magic Shows Occultic?

Another meaning for the word *magic* is the art of performing tricks or illusions by sleight of hand or other means. Magicians such as David Copperfield, Danny Korem and André Kole fall into this category. Magic shows are not necessarily occultic. The audience understands that the magician is performing tricks.

Nevertheless, some con games can be used to fool people in believing the paranormal.[20] Occult practitioners make a profit from these fraudulent means. Christian magician Danny Korem has exposed fraudulent aspects of the occult.[21] Almost all forms of the occult and paranormal can be faked, especially fortunetelling, palm reading, astrology, psychic healing, mediumship and telepathy (see answer 81). We will look at some frauds that are particularly commonplace:

Subliminal messages. Subliminal messages are recorded on cassette tapes recorded at such low frequencies that, supposedly, only the subconscious mind can pick them up. These tapes often claim to improve memory, character, looks or what have you. But they offer no generally accepted scientifically verifiable benefit to the listeners.[22] A more occultic subliminal variation is backward masking on tapes, which is said to promote Satan and the occult. Demonstrable results from listening to such tapes have yet to be achieved. Let's worry less about what a tape may or may not say when played backward and more about what it says when played forward!

Fire walking. Fire walking is the ability to walk over hot coals without getting seriously burned. Eastern mystics and human potential personalities use it to allegedly demonstrate mind and spirit over matter. But there is probably nothing supernatural going on, since coals, like the inside of ovens, are poor conductors of heat. (Ever wonder why no one tries to walk on top of a long, white-hot sheet of metal?) Sweat and speed also help the fire walker avoid getting burned.

Numerology. The practice of numerology involves the ability to predict the future or understand hidden messages through numbers. It is often used with cabala (a body of mystic Jewish teaching), pyramidology and end-time prophecy speculation. Charles Taze Russell, founder of the Jehovah's Witnesses, supported his belief that the end of the world would take place in 1914 by calculating the size of the Great Pyramid in Egypt.[23]

Biorhythm. Biorhythm machines or computers supposedly record personal highs and lows in reference to success, sex, health, driving safety and so forth on a daily basis. Biorhythm is often used like a horoscope and has a similar lack of scientific support.

The practices mentioned above are shot through with fakery, but that does not exclude the possibility that demonic forces can work through these activities to accomplish their ends. Before I became a Christian, I followed biorhythm cards that seemed to predict my future with incredible accuracy. This could have amounted to coincidence based on uncritical scrutiny of the cards, but it is also possible that supernatural forces were at work manipulating circumstances to draw me deeper into the occult. If so, they succeeded to the extent that I graduated from horoscopes and biorhythm cards to fortunetellers and tarot cards. My fascination with the occult ended when I began to read what the Bible predicted instead of what the palm reader predicted.

The Bible warns against false prophets who seduce people for personal profit and gain (Acts 20:28-35; Rom 16:17-18; 2 Cor

11:13, 20; 2 Pet 2; Jude 11). Scripture warns, "But evil men and seducers shall wax worse and worse, deceiving and being deceived" (2 Tim 3:13 KJV). In this verse the Greek word translated "seducers," *goētes,* was commonly used for charlatans and magical frauds.[24]

Question 86: What Is PSI?

Fundamental to the occult is the belief that humankind can tap into a secret force in the universe for power, divination, healing and so forth. This force is known as PSI (after the Greek letter *psi*). Occultists often consider this force neutral. It is neither good nor evil, but can be manipulated by humans for good or evil purposes. They often believe it is eternal, can heal, and can be stored and highly concentrated in objects. In Eastern mystic and paranormal circles, it goes by various names.[25]

Name	Affiliation	Force
Helen Blavatsky	Theosophy	Astral light
Robert Fludd	Rosicrucianism	Spiritus
Monte Kline	Holistic health	Bioenergy
Lao-tzu	Taoism	Tao
Franz Anton Mesmer	Hypnotism	Animal magnetism
Charles Reicher	Psychic research	Ectoplasm
J. B. Rhine	Parapsychology	PSI faculty
Rudolf Steiner	Anthroposophy	Etheric formative forces
N/A	Eastern philosophy	Yin-yang
N/A	Animism	Mana
N/A	Hinduism	Prana
N/A	Zen, certain martial arts	Chi/ki

Biblical scripture does not commend a neutral psychic force that can be manipulated by humans. It affirms that God alone is eternal, creating all things visible and invisible, and he cannot be manipulated (Gen 1:1; Jn 1:1-3; Col 1:15-18). Nor should we connect psychic forces with the power of the Holy

Spirit. The Holy Spirit, who is God (Acts 5:3-4), cannot be coerced and does not bestow any universal power that is available to nonbelievers (Acts 8:18-24; Rom 8:9).

Some affirm that Adam and Eve originally had psychic abilities, which became latent after the Fall but are potentially available to everyone. Demons can use these abilities, but God has now forbidden them to humans. This perspective has some problems. Only a few people are able to develop PSI powers. The Bible shows us that power and salvation come from above, not from within (Jn 3:3:1-8; Jn 17:1; Acts 1:9-11; Lk 24:49; Acts 2:2-4).[26] It is more likely that "genuine" psychic forces originate in the spirit realm. There may be centers in the human nervous system that can link us to spiritual forces. Perhaps demonic forces can stimulate these centers "by the direct infusion of a spirit's energy, much as a radio is activated simply by plugging it in."[27]

At any rate, true power comes from being filled with the Holy Spirit (Acts 2:4, 38-39; 4:31; 1 Cor 12; Eph 5:18-20). Our God-given ability to work in the supernatural does not come through manipulating powers; it comes from belonging to Christ and totally depending on him; we are helpless within our own strength (Gen 41:14-16; Dan 1:17-20; 2:27-30; Mk 9:28-29; Acts 3:12; 14:3).

Question 87: Is Astrology Occultic?

Your local newspaper probably runs a daily horoscope that claims to predict the future. Horoscopes are based on the ancient practice of astrology, which studies the twelve signs of the zodiac. From ancient times people have believed that stars can influence human affairs. But the Bible denounces those who try to read their fate or future in the stars— astrology is a worthless endeavor (Is 47:13-14; compare 65:11; Jer 10:2; Dan 2:2). Astrology is often considered occultic because it claims to know the future through powers other than God. The Bible claims that no one but God knows the entire future, and he doesn't speak to anyone by means of astrology (Deut 29:29; Is 41:26; Mt 24:36; Acts 16:16). Shouldn't we trust in him for our future rather than a silly human-made horoscope?

Astrology is also filled with contradictions. First, those who follow it are not able to explain scientifically how stars, most of them unspeakably distant from the earth, can determine human fate. Second, astrology is based on the fallacious and archaic notion that the universe revolves around the earth. Third, astrology leaves no horoscope for Scandinavians, Eskimos and other people who live above 60 degrees of latitude. In this region, the signs of the zodiac do not appear. Fourth, we also have the twin paradox. How is it possible that twins who are born on the same day and under the same zodiac sign can live completely different lives? Finally, horoscope readings are usually vague enough to mean practically anything; on the other hand, if two horoscopes from different sources dare to be specific, they often contradict each other. The Bible reasonably declares that astrology is futile.[28]

Question 88: Is Reincarnation Compatible with Christianity?

Many New Age groups, Eastern Mystics and occultists claim that reincarnation (the belief that the spirit of a creature or human can enter into a different creature or human after death) and Christianity are perfectly compatible. They say that John the Baptist claimed to be Elijah reincarnated, and that being "born again" refers to reincarnation! They also claim that the Bible originally taught reincarnation, but the church suppressed and destroyed these scriptures in the third and fourth centuries.

There is no evidence that the church fathers ever suppressed biblical scriptures about reincarnation. Reincarnationists should look into Greek New Testament manuscripts dating back to the fourth century or earlier, such as the Codex Sinaiticus, Codex Vaticanus, Codex Alexandrinus and numerous papyri and fragments. These writings unanimously affirm that nothing in favor of reincarnation was included in Scripture before the church allegedly suppressed it. Beginning with the first-century apostles, the church has consistently rejected reincarnation.[29]

The born-again experience has nothing to do with reincarnation. Jesus flatly denied that people can be born a second time in the womb. The born-again experience is a spiritual regeneration. At conversion, the Christian believer inherits eternal life and is baptized in the Holy Spirit into the invisible church of Christ (Jn 3:3-8; 7:37-39; 1 Cor 12:13; Tit 3:5; 1 Jn 5:1). Moreover, if Jesus had been teaching reincarnation, Nicodemus and the other Jewish leaders would have charged him with heresy.

John the Baptist came in the spirit of Elijah (Lk 1:17), but as we noted earlier (see answer 76), the word *spirit* has a variety of meanings. It does not always refer to the soul of a human or a demon. In Luke's context the word *spirit* signifies character. John the Baptist came in a character or a personality that was similar to Elijah. Not that John was the reincarnation of Elijah—he flatly denies a literal association with Elijah in John 1:21: "They [the priests and Levites] asked him [John], 'Then who are you? Are you Elijah?' He [John] said, 'I am not.' "[30] Moreover, Scripture says that Elijah never experienced death; he was taken up to heaven by a whirlwind (2 Kings 2). It would be extremely difficult, even for a reincarnationist, to believe that John could possess the spirit of a person who never died!

Reincarnation is not compatible with Christianity. The Bible teaches resurrection, not reincarnation. Death is real, and we die only once. After death we are judged and will be sentenced to either heaven or hell (Heb 9:27; Jn 5:28-29; 1 Cor 15:20-26; Rev 20:4-6, 11-15). There are many other reasons why reincarnation is incompatible with Christianity. We will consider a few of them.[31]

Reincarnation knows nothing of divine forgiveness because

it traditionally presupposes the law of karma. Karma is essentially the Eastern term for getting what we deserve. It is similar to the idea of reaping what we sow. For example, karma allegedly dictates that when a wife beater dies, in his next life he will probably be reincarnated into a wife who is beaten by her husband. Karma mandates that a murderer who later repents still has to suffer being murdered in his next life. Reincarnation also leads to moral inconsistencies. Why should anyone help a drowning child or a blind beggar? Aren't they suffering for misdeeds in a previous life? If we do help them, aren't we interfering with their karma? Reincarnation does not alleviate the problem of sin and evil, it only perpetuates it. There is no final forgiveness and no final judgment, just an endless recycling of karma.

Question 89: Is Rock Music Satanic?

We often hear about rock lyrics that glorify Satan and blaspheme God. No genuine Christian should want to listen to such music, any more than a Satanist would want to listen to gospel music. Not all rock groups blaspheme, though, and some actually intend to glorify God through their lyrics. So is the music inherently evil? Some fundamentalists claim that rock rhythms come from pagan religious rituals. In fact, however, rock music derives from rhythm and blues, which came from gospel music!

Any form of music, as long as it does not promote total chaos and confusion, is not intrinsically bad. If the lyrics to a song blaspheme God or glorify Satan, sin or the occult, then a Christian should not want to listen to it. Christians should not esteem any music star, or any other media icon for that matter, whose message and lifestyle promotes drugs, promiscuity or occultism.

Question 90: Is the New Age Movement Occultic?

The New Age movement is an eclectic, networked group of

people and organizations working to influence the world in all areas of life with an Eastern, mystic worldview in the so-called Age of Aquarius.[32] Its goal is the unity of humanity as one consciousness or "global brain" that some call Gaia. Many New Agers get involved with occult and Eastern mystic beliefs and practices like reincarnation, yoga, astrology, transcendental meditation and so forth. The New Age worldview is contrary to the Christian worldview. New Age philosophy is almost indistinguishable from general occult philosophy, believing that all is one (monism), God is all (pantheism), man is God or part of God, and we create our own reality.[33] Many New Agers believe sin is caused by the ignorance of not realizing our human potential.

The Bible gives us a completely different picture. Sin is not merely ignorance, but it is believing or doing something contrary to the standards, will or character of God (Gen 3; Mt 7:21; Rom 3:23; 14:23; Jas 4:17; 1 Jn 3:4; 5:17). The common New Age conception that sin is ignornce, morality is relative, and humans create their own reality raises vexing inconsistencies.[34] Can we say that Hitler was wrong for annihilating six million Jews if, in his moral opinion, Jews ought to be exterminated? Should we commend our daughter for getting an F in math because, according to *her* reality, one and one ought to make three? These rather extreme examples make a point: we cannot live consistently with our practices if we think that truth and morality are entirely subjective and our own reality is the only one that really matters.

Contrary to the New Age concepts of monism and pantheism, biblical scripture teaches that God is distinct from his creation, and he created all things ex nihilo, or out of nothing (Gen 1:1; Heb 1:2; Col 1:15-18). Behind the New Age assumption that God is all is the belief that God is an impersonal force, which is often equated with the alleged eternal mana, or psychic force of the universe. Since real New Agers do not

communicate with a personal God, they often wind up attempting communication with personal spirits. Scripture,
however, states that God is a personal being with intellect,
emotion and will (Ex 2:20; Jer 29:11-13; Jn 3:16). Moreover,
humans are not God; rather, they were created in God's image,
possessing moral, rational and spiritual qualities (Gen 1:26-27;
Is 43:10; Gal 4:8).

Question 91: Satan Working Through the New Age Movement?

Contrary to the worst dream of many panic-stricken Christians, there is no New Age or New World Order conspiracy.
New Agers are not secretly organizing to take over the world
and unveil the antichrist.[35] The New Age seems to be losing
the popularity it experienced in the 1980s. A growing number of secularists think that New Agers are strange, even
kooks or weirdos. The tragedy in San Diego (Rancho Santa
Fe) with the Heaven's Gate cult is beginning to cause some
to consider that certain New Age beliefs can be dangerous.
New Agers are now focusing on more publicly respectable
means of transmitting their message, like writing novels (for
example, James Redfield's *Celestine Prophecy*), discussing
holistic health (Deepak Chopra), supporting environmental
and ecological issues, creating paranormal Web sites, and of
course talking about angels.

If Satan's plan was to make the entire world New Age, I think
he failed. The occult philosophy behind the New Age movement, however, is pervasive. This philosophy includes antago-
nism toward or reinterpretation of authentic Christianity. As
noted in the last answer, the traditional Christian understanding of the Bible opposes New Age ideas. And so does the
biblical Christ.

The New Age generally believes that Jesus alone was not
the Christ, but he was the human vehicle in which the "cosmic
Christ" dwelled.[36] Jesus is a human vessel, and the Christ is a

cosmic impersonal force. In New Age terms Christ was one of many avatars who obtained the "Christ consciousness" (other avatars include Muhammad, Buddha, Krishna, Gandhi). The ultimate goal for some New Agers is to achieve their own "Christ consciousness," or self-awareness that they themselves are Christ. Thus Jesus was *a* way show-er to help us seek our own christhood. As Jesus was, so we could become.[37]

To accept the New Age Christ is to deny the genuine Christ of the Bible (1 Jn 2:22-23). Jesus Christ's historical life is recorded in four historical writings known as the Gospels. Although some biblical scholars contest minor points of these records, the majority affirm that the Gospels do portray the historical ministry of Christ.[38] In these records Jesus affirms that he is the Messiah, the Son of God and the Savior of the Jewish people. He proves his messianic power by his resurrection from the dead. His actual, historical resurrection sets him apart from all other religious leaders. Since Christ lived a perfect moral life and is the only person in history who has conquered death, we ought to believe what he says. He affirms that he is the Christ, the Son of God; God incarnate in human flesh, and the *only* way to God the Father (Jn 14:6; Mt 11:27; 16:16-17; 26:63-64; Jn 4:25-26; 5:18; 10:30, 36; compare Mt 1:23; Acts 4:12; 1 Tim 2:5; Rev 2:18). He was not one among many avatars; he alone of humankind is God. He died for the sins of others and rose again (Jn 1:1-14; 8:24-58; 1 Cor 15:1-3; compare Ex 3:14 with Is 43:10-11; Deut 6:4; Gen 1:1).

Question 92: Are UFOs a Work of Satan?

In 1947 an Idaho businessman named Ken Arnold spotted nine bright discs flying at tremendous speeds. As a result of his experience he coined the term "flying saucer." Since World War II, millions have reported seeing UFOs, or unidentified flying objects.[39] The mecca of current UFO enthusiasts is Area 51, a base in Nevada where many believe a UFO crashed. UFOs and space aliens have been popularized by a number of movies such as *E.T.* and *Independence Day*, by TV programs like *The X-Files*, by books such as Erich von Daniken's *Chariots of the Gods?*[40] and Whitley Streiber's *Communion*, and by occult groups such as the New Age movement, the Urantia Foundation and, in 1997, the eclectic suicide sect called Heaven's Gate. Are UFOs the work of the devil?

Close encounters of the third kind? UFO sightings may be classified into three levels of encounter: (1) close encounters of the first kind (the UFO is observed at close range); (2) close encounters of the second kind (the UFO is observed and leaves behind physical evidence); (3) close encounters of the third kind (aliens are observed in the UFO). Alleged alien abductions occur in this third category. Some of the most popular abductions are those reported by Betty and Barney Hill, Brian Scott and Whitley Streiber. People who have been abducted generally claim that they were taken inside the spaceship, examined and released. They sometimes recall their encounter under hypnosis.

Many UFO sightings can be explained through natural phenomena such as abnormal lights, gas, hallucinations and so forth. One source claims that close to 90 percent of all UFO sightings fall into this category.[41] The other 10 percent of UFO sightings may be genuine. Some within this smaller percentage have been observed on radar screens, they emit electromagnetic charges, they leave physical evidence such as charred ground and foul odors, and they disturb both animals and humans. Some have suggested that these sightings involve classified aircraft. But this does not seem to be true in every case, and some sightings defy the laws of physics: (1) UFOs move at high speed without causing a sonic boom; (2) UFOs seem to turn at right angles or stop in midair at speeds up to 16,000 mph; (3) UFOs adapt to human perception, so that in the nineteenth century they appeared as flying sea ships or arrows; (4) UFOs can seemingly vanish into thin air; (5) UFOs sometimes cannot be detected by radar, photos, or other devices of detection; (6) UFOs can seemingly change shape, size or color at will. Of course, some may suggest that the government has advanced spacecraft built on secretive scientific laws and the general public has been led to believe that our technology is far less developed than what it really is. But this kind of conspiracy-theorizing lacks evidence and gets us nowhere. You would think that at least one scientist or government defector would live to tell us about it!

Chariots of fire: Flying saucers? The Bible is virtually silent regarding extraterrestrial life. Some have considered the "sons of God" (Gen 6:1-5), Ezekiel's vision (Ezek 1) and Elijah's "chariot of fire" (2 Kings 2) as UFOs or space aliens. However, UFO interpretations of these passages suffer a number of problems. First, Elijah was taken up to heaven in a whirlwind, not the chariot (2 Kings 2:11). We would expect him to have entered the chariot and flown away, if this were a flying saucer. It also seems silly to interpret the "horses of fire," which carried the chariot, as UFOs. What are the odds of physical horses, let alone flaming ones, living on other planets? We would think that such advanced aliens could think of designing their physical ship into something better than an archaic earthly type of transportation.[42] Clearly, Elijah saw an angelic vision or manifestation from God.

Second, Ezekiel's vision was also angelic (compare Is 6; Rev 4), which would make the whirling objects he saw spiritual or metaphysical in nature, not physical aircraft. Also, the cherubim angels that Ezekiel saw prepared the way for his revelation from God. As we shall note below, the messages commonly given by UFO aliens today are not from God.

Third, "sons of God" in Genesis 6 (see answers 29-30) may refer to angelic beings or fallen angels who manifested themselves in physical form. Even here we run into problems with the popular understanding of UFOs as space aliens from another planet. It is better to understand the "sons of God" as fallen supernatural beings rather than *physical space aliens.*

And we find no spaceships or "chariots of fire" in the Genesis 6 account.[43]

Alien abductions? Does intelligent life exist on other planets? Frankly, I do not know. *If* there is, I am not convinced that physical life forms, no matter how intelligent, could travel millions of light-years across the universe as fast as or faster than the speed of light and live to tell us about it. But more significant for my conclusion is that out of the millions of UFO sightings, not one alien has attempted to communicate with humankind on a mass scale. Even the *Star Trek* crew always seem to violate their "primary directive" not to interfere with the evolution of other planetary societies![44] I can only conclude that it is highly improbable that UFO aliens are actually physical beings from other planets. This leaves only one other reasonable alternative at this time: they are immaterial or supernatural—in other words, spirits, angels or demons.

The people who report being abducted by UFO aliens often tend to be involved in the occult or interested in mysticism. Many people claim that they can contact these UFOs by means of channeling, ouija boards or other occult phenomena. Certain occult practitioners, such as Uri Geller, claim they received their powers from these UFOs. Moreover, UFO abductees often have psychological, emotional and mental problems that are similar to what people involved in the occult have.[45]

Perhaps most conclusive of all the evidence for me is the message these aliens bring to humankind. UFO aliens tend to deny the deity of Christ and his atonement for our sins. They often affirm occult or New Age beliefs such as pantheism, universalism and self-potentialism. Thus if there is such a thing as authentic UFO *aliens,* they could be demonic forces passing themselves off as extraterrestrials in order to draw people away from the God of the Bible. This would be an excellent tactic to persuade people who do not believe in demonic powers to believe in their doctrines nonetheless!

John Keel, a self-proclaimed agnostic, writes that UFOs may actually be "a joke perpetrated by invisible entities who have always delighted in frightening, confusing and misleading the human race."[46]

Question 93: Should I Allow My Children to Participate in Halloween?

Halloween, originally known as "hallow's eve" or "holy evening," was the evening before All Saints Day (Nov. 1). This was a time for commemorating the saints for their faith and martyrdoms. Apparently it was celebrated at this time of year to combat a pagan harvest celebration occurring at the same time. In northern Europe and the British Isles, All Saints Day replaced the pagan holiday of Samhain (pronounced "sah ween"), but the non-Christian customs of the holiday survived. It was believed that spirits wandered about on this day pestering households. According to certain traditions, the roaming spirits were appeased by "treating" them, lest they pull a "trick." Some were warded off by sticking a candle into a root vegetable or turnip.[47] We see vestiges of these traditions in the present-day celebration of Halloween.

So what is the Christian approach to a "backslidden" Christian holiday that is now steeped in occult elements such as witches and spooks? I believe there are several options. People should decide for themselves which one or which combination is best for them and their families.

1. *Restore Halloween to a holy evening.* Christian families can once again commemorate the lives of saints or commemorate Martin Luther's Reformation Day. (Traditionally, October 31 is considered the day that launched the Reformation. Christian families could give gospel literature along with candies to children. Their children can also dress up in biblical costumes and collect charity funds from other homes in the neighborhood.

2. *Provide an alternative for Halloween.* Churches can organ-

ize Halloween or harvest parties where children can get dressed up in nonoccultic customes, eat and play games.

3. Ignore Halloween. Families can simply ignore Halloween, not giving treats and not allowing their children to participate in any celebration. Parents who go this route should also make sure they give an acceptable explanation to their children for why they are not celebrating.

4. Participate in Halloween with precautions. As long as the local community is safe, parents supervise their children, and the children's costumes do not promote the occultic aspects of Halloween, I personally do not believe children should be made to feel guilty about going door to door to get candies. Discernment specialists Bob and Gretchen Passantino dissolve some common myths about Halloween when they write:

> It is not true that poisoning or sabotaging of Halloween treats is a significant risk if the parents take sensible precautions. Most of the horror stories are unsubstantiated rumors that quickly cross the country, gaining embellishments, and unnecessarily frightening parents. If parents are careful about restricting their children's treats to ones from people they know and trust, or from a formal program run by a church, community group, or merchant association, they should be fairly safe. In many communities, local hospitals and/or police stations will screen treats free of charge.[48]

Question 94: Should I Allow My Children to Listen to Fairy Tales?

Some fundamentalists Christians feel it is wrong to allow children to listen to popular fairy tales. They believe that exposing children to witches, fairies and so forth is introducing them to themes in the occult. I once had to counsel a woman who was influenced by a popular fundamentalist author to throw away all her books of children's fairy tales. She was afraid of the negative influence they might have on her children. Generally speaking, we should not discourage our children from fairy tales, for many fairy tales can actually provide children with avenues for comprehending the gospel message. Stories such as "Snow White and the Seven Dwarfs," "Sleeping Beauty" and the Lord of the Rings trilogy involve archetypal characters such as kings, witches, knights and princesses who represent opposing forces, the good always conquering the evil. Quite often in these stories, a Christlike figure appears who saves people from a witch or a warlock's oppression.[49]

An excellent example of how fairy tales can be used to present the gospel is C. S. Lewis's *The Lion, the Witch and the Wardrobe.* In this story four children (who are called sons of Adam) go through a closet wardrobe (perhaps representing faith) that leads them into another world called Narnia, where a witch (that is, devil) causes winter weather throughout the year (that is, the cursed creation due to the Fall). One of the children, Edmund, is seduced by the witch when she offers him a candy called Turkish Delight (that is, the lust of the flesh). The witch intends to kill the sons of Adam because she has heard of an ancient prophecy that the children will one day rule Narnia (that is, the age of reconciliation). But Aslan the lion (that is, Christ as the "lion of Judah") rescues the unworthy Edmund from the witch by offering his life for Edmund's (that is, Christ's atonement). But Aslan rises from the dead after the stone slab on which he was killed cracks (that is, resurrection and empty tomb). Meanwhile, the children and Aslan's forces fight the witch and her forces (that is, spiritual warfare in the church era). But the witch is not completely destroyed until Aslan returns (that is, the Second Coming of Christ).

Question 95: Should I Allow My Children to Play with Trolls, Monsters or Other Dolls That Resemble Occult Figures?

Troll dolls are those smiling figures with big bellies and long, long hair. In Scandinavian tradition trolls are imps or dwarfs that live underground. (Dolls that look something like trolls but are blue, wear white caps, and have shorter hair are called Smurfs.) In older mythology the trolls were wicked fairies that sometimes ate humans. In later traditions they are more amiable, consuming bananas and cream instead of humans.[50]

When people avoid celebrating holidays with pagan origins, or stop eating Lucky Charms cereal just because a leprechaun is pictured on the cereal box, they commit what is known as the *genetic fallacy.* This fallacy is committed every time we condemn something because of its origin rather than what it represents *today.* We certainly would not want to discourage our children from learning the days of the week or the months of the year because they are named after pagan gods!

We always need discernment in regard to our children's toys. But no toy dolls possess demons. We should be more concerned with what the doll represents to our children than with its appearance. The grotesque-looking Incredible Hulk, for instance, is an unfortunate man distorted into a green monster by gamma rays. But he happens to be a "good-guy" superhero to many of our kids. On the other hand, a Barbie doll may look innocent enough, but if our daughter wants to have an unrealistic figure like Barbie's or imagines her participating in promiscuous relationships with Ken or G.I. Joe, isn't there something wrong? Let's set our priorities straight in raising our children. As the Christian Research Institute asserts, "There are simply too many far more serious and difficult issues facing our young people today that require thoughtful and prayerful attention than scrutinizing troll dolls. If we are to communicate anything meaningful to our kids today we must be consistent in our reasoning, or it will certainly backfire on us."[51]

Question 96: What Is Witchcraft?

The word *witch* comes from the English word *wicca.*[52] The noun form of this word means "sorcerer," and the verb form means "to cast a spell." Witchcraft is known as "the craft of the wise." It is also known as ancient sorcery. In various cultures witches are considered social deviants, but they are not always evil. Witch doctors can play positive roles in some Third World cultures.

Witches often worship the mother goddess and the male horned god.[53] The mother goddess represents the moon, and the horned god represents the sun. Covens often meet on new and full moons to attune or "relink" themselves with natural forces. "Drawing down the moon" is a ritual that involves the goddess's possessing a practitioner. In Western culture popular witches are Alister Crowley, Margaret Murray, Gerald Gardner, Sybil Leek and Margot Adler. Witches claim that their craft is older than Christianity. It is the "Old Religion," or a restored paganism, hence, "neopaganism." Experience is an important, if not the most important, factor in their beliefs. Witchcraft is not the same thing as Satanism, nor should it be equated with the New Age movement. There are notable distinctions between the three groups, but there may be some overlap.

New Age	Witchcraft	Satanism
Self-adoration and pantheism	Mother goddess adoration and polytheism	Devil adoration and dualism
Considered socially acceptable	Considered socially deviant but tolerable	Considered socially deviant and generally unacceptable
Non- or pseudo-Christian	Pre-Christian	Anti-Christian
Few rituals	Many rituals	Rituals and some sacrifices
Denies Satan and hell	Denies Satan and hell	Affirms Satan and hell

Like other occultists, witches hold to psychic forces that they claim as neutral forces used for purposes that are either positive (white magic) or negative (black magic). Like New Agers, witches emphasize tolerance and relativism (although they can be very intolerant when it comes to the beliefs of Christians). Many witches associate Christianity with the Inquisition and images of "Christian" statesmen burning witches and other "social misfits" at the stake.

Christians should not convey an attitude of hatred and violence toward witches.[54] Instead, they should exemplify the love, mercy and forgiveness of Christ of the New Testament.

Question 97: What Are Some Good Ways I Can Begin a Productive Dialogue with Those Involved in the Occult?

Christians may wish to look for opportunities to dialogue and share their faith with occultists.[59] Prayer and discernment are vital prerequisites. It is not enough to bombard occultists with the gospel and then run. You must be willing to love them with the love of Christ, reason patiently with them and introduce them to your Christian community. So first, you should genuinely love and understand the people you are trying to help. Then you should try to determine something about them. Does their interest in the occult go no further than reading their daily horoscope? Could they be Christians with a misguided belief in reincarnation? Are they New Agers, witches or something else?

Second, you should speak the truth in love with a compassionate attitude (Eph 4:15). Some people involved in the occult do not realize that the Bible speaks against their practices. You should therefore show them what the Word of God says regarding occult activities (Deut 18:10-12; Acts 13:4-12; Gal 5:19-21). We should emphasize the danger of interacting with demonic forces. People who tap into psychic forces frequently experience emotional or mental breakdowns, and some attempt suicide. And anyone who is involved with the occult is a prime candidate for demon possession. You should dispel any misconceptions they may have about their own practices. White as well as black magic can be manipulated by demonic powers, all good intentions to the contrary.

Third (as noted in answer 90), you should show the occultist the inconsistency of holding to a worldview that rests in relativism and pantheism. From their perspective, if good and evil come from the same force, then isn't the mother goddess or an ultimate psychic force the cause of all evil and suffering? If they fail to distinguish between good and evil, then why do they think it is wrong for Christians to burn witches or take away their crystal balls? Some occultists may deny the problem of evil, but like it or not, evil still exists in the world, and our worldview should attempt to reconcile what we believe and what we practice.

Fourth, you should study to address any misconceptions occultists may have about Christianity. They often point out the faults of Christians or the mistakes people have made in the name of Christendom throughout the centuries. You should inform them of the distinction between the failings of Christians (or pseudo-Christians) and the life of Christ as a perfect role model. Stick to the gospel of the Christ in the Bible, emphasizing his life, death and resurrection, and eternal life through faith in him (1 Cor 15:2-3; Jn 3:16-18; Rom 3:23; 5:8; 6:23; 10:9-10). Let occultists know the benefits of the Christian life over demonic forces. The human road apart from Christ leads to separation from God and ultimate death (compare Prov 14:12). Ultimate beneficent power comes from Jesus Christ, not psychic forces. Through Christ people can have power over all demons and occult activities (Jn 1:12; 1 Jn 4:4).

Question 98: What Is Satanism?

Satanism reverses Christian values, making God evil and Satan good.[55] Satanists substitute their Satanic Bible for the Bible. True Satanists worship and invoke Satan. Some see him as a personal being similar to, if not the same as, the one found in Scripture; others see him as an impersonal force or symbol. Anton Levey, high priest of the Church of Satan in San Francisco, believes that Satan is an extension of humankind's own potential. Satan is a force or an alter ego by which humans can control their own destiny. Natural and animalistic human traits are seen as the "personification" of Satan. Thus Satanism is a means to gratify all carnal desires.[56] According to occult specialist Craig Hawkins, we can identify various classes of Satanism. Here are three of them:

1. The dabbler. These Satanists are mostly young people who experiment with satanic literature and music, but they do not take their devotion seriously. As many as 90 percent of all Satanists may fall into this category.

2. The public Satanist. These Satanists hold their beliefs as a religion protected by the First Amendment. They do not normally participate in criminal activities.

3. The individual Satanist. These Satanists do not normally affilate with organizations. They often become involved in criminal activities. Criminals like Sean Sellers and Richard Ramirez fall into this category.

Dialoguing with a Satanist requires prayer and wisdom. Just like Christians, Satanists hate to be misrepresented or stereotyped. Make sure you have your facts about them straight! What class of Satanist are you encountering? Would it be physically dangerous to dialogue with this Satanist? It definitely could be. I once knew a young girl who was a new Christian convert and wanted to witness to Richard Ramirez in prison. I discouraged her from doing so because she needed more maturity and a better understanding of what she was getting herself into. We must always exercise maturity, discernment and common sense.

Without defining your terms, it probably would not do much good to tell Satanists that they are going to hell! Some Satanists *want* to go to hell. The "dabblers" often see hell as "one big party" and heaven as a place of boredom where people strum harps and float on clouds. You can let them know that heaven is a place of joy and beauty, while hell is a place of torment and darkness, not pleasure (Lk 16:19-31; Mt 8:12; Mk 9:42-50; Rev 14:11; 20:10). Moreover, you can tell them that Satan cannot be trusted. He seeks to ensnare people with destructive vices (Jn 8:44; 10:10; 2 Tim 2:25-26). Unlike Satan, God cares about the human race and desires to give people eternal life through Jesus Christ (Ezek 33:8-11; Acts 17:25-28; Jn 3:16; Rom 5:8).

Question 99: Does Satanic Ritual Abuse Really Happen?

Satanic ritual abuse and/or crimes might on rare occasions happen, but it is highly unlikely that there is any conspiracy of underground devil worshipers who are so secretive that they never leave a trace of evidence from generation to generation. The Satanic conspiracy idea was popularized by Michelle Smith and Lawrence Pazder's *Michelle Remembers*, Mike Warnke's *Satan Seller*, Lauren Stratford's *Satan's Underground* and Bob Larson's novel *Dead Air*. The testimonies included in the first three books listed have been shown to be inconclusive and fraudulent.[57] Many of the supposed survivors of Satanic ritual abuse (SRA) have been diagnosed as suffering from multiple personality disorder (MPD). Their testimonies often lack credibility. The alleged victims are often told by counselors that they have repressed traumatic experiences they had as children. Satanic ritual abuse experiences are then surfaced by questionable therapeutic techniques, such as hypnosis or visualization.

We ought to show compassion and comfort to those who claim to have suffered from such abuse, but we should also be skeptical about all SRA stories. Claims that babies are bred to be eaten or sacrificed lack supporting evidence, as do the claims that a number of daycare centers are run by closet Satanists. Many cases of missing children involve domestic disputes, not ritual sacrifice. Kenneth Lanning, supervisory special agent of the FBI Academy's Behavioral Science Unit, has said:

> [A] Satanic murder can be defined as one committed by two
> or more individuals who rationally plan the crime and
> whose primary motivation is to fulfil a prescribed satanic
> ritual calling for the murder. By this definition, the author
> has been unable to identify even one documented murder
> in the United States. Although such murders may have and
> can occur, they appear to be few in number. In addition, the
> commission of such killing would probably be the beginning
> of the end for such a group. It is highly unlikely that they
> could continue to kill several people, every year, year after
> year, and not be discovered.[58]

Appendix: List of Questions

1. Why Are So Many People Intrigued by Angelic Beings? _____ 11
2. What Does the Word *Angel* Mean? _____ 18
3. What Are Angels? _____ 19
4. When Were the Angels Created? _____ 21
5. What Do Angels Look Like? _____ 22
6. Are Angels Gendered? _____ 23
7. What Position Do Angels Occupy in the Scheme of Things? _____ 23
8. Do Humans Ever Become Angels? _____ 24
9. Are There Different Classes of Angels? _____ 25
10. What Are the Archangels? _____ 28
11. Is Jesus Michael the Archangel? _____ 29
12. Is Jesus the Angel of the Lord in the Old Testament? _____ 30
13. Who Is the Commander of the Army of the Lord of Hosts? _____ 31
14. How Many Angels Are There? _____ 32
15. Do Guardian Angels Exist? _____ 33
16. Do Angels Protect the Nations? _____ 37
17. Do Angels Attend Church Services? _____ 38
18. Is It Wrong to Communicate with Angels? _____ 38
19. What Are Some Works That Angels Do? _____ 40
20. Do Angels or Demons Bring Calamity on the Wicked? _____ 42
21. How Were Angels Involved in the Life of Christ? _____ 44
22. Can Angels Reveal the Second Coming of Christ? _____ 45
23. How Will Angels Assist God During the End Times? _____ 46
24. Are There Any Contemporary Examples of Angels
    Visiting Humans? _____ 47
25. What Is a Good Way to Remember the Activities of Angels? _____ 49
26. Do Demons Actually Exist? _____ 51
27. What Concepts Are Used to Describe Demons in Scripture? _____ 53
28. What Are Demons? _____ 55
29. What Is the Origin of Demons? _____ 57
30. Who Are the "Sons of God" in Genesis 6? _____ 60
31. Why Are the Offspring of the Sons of God Called "Giants"? _____ 65
32. Do Descendants of the Giants Exist Today? _____ 67
33. Are Demons Ghosts? _____ 68
34. What Is the Difference Between Gargoyles, Goblins,
    Poltergeists and Demons? _____ 69
35. Are There Different Ranks Within the Kingdom of Darkness? _____ 71
36. How Many Demons Are There? _____ 73

37. Can Demons Materialize? _____ 74
38. What Does Christ's Power over Demons Signify? _____ 74
39. What Are the "Doctrines of Demons"? _____ 76
40. Are Demons the Cause of Sickness and Disease? _____ 77
41. Was Satan Once a Beautiful Angel Named Lucifer? _____ 80
42. How Did Satan Fall? _____ 83
43. Why Did God Allow Satan to Fall If He Foreknew the Evil and
    Suffering That Would Follow? _____ 88
44. Was Satan Literally the Serpent in the Garden of Eden? _____ 89
45. Why Is Satan Called a Leviathan Dragon? _____ 91
46. What Are the Devil's Titles? _____ 92
47. Did the Biblical Concept of Satan Come from Zoroastrianism? ____ 95
48. Was the Biblical Idea of Satan as Belial Influenced by the
    Dead Sea Scrolls? _____ 97
49. What Is the Connection Between Satan and Azazel, the
    Scapegoat? _____ 97
50. What Does the Word *Beelzebub* Mean? _____ 98
51. Does Satan Know Our Thoughts? _____ 99
52. How Powerful Is Satan? _____ 100
53. Does Satan Live in Hell? _____ 101
54. Why Is the Devil Portrayed with Red Skin, Horns and a
    Pitchfork? _____ 102
55. Why Doesn't Satan Repent? _____ 103
56. Did Satan Cooperate with God in Having Christ Crucified? _____ 105
57. Why Did Satan Influence Peter to Discourage Christ from
    Being Crucified If He Later Influenced Judas to Betray Him? ____ 105
58. Did Jesus Confront Satan Between His Death and His
    Resurrection? _____ 106
59. What Was Paul's Thorn in the Flesh Given by Satan? _____ 109
60. What Is the Relation Between Satan and the Antichrist? _____ 110
61. What Works Will Satan Do Before Christ Returns? _____ 111
62. What Is Spiritual Warfare? _____ 113
63. What Are Some of the Strategies of the Devil? _____ 114
64. How Do the Demons Undermine the Work of Christians? _____ 116
65. Do Christians Have Authority to Rebuke Satan and His
    Demons? _____ 116
66. What Is "Binding and Loosing"? _____ 118
67. How Do We Resist Satan and His Demons? _____ 120
68. Do Territorial Spirits Exist? _____ 125
69. Was Jesus an Exorcist? _____ 126
70. Do Generational Spirits Exist? _____ 127
71. What Are the Indications of Demon Possession? _____ 128
72. How Do We Distinguish Between Demon Possession and
    Mental Illness? _____ 129
73. Can a Christian Be Demon Possessed? _____ 130

74. What Is the Difference Between Demon Possession and Demon Oppression? _____ 133
75. How Is an Exorcism Performed? _____ 133
76. Are the Spirit of Fear, the Spirit of Cancer and Related Entities Demonic Spirits? _____ 135
77. Can Satan Intercept Our Prayers? _____ 136
78. Are Phenomena like Speaking in Tongues, Getting "Slain in the Spirit" and Convulsing of the Devil? _____ 137
79. How Do We Discern Whether a Supernatural Event Is of God or of the Devil? _____ 139
80. What Is the Occult? _____ 140
81. What Are Some Occult Practices? _____ 142
82. What Does the Bible Say About the Occult? _____ 145
83. What Objects Are Used in Occult Practices? _____ 147
84. What Is Magic? _____ 149
85. Are Magic Shows Occultic? _____ 150
86. What Is PSI? _____ 152
87. Is Astrology Occultic? _____ 153
88. Is Reincarnation Compatible with Christianity? _____ 154
89. Is Rock Music Satanic? _____ 156
90. Is the New Age Movement Occultic? _____ 156
91. Is Satan's Working Through the New Age Movement? _____ 158
92. Are UFOs a Work of Satan? _____ 159
93. Should I Allow My Children to Participate in Halloween? _____ 163
94. Should I Allow My Children to Listen to Fairy Tales? _____ 164
95. Should I Allow My Children to Play with Trolls, Monsters or Other Dolls That Resemble Occult Figures? _____ 165
96. What Is Witchcraft? _____ 166
97. What Are Some Good Ways I Can Begin a Productive Dialogue with Those Involved in the Occult? _____ 168
98. What Is Satanism? _____ 169
99. Does Satanic Ritual Abuse Really Happen? _____ 171

Notes

Chapter 1: The Angel & Demon Craze

[1] Barbara Graham, "Talking with . . . Joan Wester Anderson," *People Weekly*, April 11, 1994, p. 25.

[2] Nancy Gibbs, "Angels Among Us," *Time*, December 27, 1993, p. 56.

[3] Barbara Kantrowitz with Patricia King, Debra Rosenberg, Karen Springen, Pat Wingert, Tessa Namuth and T. Trent Gegax, "In Search of the Sacred," *Newsweek*, November 28, 1994, p. 54.

[4] Gibbs, "Angels Among Us," p. 56.

[5] Ibid.

[6] Rick Marin, "Alien Invasion!" *Newsweek*, July 8, 1996, p. 42.

[7] Ibid., p. 43.

[8] George Gallup Jr. and Frank Newport, "Out of This World," *Sunday Tribune/Early Morning Tribune*, August 5, 1990, pp. 1, 12.

[9] The baby-boom generation includes people born after World War II through the Kennedy years. Baby busters make up the generation born during the Vietnam era, and "X generation" often refers to those born in the post-Watergate era.

[10] Marin, "Alien Invasion!" p. 44.

[11] Karl Rahner, "Angels," in *Encyclopedia of Theology: A Concise Sacramentum Mundi*, ed. Karl Rahner (London: Burns and Oates, 1975), p. 7.

[12] For a brief overview of angels in early church iconography, see C. Carletti, "Angel," in *Encyclopedia of the Early Church*, ed. Angelo Di Berardino (Cambridge, U.K.: James Clarke, 1992), 1:38-40.

Chapter 2: Questions About Angels

[1] Millard Erickson, *Christian Theology* (Grand Rapids, Mich.: Baker Book House, 1985), p. 451.

[2] *Angelos* appears most often in the Synoptic Gospels (Matthew, Mark and Luke), Acts and Revelation (Hans Bietenhard, "Angel, Messenger,

Gabriel, Michael," in *The New International Dictionary of New Testament Theology* [hereafter *NIDNTT*], ed. Colin Brown (Grand Rapids, Mich.: Regency Reference Library/Zondervan, 1986), 1:102.

[3]It could be argued that Satan, who manifested himself as the serpent in the Garden of Eden, is the first direct biblical reference to a supernatural angel (Gen 3; compare Rev 12:9). In the garden, however, Satan does not seem to function as a benevolent messenger sent by God. (Gen 3:1).

[4]We will discover more about what angels are in answer 3. Demons are fallen angels. We will discover their nature, characteristics and roles in chapters four through six.

[5]This summarized definition of Aquinas's view on angels comes from Karl Barth in *Church Dogmatics* (Edinburgh: T & T Clark, 1960), 3/3:391. Barth calls Aquinas's work *Summa Contra Gentiles* "probably the greatest angelogue of all Church history." However, he considers it a work of philosophy rather than theology, and he claims, "In its misguidedness we can compare it only with the foolish explanations which many modern theologians have given for their complete scepticism or indifference to the whole problem [of angels]" (3:391-92). Apparently Barth would blame Aquinas for the modernists' mocking assertion that medieval theologians spent their time pursuing silly questions, such as, How many angels dance on the head of a pin?

[6]Hebrews 1:7 ("who maketh his angels spirits, and his ministers a flame of fire," KJV) is often used as a proof text supporting the spiritual nature of angels. The best rendering of this text, however, is "He [God] makes his angels *winds* . . ." (compare Ps 104:4). In the context of Hebrews 1, this passage contrasts the subordinate and transitory nature of angels (portrayed as "winds" and "fire"; compare 2 Esdras 8.21; *2 Apocalypse of Baruch* 21.6; 48.8) with the superior and permanent nature of Christ (Heb 1:4-6, 8-13). In one rabbinic tradition the angels declare, "God changes us every hour . . . sometimes he makes us fire, at other times wind" (*Yalkut Shimeoni* 2.11.3).

[7]Aquinas, on the other hand, claims that although angels can rejoice, they cannot weep. They cannot experience sorrow and pain because they are in a state of heavenly bliss (*Summa Contra Gentiles* 113.7).

[8]Some early church traditions speculated that the angels are perfected by the Holy Spirit (Basil *Homilies* 32.4).

[9]Thomas Aquinas argued that angels must always be at a respective point in time and only one angel can be at any one exact location at one time. Like other creatures, they must move about from one place to another (*Summa Contra Gentiles* 50.3; 52-53). The precise nature of angels in reference to space and time, however, is very difficult to decipher. If angels are spirits, are they not extradimensional beings that are not subject to the laws of physics that apply to all human beings?

[10]One Jewish tradition claims that God created the "primeval ones"—a group of angels who offered advice to God. When God planned to create

humans, these angels rejected the idea. God destroyed two councils of angels before a third company agreed with his idea (*b. Sanhedrin* 38b; compare *3 Enoch* 4.6-10). Such fanciful ideas, however, tend to slight the benevolent character of God.

[11]The three messengers in Genesis 18 are sometimes mistakenly interpreted as a manifestation of the Trinity. God the Father and God the Holy Spirit, however, do not take on human form (Jn 1:18; 4:24). If the three messengers were the Father, Son and Holy Spirit, this would support not trinitarianism but tritheism. Three *separate individuals* would make three gods (tritheism), not one God who is three Persons (trinitarianism). While it is true that in Genesis 18:16-33 one of the three messengers appeared to be a manifestation of the Lord (perhaps the preincarnate Christ), the other two messengers were angels (compare Gen 18:2, 16; 19:1).

[12]Some have suggested that the face of the cherub in Ezekiel 10:12-14 would be similar to, if not the same as, the face of an ox (Ezek 1:10; 2 Chron 4:4; Rev 4:6-8). Either that or we have a gloss with the original text having "ox" instead of "cherub."

[13]The notion of circumcised angels may sound rather silly to us, but this is because Christians do not normally associate circumcision with holiness, as do the Jews. Their perspective suggested that if the men who ministered in the temple and the synagogues were circumcised, then the angels who ministered in the presence of God also had to be circumcised.

[14]Some would argue, however, that the angels in Genesis 6 were punished *because* they left their former state of sexlessness and cohabited with earthly women (2 Pet 2:4; Jude 6). We will discuss this topic again in chapter four. At any rate, in the current Christian era angels do not manifest themselves to have sex with humans.

[15]In the patristic era Tertullian (160-225) believed that angels prepared the way for the Holy Spirit whenever an individual was baptized (*De Baptismo* 4-6).

[16]Compare Joseph Fitzmyer, "A Feature of Qumrân Angelology and the Angels of 1 Cor. XI.10," *New Testament Studies* 4 (1957-1958): 56-58. Biblical scholar Dale Martin argues that both disorder and sexual vulnerability are in view in 1 Corinthians 10:11 (Dale Martin, *The Corinthian Body* [New Haven, Conn.: Yale University Press, 1995], pp. 242-48.

[17]The origin of these words is difficult. The word *seraphim* (*śᵉrāp̄îm*) may come from a Hebrew root word denoting "fire" (Is 30:6) and could indicate the darting motion of the creatures (Ezek 1:13; 28:16). For a list of possible origins of the term, see George A. Barton, "Demons and Spirits (Hebrew)," in *Encyclopaedia of Religion and Ethics* [hereafter *ERE*], ed. James Hastings (New York: Scribner's/Edinburgh: T & T Clark, 1911), 4:595.

The word *cherubim* (*kᵉrûḇîm*) may be a loan word from the Babylonian spirits called *kuribu*, which were associated with wind and storm (Walther Eichrodt, *Theology of the Old Testament* [London: SCM Press, 1967], 2:203). Some suggest the cherubim may be similar to the hybrid beasts in ancient Near Eastern cultures that had the bodies of lions and the wings of eagles. In these cultures the lion represented the roar of thunder, and the eagle's wings represented the wind (Theodore Hiebert, "Theophany in the OT," in *Anchor Bible Dictionary* [hereafter *ABD*], ed. David Noel Freedman [New York: Doubleday, 1992], 6:510; William F. Albright, "What Were the Cherubim?" *Biblical Archaeology* 1 [1938]: 1-3). *First Enoch* describes a third group of angels called the *'ōpannîm* ("wheels"), which are depicted as the chariot wheels in Ezekiel's vision (*1 Enoch* 71:7; compare Ezra 1:21).

[18]There are various interpretations of what the four faces symbolize. The church fathers often related them to the four Gospels. The man represented the Gospel of Luke (indicating Christ's perfect humanity), the lion represented the Gospel of Matthew (Christ as the son of David—the lion of Judah), the eagle represented the Gospel of John (the deity of Christ) and the ox represented the Gospel of Mark (often depicting Christ as a servant). It seems unlikely, however, that the four faces were originally intended to represent the four Gospels. There is no agreement among the early church fathers on this issue. Irenaeus, for instance, equated the lion to John, the ox to Luke, the man to Matthew, and the eagle to Mark. More likely, the four faces represented certain characteristics of the angels or of God, or both. For instance, the "blessing" (man), "honor" (lion), "glory" (eagle), and "power" (ox) the angels offer to God might be one interpretation of what the four faces represent (Rev 5:13; compare 19:1).

[19]Augustus H. Strong, *Systematic Theology* (Westwood, N.J.: Revell, 1907), p. 449.

[20]Walter Lock, *A Critical and Exegetical Commentary on the Pastoral Epistles*, International Critical Commentary (Edinburgh: T & T Clark, 1924), p. 63. There is also another way to understand this passage. The word *elect* (*eklektos*) has a variety of meanings. It could mean "selected" or "chosen," but it could also mean "choice," "excellent" or "pure," depending on the context (compare Ex 30:23 LXX). If we understand it in the latter sense, Paul is indicating that holy angels watch over Timothy's conduct.

[21]Helmer Ringgren, *The Faith of Qumran: Theology of the Dead Sea Scrolls* (Philadelphia: Fortress, 1963), p. 83. In Jewish apocalyptic literature, on the other hand, scholar D. S. Russell sees three orders of angels: angels of the presence, angels of sanctification and angels over the natural order (compare *Jubilees* 2; D. S. Russel, *The Method and Message of Jewish Apocalyptic: 200 B.C.-A.D. 100* [London: SCM Press, 1964], p. 241).

[22]In the pseudepigrapha the hierarchy of angels is one of the central themes of the books of Enoch. *First Enoch* 61.10 lists "all the holy ones above, and the forces of the Lord—the cherubim, seraphim, ophanim,

all the angels of governance, the Elect One, and the other forces of earth (and) over the water." *First Enoch* 69 gives a list of the names of fallen angels that would raise even Milton's brows; *2 Enoch* 3—20 lists various angelic functions in the "seven" heavens; the entire book of *3 Enoch* is a list of various classes of angels.

Pseudo-Dionysius's angelic hierarchy became influential in the medieval church. He listed nine angelic choirs in three triads. The highest level consisted of seraphim, cherubim and thrones. The second triad was composed of "dominions" *(kyriotētes)*, "powers" *(dynameis)* and authorities *(exousiai)*. The lowest level consisted of "principalities" *(archai)*, archangels and regular angels (*De Hierarchia Coelesti* 6).

[23]Gustav Davidson, *A Dictionary of Angels* (New York: Free Press/London: Collier-Macmillan, 1967), pp. 51, 338, 342. In Jewish mysticism twelve chief angels are equated with the signs of the zodiac, and the Cabala lists ten. The Qur'an lists four but names only two: Jibril (Gabriel), the angel of revelation, and Michael, the warrior angel. In *1 Enoch* 20, each of the archangels has a particular function. For example, Michael is set over a portion of humankind and over chaos; Gabriel is set over Paradise, serpents and cherubim; Raphael is set over the spirits of humans.

[24]In 1 Thessalonians 4:16, the "voice of the archangel" and the "trumpet" both appear to be further descriptions of the "shout." Either the "shout" is directed toward the dead, commanding them to rise up (Jn 5:28-29; 11:43-44; Rev 11:12), or it is a general announcement heralding the second coming of Christ (Rev 11:15).

[25]In the Old Testament the word LORD designates the Tetragrammaton, *YHWH*, or the English rendering "Jehovah."

[26]J. M. Wilson, "Angel," in *International Standard Bible Encyclopedia* [hereafter *ISBE*], ed. Geoffrey Bromiley, rev. ed. (Grand Rapids, Mich.: Eerdmans, 1979), 1:125. Eichrodt writes that the angel of the Lord can be seen as a protector (Gen 24:7; 1 Kings 19:5; 2 Kings 1:3, 15), an assassin (2 Sam 24:26; 2 Kings 19:35) or a judge (2 Sam 14:17; Zech 3:1). *Theology of the Old Testament*, 2:23-24.

[27]Theodore Hiebert, "Theophany in the OT," in *ABD*, 6:505.

[28]In reference to the Lord's angel in Exodus 32:30-34, 33, Gerhard von Rad suggests that as a consequence of Israel's idolatry, God established three mediating institutions: the angel of YHWH, the tent of meeting and the face *(pānîm)* of God (Gerhard von Rad, *Old Testament Theology: The Theology of Israel's Historical Traditions* [Edinburgh: Oliver and Boyd, 1962], 1:288).

[29]This view may resolve the Old Testament paradox of two persons who are both called "the LORD" or YHWH (Gen 19:23-24; Zech 3:2). In trinitarian terms, this would refer to both the Father and the Son. If the angel of the Lord is understood in this sense, then he is not a true angel by nature, but God himself. Hence "messenger of YHWH would be the

correct way to interpret the phrase.

[30]Eichrodt, *Theology of the Old Testament*, 2:28.

[31]Carol A. Newman, "Angels," in *ABD*, 1:252; Russell, *Method and Message*, p. 244.

[32]*First Enoch* 71:8 (compare 1:10; 60:1) claims a "countless" number of angels, but then gives the number at "a hundred thousand times a hundred thousand, ten million times ten million."

Chapter 3: Questions About the Activities of Angels

[1]Barbara Graham, *People Weekly*, April 11, 1994, p. 25.

[2]Hugh Pope, "Guardian Angel," in *The Catholic Encyclopedia* [hereafter *CE*], ed. Charles G. Herbermann, Edward A. Pace, C. B. Pallen, Thomas J. Shahan, John J. Wynne (New York: Encyclopedia Press, 1913), 7:49.

[3]For a list of Jewish sources, see W. D. Davies and Dale Allison, *The Gospel According to Saint Matthew*, International Critical Commentary (Edinburgh: T & T Clark, 1991), 2:770.

[4]Augustine's view was perhaps colored by his doctrine of predestination, which seemed to mitigate the necessity of believers' being under constant angelic surveillance. He did not believe that everyone was assigned a guardian angel (H. L. Pass, "Demons and Spirits (Christian)," in *ERE*, 4:580.

[5]Jerome as cited by Pope, "Guardian Angel," 7:49.

[6]On a similar note, Origen (185-254) believed that the soul of every newly baptized convert was assigned a guardian angel. If the soul falls for some reason, it comes under the power of a wicked angel (*Homelia in Lucam* 12-13).

[7]For a brief refutation of the so-called guardian angel passages, see William Hendrickson, *The Gospel of Matthew*, New Testament Commentary (Edinburgh: Banner of Truth Trust, 1973), pp. 692-94.

[8]Donald Guthrie, *New Testament Theology* (Downers Grove, Ill./Leicester, U.K.: InterVarsity Press, 1981), p. 136.

[9]In this passage Christ demonstrates that even those of low status—the "little children"—are immeasurably precious to both God and the highest angels who constantly abide in God's very presence. Ironically, Thomas Aquinas believed that only the lowest-ranking angels were human guardians (*Summa Contra Gentiles* 113:1-3).

[10]For more examples see Russell, *Method and Message*, p. 242.

[11]According to the Hebrews' tradition, Abraham, the father of the Jewish nation, was called centuries after the Tower of Babel incident.

[12]The New Testament agrees with the Dead Sea Scrolls that the number of Israelites who entered Egypt was seventy-five, not necessarily seventy (Acts 7:14). Scholars who support the seventy nations theory arrive at this number by counting fourteen nations from the sons of Japheth (Gen 10:1-5), thirty nations from the sons of Ham (Gen 10:6-20) and twenty-six nations from the sons of Shem (Gen 10:21-31). However, they

often assume Nimrod as the father of one nation instead of counting him as the father of six or possibly nine city-states (Gen 10:9-12). An alternative interpretation is that there are seventy angels who watch over seventy nations (1 Enoch 89.59ff.; 90.22ff.).

[13]The Septuagint derives its name from the seventy scholars who translated the Hebrew Scriptures into Greek under the auspices of Ptolemy Philadelphus, king of Egypt (250 B.C.E.).

[14]Compare Job 1–2 with the Manual of Discipline (11.5), Hymns of Thanksgiving (10.9) and Damascus Rule (2.9). See also Geza Vermes, The Dead Sea Scrolls: Qumran in Perspective (Philadelphia: Fortress, 1977), p. 205.

[15]Contrariwise, Gregory of Nyssa and Thomas Aquinas believed that national guardian angels, including the prince of Persia, were good angels (Barth, Church Dogmatics, 3/3:398). Answer 68 will demonstrate more reasons why I believe these angels are mostly evil.

[16]Ambrose De Viduis 9 (compare Augustine Contra Faustum 20.21). Citation from Pope, "Guardian Angel," 1:477.

[17]Some claim that this passage is not speaking against worshiping angels; rather, it is forbidding humans to take part in a visionary angelic liturgy (compare 4Q400-407; 3 Enoch 1). They argue that the Greek words tōn angelōn ("of [the] angels") should not be understood as an objective genitive (worship toward angels) but as a subjective genitive (worship led by angels) (Daniel G. Reid, "Angels, Archangels," in Dictionary of Paul and His Letters [hereafter DPL], ed. Gerald F. Hawthorne, Ralph P. Martin and Daniel G. Reid [Downers Grove, Ill./Leicester, U.K.: InterVarsity Press, 1993], p. 22). If the New Testament speaks even against worshiping with angels, we are hard-pressed to find a justification for worshiping angels.

[18]We may wonder why John, a faithful servant of God, would worship an angel in the first place. Perhaps he somehow mistook the angel for the glorified Christ whom he saw in Revelation 1. In a similar Jewish account Zephaniah bows down to an angel, accidentally thinking it a manifestation of God. Similar to what happened to John, the angel tells Zephaniah not to worship him (Apocalypse of Zephaniah 6.11-15).

[19]In Revelation John asks an angel to give him the little scroll in the angel's hand, but this is because God commanded John to do so (Rev 10). We cannot conclude from this that we should do the same thing John did in this unique situation.

[20]But after the death of the rich man, (traditionally known as Dives, who was indifferent to Lazarus, no angelic transportation is mentioned. Dives ends up in the flames of Hades!

[21]Contrary to popular belief, the fourth person was not the preincarnate Christ. Later on in the same narrative, Scripture affirms that an angel protected the three Hebrews (Dan 3:28). The pagan Nebuchadnezzar could hardly be referring to the "Son of God" in the New Testament sense hundreds of years before the New Testament was written. The text is

best rendered "a son of the gods" (*ŕbar-ʿᵉlāhîn*).

[22]In Ezekiel 9:4 the word *mark* in Hebrew is *tāw,* also the last letter of the Hebrew alphabet. In ancient script it was written as a cross (X). Some have argued that this passage might be prophetic, describing special protection to Christians, who in a spiritual sense wear the sign of a cross.

[23]I am indebted to Maxwell J. Davidson, from whom I derived much information. See Maxwell J. Davidson, "Angels," in *Dictionary of Jesus and the Gospels* [hereafter *DJG*], ed. Joel B. Green, Scot McKnight and I. Howard Marshall (Downers Grove, Ill./Leicester, U.K.: InterVarsity Press, 1992), pp. 8-11.

[24]Ibid., p. 11.

[25]For more information on the vanishing hitchhiker, see B. J. Oropeza, *99 Reasons Why No One Knows When Christ Will Return* (Downers Grove, Ill.: InterVarsity Press, 1994), pp. 137-39.

[26]The fact that these angels were bound, however, indicates they may be fallen angels let loose to bring destruction on humankind.

[27]Interestingly enough, the angel who binds Satan is not even designated as a mighty angel, as are some of the other angels (Rev 5:2; 10:1).

[28]The acrostic is adapted from Hendrickson, *Gospel of Matthew,* p. 694.

Chapter 4: Questions About Fallen Angels

[1]Rudolf Bultmann, "The New Testament and Mythology," in *Kerygma and Myth,* ed. H. W. Bartsch (London: SPCK, 1953), 1:5.

[2]Other witnesses were with me when this "haunting" took place (summer 1984). I heard the hostile spirit's voice as though it were speaking right in my ear. (I do not care to repeat the foul language it used.) After Marty, Tony and Nick (the friends who were with me) and I prayed for thirty minutes or so, we sensed that the presence had departed from our home. For various poltergeist reports, genuine and fake, consult Frank Smyth, *Ghosts and Poltergeists* (London: Aldus Books/Danbury, 1975); George Colin Wilson, *Poltergeist* (St. Paul: Llewellyn, 1993). Also helpful on spiritual/occultic encounters is Richard Cavendish, ed., *Man, Myth and Magic,* 3 vols. (New York: Marshall Cavendish, 1970). On the World Wide Web, consult the extended annotated bibliography called "Borely Rectory Selected Bibliography" linked to "Archive X" [www:crown.net/x/].

[3]S. E. McClelland, "Demon, Demon Possession," in *Evangelical Dictionary of Theology,* ed. Walter Elwell (Grand Rapids, Mich.: Baker Book House, 1984), p. 308.

[4]Those who do not believe in the reality of demons often reply that Jesus' disciples, who wrote the Gospels, made up the idea that demons knew Jesus as the Son of God and inserted these stories into the narratives. It seems that those who wish to deny the existence of demons are reading into passages their own preconceived notions, arbitrarily erasing the reality of demons because this idea insults their modern intelligence.

They also seem to turn a deaf ear to numerous missionary reports of demonic encounters. Yet even ancient nonbiblical sources support the idea of Jesus as an exorcist, as I note in the main text. This lends credibility to the notion that the Christ actually confronted the genuinely demon possessed.

[5]David Aune, "Demonology," in *ISBE*, 1:923; Craig Evans, "Jesus in Non-Christian Sources," in *DJG*, pp. 364-68.

[6]The non-Christian *Great Paris Magical Papyrus* (4.3019), for instance, uses this formula: "I adjure you by the God of the Hebrews, Jesus, Iaba, Iae, Abroath" (cited from J. Stafford Wright, "Satan, Beelzebul, Devil, Exorcism," in *NIDNTT*, 3:476).

[7]C. G. Jung, *Collected Works*, cited in J. Bruce Long, "Demons: An Overview," in *The Encyclopedia of Religion*, ed. Mircea Eliade (New York: Macmillan/London: Collier Macmillan, 1987), 4:287.

[8]W. H. Kent notes that the word *daimōn* may come from *daiō*, which means "to divide" or "to apportion," suggesting an order of divine beings that came between humans and the gods (W. H. Kent, "Demon," in *CE*, 4:710).

[9]Werner Foerster writes, "According to popular belief demons are . . . 'shades' which appear in all kinds of places, especially the lonely, at all possible times, expecially at night, and in the most varied forms, especially those of uncanny beasts" (Werner Foerster, "δαίμων κτλ.," in *Theological Dictionary of the New Testament* [hereafter *TDNT*], ed. Gerhard Kittel and Gerhard Friedrich, 10 vols. [Grand Rapids, Mich.: Eerdmans, 1964-76], 2:6; compare 2:2, 2:8).

[10]The Dead Sea Scrolls sometimes call an evil spirit *daimōn* (1QS 3.18; 1QM 13.10).The pseudepigrapha also uses the term in reference to evil spirits. Josephus distinguishes between *daimonia*, which he considers an evil spirit, and *daimōn*, which he uses for the Greek idea of a protective spirit. Likewise, Philo also understood the term to refer to a protective spirit.

[11]The origin of the word *šēḏîm* is uncertain. The word is possibly related to the *shidu*, the Assyrian bull-colossi, or one of the Canaanite deities (cf. S. R. Driver, *A Critical Exegetical Commentary on Deuteronomy*, International Critical Commentary [Edinburgh: T & T Clark, 1965], pp. 362-63; C. A. Briggs, *A Critical Exegetical Commentary on the Book of Psalms*, International Critical Commentary [Edinburgh: T & T Clark, 1907], p. 353).

[12]Eichrodt, *Theology of the Old Testament*, 2:224.

[13]Another creature, the leech or horse leech *("ᵃlûqâh)* in Proverbs 30:15, was often associated with a demonic vampire. However, this passage probably refers to some type of blood-sucking animal without clear demonic connotations. For a list of other possible words related to demons, see Aune, "Demonology," 1:919.

[14]The Sumerian word for wind is *lil*.

[15]Eichrodt, *Theology of the Old Testament,* 2:224.

[16]Magic and superstition surround the *lilit.* Lowell Handy notes that certain ancient Near Eastern and Jewish communities wore amulets or recited incantations to ward off the *lilit.* Sometimes Mesopotamians invoked the demon Pazuzu, king of the *lilu,* to protect themselves from her (Lowell K. Handy, "Lilith," in *ABD,* 4:324-25).

[17]The angels mentioned in Romans 8:38 and 1 Corinthians 4:9; 6:3 seem to refer to fallen angels.

[18]Tertullian, however, argued that even though demons have no flesh, they are not immaterial. They are made of a very light material substance (*Adversus Mareionem* 2.8.2; *De Carne Christi* 6.9). In any case, I doubt that angels or demons are by essence composed of molecules and atoms. A vacuum or an atomic bomb would not harm them.

[19]Terence Page, "Demons and Exorcism," in *DPL,* p. 210.

[20]We do not know how demons possess predictive abilities. We assume that they, as spirits, have superhuman knowledge. Given that their intelligence is higher than ours, they may be able to make better-educated guesses about the future. Also, since they have the ability to influence people, demons could influence and orchestrate non-Christian people and events to help fulfill the predictions made by a medium.

[21]Foerster, "δαίμων κτλ.," *TDNT* 2:12-13.

[22]Aune, "Demonology," 1:920.

[23]Daniel G. Reid, "Principalities and Powers," in *DPL,* p. 750.

[24]We will discover in chapter five that Isaiah 14:12 and Ezekiel 28 are most likely *not* references to the fall of Satan (compare answer 41). But even if these passages depicted the fall of Satan, they would not depict the fall of any other angel.

[25]Those who argue that according to Revelation 4:1, Revelation 12 must be *entirely* futuristic overlook the apocalyptic principle that past events can have current and future ramifications (Rev 17:1-11). To the original readers of Revelation, Satan's present and future persecution of the saints was a reality that they understood as a result of Christ's atoning work. If Revelation 12 is entirely futuristic, then the "salvation" that has "come" in 12:10 is not available in this current era.

[26]Both Jews and pagan Greeks believed Tartarus was a subterranean place—the lower part of hell (Hades), the place of the dead. In Greek mythology this is the place where the Titans who rebelled against Zeus were banished. In Tartarus God punished the wicked (*1 Enoch* 20.2; Sibylline Oracles 2:302; Josephus *Against Apion.* 2.240). Beelzeboul was said to be the only demon of the fall who escaped Tartarus (*Testament of Solomon* 6.2).

[27]In addition, the phrase *sons of God* in Genesis 6 is found in a context that is completely different from Deuteronomy 14:1. The former is a narrative text, while the latter is found in the stipulations of Moses. The former appears to be a commonly understood designation, while the

latter merely emphasizes ownership. (The context demonstrates in Deuteronomy 14:1-2 that it is because the Israelites belong to and are set apart as God's possession [they are the elect children of God] that they should not behave like the other nations surrounding them.) Furthermore, "sons of God" in Genesis 6:2 reads in Hebrew *b^enê-hā-*'lōhîm, while the phrase is "children of the LORD your God" in Deuteronomy 14:1: *banîm 'attem layhwâh '^elōhêkem.* Clearly the two phrases were not intended to be taken as parallels.

[28]Gordon J. Wenham, *Genesis 1−15,* Word Bible Commentary (Waco, Tex.: Word, 1987), p. 139.

[29]Brendan Byrne, "Sons of God," in *ABD,* 6:156.

[30]Wenham, *Genesis 1−15,* pp. 140-41.

[31]Compare Job 1−2 with the *Manual of Discipline* (11. 5), *Hymns of Thanksgiving* (10.9), *Damascus Rule* (2.9) and *Genesis Apocryphon.*

[32]Wenham, *Genesis 1−15,* p. 139.

[33]Ibid., p. 141.

[34]For references to ancient sources describing marriages between gods and humans, see Wenham, *Genesis 1−15,* p. 138. Josephus claims that the angels with women "begat sons that proved unjust, and despisers of all that was good, on account of the confidence they had in their own strength for the tradition is that those men did what resembled the acts of those whom the Grecians call giants" (*Antiquities of the Jews* 3.1). And in the late second century C.E. Justin Martyr wrote, "Whence also the poets and mythologists, not knowing that it was the angels and those demons who had been begotten by them that did these things [caused adulteries, wars, etc.] to men, and women, and cities, and nations, which they related, ascribed them to God himself, and to those who were accounted to be his very offspring, and to the offspring of those who were called his brothers, Neptune and Pluto, and to the children again of these offspring" (*Second Apology* 5).

[35]Maybe attempting to duplicate God's ability to give life was one of the reasons these angels were punished. Along these lines, the indications in Scripture that their offspring were giants implies deformity. The Genesis text might be teaching that in their attempt to replicate God's creation, the sons of God could only ape God's abilities.

[36]Wenham, *Genesis 1−15,* p. 143. Philo taught that Nimrod, the great warrior of Genesis 10:8, was one of the giants (*De Gigantibus* 58-65).

[37]The NIV version of this passage, in my opinion, is poorly translated. The parentheses after "we saw the Nephilim there" make the following comment seem to have been inserted by the biblical writer, "(the descendants of Anak come from the Nephilim)," to give the reader a better understanding of identity of the Nephilim. In Hebrew, however, no parentheses appear in the text. A more literal reading in Hebrew would be, "And there we saw the Nephilim (the) sons of Anak of the

Nephilim" (w°šām rā'ínû 'et-hann°pîlîm b°nê °nāq min-hann°pîlîm). The Hebrew reading supports the phrase as having been spoken by the exaggerating spies, not Moses or a later writer.

[38] The Dead Sea Scrolls exaggerate by claiming the giants who fell were like cedars and mountains in size (CD 2.18). First Enoch 7 claims they were three hundred cubits high. In 1 Enoch (7–10) the giants ate all the produce in the land, so the people would not give them anything else to eat. The giants then began eating people! They also drank blood, ate unclean animals and introduced humans to weapons, armor, cosmetics, jewelry and so on. Many of them were wicked. The people groaned, and the good angels requested that God do justice. So God sent the flood and bound them for seventy generations underneath a rock until the day of judgment. At that time they will be tormented with fire.

[39] Some scholars interpret the phrase "and also afterward" in Genesis 6:4 as referring to a time after the flood, anticipating the Numbers 13:33 mention of the Nephilim. But this interpretation is hard to reconcile with the context of Genesis 6–9, which depicts the flood as wiping out all human life (Gen 6:5–7:23). See explanation 3 in note 40, below.

[40] There are some other explanations:

1. The Nephilim in Genesis 6 and Numbers 13 are two unrelated peoples who happen to have the same name. But this seems unlikely, given the great stature of both races.

2. The Nephilim in Numbers 13 are descendants of the older Nephilim only in the sense that they shared certain characteristic(s): great size, apparent deformities, immoral behavior or whatever other unknown meanings the term Nephilim might suggest. Hence they are followers but not literal descendants. This alternative explanation also resolves the two accounts of Nephilim in Genesis 6 and Numbers 13.

3. The Nephilim existed before the children born to the "sons of God." This view emphasizes the words "and also afterward" in Genesis 6:4 to suggest that Nephilim were on earth prior to the sons of God. The children of the sons of God would simply be another species of the genus Nephilim. Specifically, they were the heroic variation of the Nephilim. However, since Genesis 6–9 stresses the universality of the flood, the flood would seem to have wiped out all the different species of the Nephilim, unless the term was used nonspecifically for any tall, wicked people. This takes us back to view 2. The rabbis understood the phrase "and afterward" as referring to the 120-year period before the flood (Gen 6:3). Thus a clearer paraphrase of the early verses in Genesis 6 might read: "In the days when the population increased, the angels married women. The Nephilim were born to them at that time, and also afterward—over the span of 120 years before the flood—whenever the sons of God had sex with women, Nephilim were born. These Nephilim were the heroes of old."

[41] Timothy R. Ashley, The Book of Numbers, New International Commen-

tary on the Old Testament (Grand Rapids, Mich.: Eerdmans, 1993), p. 243.

[42]*The New Encyclopaedia Britannica: Micropaedia*, 15th ed. (Chicago: Encyclopaedia Britannica/University of Chicago, 1975), 4:524.

[43]Some claim that a demon impersonated Samuel in this account. But the passage seems to affirm it really was Samuel who appeared to Saul. First, without qualification, 1 Samuel 28:12, 15 states, "When the woman saw Samuel" and "Samuel said to Saul" (compare 28:16, 20). Second, Samuel's prophecy about Saul came to pass (28:17, 19). The next day Saul and his sons died in battle, and David was given Saul's kingdom (1 Sam 31; 2 Sam 1–5). It is hard for me to accept that a demon would have accurately predicted something as crucial as the death of the king of God's people and the enthronement of righteous king David. Third, it is also difficult to believe a demon would have declared to Saul that he was going to be punished because of his disobedience to God (28:18). Finally, that the medium cried out in 1 Samuel 28:12 might indicate she was surprised to see a genuine apparition—no phony-baloney séance this time!

[44]At best, Luke 16:19-31 indicates only that those who die in a state of wickedness (in this case, the rich man) cannot visit the living. This passage says nothing about whether dead believers can revisit the living.

[45]*The New Encyclopaedia Britannica: Micropaedia*, 4:591.

[46]R. Campbell Thompson, "Demons and Spirits (Assyr.-Bab.)," in *ERE*, 4:570-71.

[47]J. Stafford Wright, *Mind, Man and the Spirits* (Grand Rapids, Mich.: Zondervan, 1971), p. 117.

[48]John Weldon and Clifford Wilson, *Psychic Forces and Occult Shock* (Chattanooga: Global Publishers, 1987), pp. 446-53.

[49]Wright, *Mind, Man and the Spirits*, p. 118.

[50]I am indebted to Daniel G. Reid, from whose article "Principalities and Powers" I have drawn much insight regarding this question (*DPL*, pp. 746-52).

[51]We should also mention the "elemental spirits of the world" *(stoicheia)*. In ancient literature the elemental spirits are associated with the star gods and the signs of the zodiac. In Hebrews 5:12, however, they seem to be nothing more than basic principles of religious belief. In 2 Peter 3:10-12 they seem to represent the basic material elements of the universe, such as fire, water, earth and air. Paul uses *ta stoicheia* in reference to religious rules that Christians no longer follow (Gal 4:3, 9; Col 2:8, 20). The Galatian and Colossian saints may have believed that spirits influenced the teaching of these rules or controlled the stars. The Galatians had once served false gods (Gal 4:8-11), and the Colossians were being tempted to religious legalism involving the worship of angels (Col 2:18). Both groups observed special days connected with the

observance of the moon and the stars. The Colossians, who apparently believed the *stoicheia* controlled the fate of humans, placated these influences through ascetic practices (Col 2:16-23). Since Paul claims that Christ defeated the "principalities and powers" on the cross, he assures the Colossians that they should no longer be enslaved to their old religious practices, including the fear of the elemental spirits (Col 2:13-15). It is not clear, however, whether Paul himself believes that these are real demonic spirits.

Other possible classes of demons are found in the lists that Paul combines with the "principalities and powers" (Col 1:16; Eph 1:21; 6:12). These particular manifestations of power include dominions *(kyriotētes)*, thrones *(thronoi)* and cosmic rulers *(kosmokratētes)*. Their precise nature and activities are harder to identify, and they may be the names for impersonal forces or ideas, not necessarily demons. (For some possible explanations regarding the nature and activities of some of these powers, see Reid, "Principalities and Powers," p. 749.)

[52]Daniel Reid notes that while the Septuagint (LXX) uses *stratēgos*, Theodotion uses *archōn* to refer to the princes of Persia and Greece in Daniel 10 ("Principalities and Powers," p. 748). It is possible that *archontes, archai, exousia* and similar magisterial terms may be Paul's way of identifying some rulers in his day whom he believed were influenced by demonic powers. After all, the decisions of those in authority over provinces or nations would often have repercussions on the way people lived or believed in those communities. Such decisions also influenced societal attitudes toward the Christians of those communities, and they would have definitely affected Paul and his colleagues (see Acts 18:2; Rev 2:13).

[53]Colossians 2:15 speaks of Christ's resurrection victory in imagery related to a warrior leading a triumphal procession of bound and defeated foes.

[54]Reid, "Principalities and Powers," p. 748.

[55]Hans Bietenhard, "Angel, Messenger, Gabriel, Michael," in *NIDNTT,* 1:451.

[56]For more information on demon possession, see answers 71-75.

[57]James Dunn writes that the " 'Kingdom of God' was one, though only one, of Judaism's ways of speaking about the hoped for new age, the eschatological age, when God's rule would be fully realized, his people Israel vindicated, and his enemies judged . . ." (James D. G. Dunn, *Jesus and the Spirit: A Study of the Religious and Charismatic Experience of Jesus and the First Christians As Reflected in the New Testament* [London: SCM Press, 1975], p. 47). For the relationship between the Holy Spirit and the "hand" or the "finger of God," compare Luke 11:20 with Matthew 12:28 (also Ex 8:6-19; Ezek 3:14; 8:1-3; 37:1).

[58]Aune, "Demonology," 1:923.

[59]Dunn, *Jesus and the Spirit,* p. 48.

[60]Ibid., p. 49.

[61]For early Jewish references to sinful vices associated with demons, see George A. Barton, "Demons and Spirits (Hebrew)," in *ERE*, 4:599.

[62]Likewise, the early rabbis claimed that not all diseases can be attributed to demons (Foerster, "δαίμων κτλ.," 2:13).

[63]Foerster, "δαίμων κτλ.," 2:17.

Chapter 5: Questions About Satan

[1]Jeffrey Burton Russell, *Lucifer: The Devil in the Middle Ages* (Ithaca, N.Y./London: Cornell University Press, 1984), p. 66.

[2]Another passage sometimes cited in support of the Satan/Lucifer theory is 2 Corinthians 11:14. The context refers to Satan as an "angel of light" because of his shrewd ability to deceive. The passage says nothing about how he fell or whether he was *originally* a virtuous and beautiful "light-bearing" angel called Lucifer. Likewise, Satan falling as "lightning" in Luke 10:18 seems to refer to the suddenness of his fall in relation to Jesus' ministry of establishing God's kingdom here on earth (compare Foerster, "ἀστραπή," *TDNT* 1:505). It is unlikely that either passage was meant to allude to Lucifer in Isaiah 14:12.

[3]See, for example, Walther Zimmerli, *Ezekiel 2: A Commentary on the Book of the Prophet Ezekiel Chapters 25–48*, Hermeneia (Philadelphia: Fortress, 1983), p. 95.

[4]Scholars have suggested parallel fallen god accounts from both Greek and the ancient Near East. In the Greek myth Phaethon is the son of Eos, the Venus star. Eos gives birth to the "morning star" (*eosphoros*; compare Is 14:12 LXX). The morning star attempted to ride his father's chariot, the sun, through the clouds. But Zeus, the king of the gods, struck him to earth with one of his lightning bolts. See John D. W. Watts, *Isaiah 1–33* (Waco, Tex.: Word, 1985), p. 210.

The Ras-Shamra texts of ancient Ugarit (2000 B.C.E.) show Baal sitting on Mount Sapon when the question is raised if someone else could sit on his throne. "Athtar, the Venus-star, is proposed. He is, however, too small to fill the throne and must come down to the earth and reign 'god of it all' " (J. Gray, "Day Star," in *ISBE*, 1:785). These accounts are similar to Isaiah 14, but Isaiah may be using a clearer parallel than we have access to today.

[5]The best explanation of this kind is to apply the prophetic principle of *Urzeit wird Endzeit* (primeval time becomes end time). Prophecy sometimes alludes to past events as well as future ones. (The whore of Babylon in Revelation 17, for instance, seems to be an allusion to the ancient and future Rome as well as ancient Babylon.) But if we apply this principle to Isaiah 14, the passage would resemble more the future fall of the antichrist—who at least is a man—than any archaic fall of Satan. In any specified sense, however, this passage refers to neither Satan nor the antichrist. Better to leave it portraying the one it intends

to portray—the king of Babylon.

[6]Some affirm that 2 *Enoch* gives the first reference to Lucifer as Satan. This Jewish document, however, may have been completed as late as the seventh century C.E. If this document is based on an older Greek text from the first century, we do not know if that version included the fall of Satan. See John Burton Russell, *Satan: The Early Christian Tradition* (Ithaca, N.Y.: Cornell University Press, 1981), p. 130. The book was perhaps written in Greek and Latin around 400 C.E. M. D. Johnson, however, suggests that the text is based on an older Hebrew version that may date back to 100-200 C.E. (J. H. Charlesworth, ed., *The Old Testament Pseudepigrapha* [Garden City, N.Y.: Doubleday, 1985], 2:252). *Second Enoch* 29 claims that "Satanael was hurled from the height, together with his angels" on the second day of creation. He was an archangel who contemplated the impossible—placing his throne above the clouds, becoming equal to the one who later cast him out of heaven. This text probably alludes to Isaiah 14. However, the devil's name here is Satanael, not Lucifer. Satanael was the early Jewish name for Satan prior to his fall (*3 Apocalypse of Baruch* 4.7-9). He lost the "-el" ("-God") part of his name when he fell. A second possible candidate for the oldest allusion to the fall of Satan in reference to Isaiah 14 is *The Life of Adam and Eve.* It, however, does not use the name Lucifer (*Adam and Eve* 15:1-3; compare 12:1-2; 16:1).

First Enoch 86 and 88 may depict fallen angels as fallen stars, similar to Revelation 9:1. This is perhaps the closest we can get to a Satan = Lucifer theory around the time of the first century. Old Testament scholar John D. W. Watts writes, "It is significant that the account of the fall of Satan (Rev 12) makes no reference to Isa 14" (Isaiah 1—33, Word Biblical Commentary [Waco, Tex.: Word, 1985], p. 212). It is possible that Origen is alluding to an earlier Jewish source, but I am not aware of any extant copies of such a source that clearly demonstrate Satan as Lucifer. Origen seems responsible for first popularizing the Lucifer-as-Satan theory among Christians.

[7]See F. L. Cross, and E. A. Livingstone, eds., *The Oxford Dictionary of the Christian Church,* 2nd ed. (London: Oxford University Press, 1974), pp. 841-42. Joseph Jensen and William Irwin in *The New Jerome Biblical Commentary* rightly note that "since some patristic writers [church fathers] saw in this piece [Is 14:12] an account of the fall of Satan, Lucifer came to be a name for the devil" (*The New Jerome Biblical Commentary,* ed. Raymond E. Brown, J. A. Fitzmyer and Roland E. Murphy [London: Geoffrey Chapman, 1990], p. 239).

[8]John N. Oswalt, *The Book of Isaiah: Chapters 1—39* (Grand Rapids, Mich.: Eerdmans, 1986), p. 320.

[9]So also Gerhard von Rad and Werner Foerster, "διαβάλλω, διάβολος," in *TDNT,* 2:75-76. Von Rad notes that according to Jewish literature the demons submitted to Satan independently of the Genesis 6 account (*1*

Enoch 54.6). Satan, as "Mastema," had "nothing to do with the fall of angels or the judgment of fallen angels, though he uses them as his instruments" (compare *Jubilees* 10.8).

[10]Some argue, however, that Satan is not one of the "sons of God" in Job 1—2 who sat in the heavenly council and presented themselves before God. Rather, he is an intruder "who also came with them" (Job 1:6). Whether or not he is considered one of the "sons of God," one fact remains: in the Old Testament he plays the role of the accuser in the heavenly council (Zech 3:1-4; 1 Kings 22:19-22).

[11]Compare Werner Foerster, "σατανᾶς," *TDNT,* 7:157.

[12]The King James Version's "abode not in the truth" can be misleading. The past-tense "abode" could be read as implying a time when Satan *did* abide in truth. The NIV and the Greek text imply no such thing.

[13]Compare Walter Lock, *The Pastoral Epistles,* International Critical Commentary (Edinburgh: T & T Clark, 1966), p. 39. What kind of condemnation is Paul referring to? Although Satan may no longer have access to accuse believers (compare Rev 12:9-11), he still has access to attack them through the accusations and slanders of unbelievers (1 Tim 5:14; Tit 2:8; Prov 6:24; compare Sirach 51.2). Sin provides an opportunity for the devil to attack God's people (Eph 4:26-27; 1 Tim 1:19-20). In 1 Timothy 3:6-7, the sin of a Christian leader allows Satan to instigate such accusation and slander. (This would seem to be similar to the scandals caused by televangelists Jim Bakker and Jimmy Swaggart in the 1980s.

[14]Anselm, Albert the Great and Thomas Aquinas taught that the devil knew it was impossible to be equal to God (Jas 2:19), but he, contrary to God's will, sinned in wanting to receive a "natural beatitude" obtained by his own power. Duns Scotus and the Franciscans, on the other hand, believed that angels could desire the impossible, so the devil did desire equality with God. The angels did not commit one sin in the beginning; they committed various sins before they became totally hardened to doing evil (Cross and Livingstone, *Oxford Dictionary of the Christian Church,* p. 397; W. H. Kent, "Demon," in *CE,* 4:765).

[15]Daniel G. Reid notes an interesting twist when comparing 2 Corinthians 4:4 with *Life of Adam and Eve* 12-16. The latter recounts Satan's refusal to worship the image of God in Adam. The former depicts Christ, the second Adam in the image of God, heralding the "good news" (Reid, "Satan, Devil," in *DJG,* p. 864). Since Satan refused to bow down to the first Adam, he will have to bow down to Christ, the second Adam (Phil 2:10; Rom 14:9-11).

[16]According to the Spanish theologian Francisco De Suárez (1548-1617), the angels received a glimpse of the future incarnation of Jesus Christ, the man who was God. Seeing a lower nature than themselves (a human) become the Son of God was the occasion for Satan's pride (*De Angelis* 7.13). This view, however, presupposes what it attempts to prove. There would be no need for a future incarnation of Christ if the devil

had not tempted Eve to sin in the first place.

[17]A special thanks to one of my old teachers, Dr. A. E. Wilder-Smith, for this insight.

[18]Wright, *Mind, Man and the Spirits,* pp. 127-28.

[19]See Lowell K. Handy, "Serpent (Religious Symbol)," in *ABD,* 5:1113-16; for other accounts (though non-Christian), see Roger Cook, *The Tree of Life: Image for the Cosmos* (New York/London: Thames and Hudson, 1995); David Maclagan, *Creation Myths: Man's Introduction to the World* (New York/London: Thames and Hudson, 1992).

[20]Handy, "Serpent (Religious Symbol)," 5:1113.

[21]For example, Satan disguises himself as a bread seller (*Testament of Job* 23.1), a beggar (*Testament of Job* 9.8—10:4) and an angel of light (*Life of Adam and Eve* 9.1).

[22]We also have modern-day examples of destroying objects that have been used for wrongful purposes. For instance, a person may break the pen of a reporter who writes slanderous articles about him, or a child, after growing up, may break an object that reminds her of an adult who mistreated her.

[23]Serpents may have always been considered shrewd due to their agility (Prov 30:19), or some suggest that this is one trait serpents lost due to the Fall.

[24]Cited from John Day, "Leviathan," in *ABD,* 4:295. See also the Mesopotamian cylinder seal in the British Museum, London. In Ugaritic literature the dragon is called "Yamm." In the Babylonian creation story, the Enuma Elish, it is known as "Tiamat," the chaos monster defeated by Marduk. Some have equated the latter with the Hebrew word *t°hôm,* "the deep," in Genesis 1:2. But Day argues there is no evidence that the Hebrew word was derived from the Akkadian "Tiamat." The Hebrew concept of Leviathan probably has more in common with the dragon myths of Canaan than Babylon (John Day, "Dragon and Sea, God's Conflict With," in *ABD,* 2:229). For Eastern dragon examples from a non-Christian perspective, see Francis Huxley, *The Dragon: Nature of the Spirit, Spirit of Nature* (New York/London: Thames and Hudson, 1992).

[25]Identifying leviathan as a crocodile in Job 41 is unconvincing, given the leviathan's enormous size, its virtual invincibility and its mouth, which apparently shoots out fire. The Institute for Creation Research in El Cajon, California, taking Job 40—41 in a rather literal sense, suggests that leviathan may be a type of dinosaur. It is compared to the bombardier beetle, which can shoot out heat above 200 degrees (ICR, Back to Genesis seminar). On the other hand, the writer of Job may be simply using poetic language to allude to a mythical creature that was popular in ancient literature. Contrary to Jerome (*Homilies* 30), the serpent in the Garden does not fit the description of the leviathan serpent (contrast Gen 3:1, 14-15 with Job 41).

[26]It seems that other ancient cultures made this creation-serpent/Paradise-serpent connection as well. They probably collapsed the two categories as explaining the origin of evil. This would give them a *cosmological* explanation for evil as chaos, darkness and catastrophe on the one hand, and an *anthropological* explanation for evil as sin, death and wickedness on the other hand. The Genesis account supports only the anthropological view of evil. The cosmological view of chaos, darkness and perhaps catastrophe would be considered part of the good creation of God (Gen 1:2-10, 31). Nevertheless, the creation-dragon-sea-chaos motif must have gradually became a referent for evil even among Jews; they eventually associated it with the serpent (Satan) in the garden. Both *dragon* and *serpent* are used to refer to Satan in Revelation 12. John Day notes the possibility that the Israelites celebrated the defeat of the leviathan chaos dragon at their new year festival (the feast of tabernacles), as did other ancient Near Eastern cultures. For the Israelites, the new year celebration commemorated the Lord's power over the sea at the beginning of creation (Day, "Dragon and Sea, God's Conflict With," 2:228-29). This tradition may have had something to do with the Jews' associating the dragon with Satan. In later Jewish tradition Satan was considered powerless on the Day of Atonement, which heralded the feast of tabernacles. The sounding of the trumpet on new year's day was said to confuse Satan. For rabbinic references, see Victor P. Hamilton, "Satan," in *ABD*, 5:988.

[27]Victor Hamilton notes that the Job and Zechariah references to Satan include the Hebrew definite article before śāṭān. In the Old Testament, only 1 Chronicles employs no definite article before Satan, making the usage a personal name. According to Hamilton, "Satan" in Job and Zechariah might be better translated as "the accuser" (Hamilton, "Satan," 5:986).

[28]An accusation can be true or false. It is different from slander, which is always false (Ibid., 5:985-86).

[29]H. E. Gaylord, "3 (Greek Apocalypse of) Baruch," in *The Old Testament Pseudepigrapha: Apocalyptic Literature and Testaments,* ed. James H. Charlesworth (London: Darton, Longman and Todd, 1983), 1:658.

[30]Werner Foerster writes, "The word of the adversary implies always an attempt of the part of the διάβολος to separate God and man. It is an open question whether the verb διαβάλλειν ['to separate'] influenced the usage" (Foerster, διαβάλλω, διάβολος," in *TDNT*, 2:73; cf. 71-72).

[31]Knut Schäferdiek, "σατανᾶς," *TDNT,* 7:163. It appears most often in the writings of the Shepherd of Hermas.

[32]Cited from Alfred Plummer, *Second Epistle of St. Paul to the Corinthians,* International Critical Commentary (Edinburgh: T & T Clark, 1915), p. 114.

[33]For some good overviews of Zoroastrianism, see Jack Finegan, *Myth and Mystery* (Grand Rapids, Mich.: Baker Book House, 1989), chap.

3; A. V. Williams Jackson, "Demons and Spirits (Persian)," in *ERE*, 4:619-20.

[34]Theodore H. Gaster, "Satan," in *The Interpreter's Dictionary of the Bible*, ed. G. A. Buttrick (New York: Abingdon, 1962), 4:226. In Persian myth there is a serpent figure called "Dahaka" that is an incarnation of the wicked spirit Angra Mainyu. Yima, the golden-age ruler, overcomes this serpent (John Skinner, *Genesis*, International Critical Commentary [Edinburgh: T & T Clark, 1930], p. 70). Some claim that the Jewish idea of Satan as the serpent arises from this myth, but we have already discussed how widespread the serpent-creation stories are. These myths, including the Persian account, may all point to an oral tradition described in Genesis 3.

[35]See John E. Hartley, *The Book of Job*, New International Commentary on the Old Testament (Grand Rapids, Mich.: Eerdmans, 1988), pp. 17-20. Hartley, however, claims that "Satan" in Job functions as a title, not a proper name. Be that as it may, we still have an accuser figure prior to the Jewish captivity.

[36]Hugh Pope presents an interesting twist to this issue. He suggests that the Persians may have borrowed from the Jews instead of vice versa. He claims the Persian angelic beings do not date back to the time of the Jewish captivity, but arrived later, during the dynasty of Sassanides: "If this be the case, . . . we should rather reverse the position and attribute the Zoroastrian angels to the influence of the Bible and of Philo" (Hugh Pope, "Guardian Angel," in *CE*, 7:48).

[37]Theodore J. Lewis, "Belial," in *ABD*, 1:654-55.

[38]The Dead Sea Scrolls emphasize Belial as an adversary of God. Paul switches the motif from God vs. Belial to Christ vs. Belial (Jerome Murphy-O'Conner, ed., *Paul and Qumran* [Chicago: Priority Press, 1968], pp. 55-56).

[39]David P. Wright, "Azazel," in *ABD*, 1:536.

[40]In biblical hermeneutics (the science of interpretation), *type* refers to an Old Testament object, practice or event that points to its greater fulfillment in the New Testament (for example, 1 Cor 10:6-11).

[41]Theodore H. Gaster, "Beelzebul," in *The Interpreter's Dictionary of the Bible*, 1:374.

[42]A messenger tells Job that the fire from heaven came from God (1:16). But surely this was a wrong assumption on the messenger's part. The context clearly suggests that Satan was behind it all.

[43]Graham H. Twelftree, "Demon, Devil, Satan," in *DJG*, p. 170.

[44]Hans Beitenhard, "Demon, Air, Cast Out," in *NIDNTT*, 1:449. The Greeks distinguished between *aer*—the lower, impure and vaporous atmosphere (compare Rev 9:12; 16:17)—and *ether*—the upper, pure air. We do not know if Paul understood the terms in the same way, but he does make distinctions between heavenly realms (2 Cor 12:2; compare *2 Enoch* 8.1-8).

[45]For a gallery of art pictures related to this subject, see Heinz Mode, *Fabulous Beasts and Demons* (London: Phaidon, 1975).

[46]In Greek mythology satyrs were half-human/half-goat creatures that followed Dionysus, the god of wine.

[47]Russell, *Lucifer,* p. 254.

[48]Ibid., p. 69.

[49]For a list of various features of the devil in art, see ibid., pp. 210-13.

[50]Ibid., p. 131.

[51]Eduard Lohse, *Colossians and Philemon,* Hermeneia (Philadelphia: Fortress, 1971), pp. 59-61; F. F. Bruce, *The Epistle to the Colossians, Philemon, and to the Ephesians,* New International Commentary on the New Testament (Grand Rapids, Mich.: Eerdmans, 1984), pp. 76, 111-12; Peter T. O'Brien, *Colossians, Philemon,* Word Biblical Commentary (Waco, Tex.: Word Books, 1982), pp. 54-57.

[52]For other references from the church fathers along these same lines, see H. L. Pass, "Demons and Spirits (Christian)," in *ERE,* 4:579.

[53]Thomas Aquinas believed that once the angels made their choice to serve or not to serve God in the beginning, their decisions forever fixed their fate. The good angels are without the imperfection of a freedom that leads them to a deviant choice; the bad angels are incapable of repentance (*Summa Contra Gentiles* 62.8; 64.2). Tatian (c. 160) held that the nature of angels is such that they are incapable of repentance (*Orations* 12, 15, 20).

[54]B. F. Wescott, *The Epistle of the Hebrews* (Grand Rapids, Mich.: Eerdmans, 1974), p. 55.

[55]William Gouge, *Commentary on the Whole Epistle to the Hebrews* (Edinburgh: James Nichol, 1866), 1:176.

[56]Foerster, "σατανᾶς," *TDNT,* 7:159.

[57]When passages mention Christ "in hell" or in "the heart of the earth" (for example, Mt 12:40; Acts 2:27), they are most likely referring to the grave. In Ephesians 4:9, Christ's descension "to the lower earthly regions" seems to be a metaphor depicting his incarnation and lowly status here on earth (compare Ps 139:15; Is 44:23; Rom 10:7). Others, however, think this may be a reference to his descension to Hades, while still others believe this passage refers to the Spirit's descension. For an elaboration on these views, see Andrew T. Lincoln, *Ephesians,* Word Biblical Commentary (Waco, Tex.: Word Books, 1990), pp. 244-47.

[58]Bruce, *Epistle to the Colossians, Philemon,* pp. 111-12. The *stoicheia,* whether real or imagined, are the spiritual powers involved in the Colossian heresy. Apparently Paul would include them in his definition of "principalities and powers" in Colossians 2:15.

[59]The word for "proclaim" in this passage in Greek is *kēryssō,* not *euangelizō.* We would expect the latter word if Jesus were preaching the gospel to these spirits. The term *spirits (pneumata)* refers to supernatural, not human, spirits (Mt 8:16; Lk 10:20; compare *1 Enoch* 15.4-10; 16.1).

In *1 Enoch*, which Petrine theology seems to be familiar with, God sends Enoch to proclaim doom to the fallen angels that sinned with women (1 *Enoch* 12:4; 15:2). The fallen angels were in prison houses (10:4-14; 13:1; 18:14-16; 21:6-10).

[60]J. N. D. Kelly, *A Commentary on the Epistles of Peter and Jude* (London: Adam and Charles Black, 1969), p. 153. Origen taught that Christ became a ransom to Satan for our sins. At his death Jesus delivered up his soul to Satan in exchange for the souls of men. The devil accepted the deal, but could not hold on to Jesus because the Son of God was more powerful than death itself. Hence Satan lost his power over death and his ability to retain the soul of Christ. But Origen's view, commonly known as the ransom theory, is far too questionable. It weakens the sovereignty of God by claiming that he had to make a deal with the devil. Moreover, some would call God's ethics into question over double-crossing Satan. Scripture affirms that Christ committed his spirit to God, not Satan, when he died (Lk 23:46). I believe the atonement is best described by a modified satisfaction theory similar to that of Anselm (see his *Cur Deus Homo*).

[61]J. Ramsey Michaels, *1 Peter,* Word Biblical Commentary (Waco, Tex.: Word Books, 1988), pp. 203-10.

[62]In 1 Peter 3:19 Michaels interprets "prison" *(phylakē)* as "refuge" (compare Rev 18:2). This refuge of demons was located in the second heaven, not somewhere under the earth (2 *Enoch* 7:1-3).

[63]Michaels, *1 Peter,* p. 210.

[64]For a list of the most prominent options, see Philip Hughes, *Paul's Second Epistle to the Corinthians* (London: Marshall, Morgan and Scott, 1961), pp. 442-48; Ralph P. Martin, *2 Corinthians,* Word Biblical Commentary (Waco, Tex.: Word Books, 1986), pp. 412-17.

[65]Clark H. Pinnock, "Thorn in the Flesh," in *ISBE,* 4:843.

[66]But G. H. Twelftree replies that Paul's reference to the Galatians' giving their eyes for him is only a figurative way of saying they would have sacrificed anything for him (Gal 4:13-14). Ancient cultures considered the eyes very delicate, and "gouging out the eyes" for another person was used as a figure of speech for friendship (Deut 32:10; 1 Sam 11:2; compare Lucian *On Friendship* 40-41; G. H. Twelftree, "Healing, Illness," in *DPL,* p. 380).

[67]Hughes suggests that this vision occurred when Paul was still in Antioch (Acts 11:26). Hughes, *Paul's Second Epistle to the Corinthians,* p. 430.

[68]For a fuller refutation of equating Satan with the antichrist, see my book *99 Reasons Why No One Knows When Christ Will Return* (Downers Grove, Ill.: InterVarsity Press, 1994), pp. 156-57.

Chapter 6: Questions About Spiritual Warfare
[1]Some claim that the sin focused on David's failure to abide by the Old Testament law of paying atonement money when taking a census (Ex

30:11-16). Unfortunately, Scripture is not explicit regarding the exact nature of the sin David committed by numbering the people.
[2]Ethelbert Stauffer, "ἐπιτιμάω, ἐπιτιμία," *TDNT,* 2:624-25.
[3]Stauffer (ibid.) notes that a nuance of "rebuke" *(epitimaō)* applies to the church (Lk 17:3; 2 Tim 4:2; compare Lk 23:40-41).
[4]This reading is based on the NIV footnote text. The regular texts read "will be bound" *(estai dedemenon)* and "will be loosed" *(estai lelymenon).* But these are literally translated as future perfects: "will have been . . ." The literal reading probably is not crucial to the meaning of the text. However, R. T. France suggests that the future perfects mean that Peter's decisions have the "prior endorsement" of the Lord in heaven (R. T. France, *Matthew,* New Testament Commentary [Leicester, U.K.: Inter-Varsity Press/Grand Rapids, Mich.: Eerdmans, 1985], p. 275). W. D. Davies and Dale Allison respond that the parallel passage of Matthew 18:18 reads, "Again, I say to you, if two of you agree on earth about anything they ask, it will be done for them by my Father in heaven." This is clearly a case where the church's decision precedes God's decision in reference to binding and loosing. The Greek texts can also use future perfects as simple future passives, as does the main NIV text (2 Kings 22:3 LXX; Is 8:17; Heb 2:13). For these and other reasons, Davies and Allison suggest that we not press the meaning of the future perfects too far (W. D. Davies and Dale Allison, *The Gospel According to Matthew,* International Critical Commentary [Edinburgh: T & T Clark, 1991], 2:638-39).
[5]In the Old Testament, as well as in Jewish and pagan literature, "gates of hell" often referred to death and dying (Job 17:16; 38:17; Ps 107:18; compare Wisdom of Solomon 16.13; 3 Maccabees 5.51). See D. A. Carson, "Matthew," in *The Expositor's Bible Commentary,* ed. Frank E. Gaebelein (Grand Rapids, Mich.: Regency Reference Library/Zondervan, 1984), 8:370.
[6]This does not mean, however, that heaven will endorse unrighteous decisions made by church leaders, no matter who they are. Jesus did not accept the authority of ministers who unjustly condemned others (Mt 15:1-20; 23:13; Jn 9:34-38). See William Hendrickson, *The Gospel of Matthew,* New Testament Commentary (Edinburgh: Banner of Truth Trust, 1973), p. 651.
[7]Andrew T. Lincoln, *Ephesians,* Word Biblical Commentary (Dallas: Word Books, 1990), p. 443.
[8]David W. Diehl, "Righteousness," in *EDT,* p. 953.
[9]Lincoln, *Ephesians,* p. 449.
[10]Daniel P. Fuller, "Satan," in *ISBE,* 4:343.
[11]Lincoln, *Ephesians,* p. 451.
[12]Ibid.
[13]The gift of discernment, for instance, would seem to include the ability to discern demonic doctrines and presences (1 Cor 12:10). Perhaps this

gift, or the gift of miracles, would include the ability of certain Spirit-filled saints to excel in casting out devils (1 Cor 2:4; 2 Cor 12:12; Gal 3:5; 1 Thess 1:5).

[14]Fuller, "Satan," 4:343.

[15]This reading is based on the NIV footnote text. For reasons why this reading is preferred, see answer 16.

[16]Tet-Lim N. Yee, " 'Put on the Armour of God': Eph. 6.10-20 as a Test Case for Genuine Unity," paper and oral presentation given in New Testament postgraduate seminar, Durham University, England, May 6, 1996.

[17]Wayne Grudem, *Systematic Theology* (Leicester, U.K.: InterVarsity Press/Grand Rapids, Mich.: Zondervan, 1994), p. 421. One further note on Grudem's fourth point: as noted in answer 67, proclaiming the gospel, in and of itself, defeats the forces of darkness. We do not necessarily have to wait for some "stronghold" to be broken in order to do this effectively. But we do need the power of the Spirit, and this often comes through worship, fellowship and prayer.

[18]Cross and Livingstone, eds., *Oxford Dictionary of the Christian Church*, p. 494.

[19]In the *Testament of Solomon* (5.12) we find the belief that demons do not like water (compare Mk 5:13).

[20]A common belief in exorcism shared by many ancient people was that the demons had to speak and thus reveal their name and nature. The exorcist, who swore by an oath or made incantations, would command the demon to leave the possessed. It was believed that the demon would also make a physical sign of its departure, such as knocking over a cup of water or causing the victim to sneeze. Drugs were also used in some exorcisms (David Aune, "Exorcism," in *ISBE*, 2:242-45). Justin Martyr believed that prayer, fasting, laying on hands, burning roots, sprinkling holy water and the name of Jesus should be used in exorcisms (*Second Apology* 6). His view reflects a combination of ideas derived from both Christianity and superstition.

[21]M. Gaster, "Divination (Jewish)," in *ERE*, 4:811.

[22]Henry A. Virkler, "Demonic Influence and Psychopathology," in *Baker Encyclopedia of Psychology*, ed. David G. Benner (Grand Rapids, Mich.: Baker Book House, 1985), p. 295. Church tradition seems a bit sweeping when it claims that demonic influence may come from practicing idolatry, eating food sacrificed to idols, or the sinful nature inherited through Adam (Clementine *Recognitions* 21.71).

[23]The last passages referenced in the main text may suggest why demons desire to possess bodies. They are used as "homes" where the demons can express themselves (Wright, *Mind, Man, and the Spirits*, pp. 132-33). Demons also wish to destroy and usurp God's creation; they are partially able to do this by possessing animals or humans.

[24]For documented cases of demon possession, see J. L. Nevius, *Demon Possession*, 8th ed. (Grand Rapids, Mich.: Kregel, 1968); see also John

Warwick Montgomery, *Demon Possession* (Minneapolis: Bethany Fellowship, 1976).

[25]The chart outline is adapted from the points made in Virkler's article "Demonic Influence and Psychopathology," p. 297.

[26]Basil Jackson, "The 'Demons' of Misdiagnosis," *Ministries,* Spring 1986, pp. 36-38.

[27]Virkler, "Demonic Influence and Psychopathology," p. 296.

[28]Merrill Unger, "Can a Christian Be Demon Possessed?" *Front Page* 7 (July 1991): 5-6; Virkler, "Demonic Influence and Psychopathology," p. 295.

[29]A "one-night" demonic attack would then be understood as just that: a demonic attack. Virkler ("Demonic Influence and Psychopathology," p. 295), drawing from Kurt Koch, asserts, "Oppression may range from a simple form of occult subjection that may go unnoticed for years until a particular event uncovers it, to a moderately intense form of oppression where a negative reaction occurs toward any form of Christian counselling, to a state where the person is continually surrounded and oppressed by the powers of darkness. . . . Since demonic temptation, oppression, and possession form a continuum rather than discrete categories, extreme forms of oppression share much in common with possession." Compare Kurt Koch, *Occult Bondage and Deliverance* (Grand Rapids, Mich.: Kregel, 1971), p. 32.

[30]Grudem, *Systematic Theology,* pp. 424-25.

[31]Some manuscripts include the word *fasting* in these verses (compare KJV). But some of the best manuscripts do not support this reading. Nevertheless, I do believe that fasting certainly helps when dealing with the demonic. The early church obviously thought so, or the word *fasting* would not have been included in these passages.

[32]So also Virkler, "Demonic Influence and Psychopathology," p. 298.

[33]As various interpreters of this passage have suggested, the prince of Persia may have simply been trying to protect his territory from an invading power or trying to hinder the work of God in a general sense, knowing that Gabriel worked for the "enemy." In addition, we are not told *how* this prince hindered Gabriel or how Michael overcame him. If we take this passage in a literal sense, I am intrigued to know how spiritual entities "fight"!

[34]Some cite 1 Corinthians 14:2, claiming that no one understands the language of those who speak in tongues. This is true; however, the context is only speaking in the categories of humans and God. No *human* can understand the one who speaks in tongues. This passage says nothing about whether or not angels can understand the one who speaks in tongues. Another passage often cited is Romans 8:26. But there is no clear evidence that this passage refers to speaking in tongues. The "groanings" of the Spirit "cannot" be uttered. Tongues, on the other hand, are utterable.

[35]For refutations of the view that tongues and other supernatural gifts

have ceased since the first century, see Grudem, *Systematic Theology*, pp. 1016-38; Jack Deere, *Surprised by the Power of the Spirit* (Grand Rapids, Mich.: Zondervan, 1993); Stanley M. Burgess, *The Holy Spirit: Ancient Christian Traditions* (Peabody, Mass.: Henrickson; 1984); Jon Ruthven, "On the Cessation of the Charismata: The Protestant Polemic of Benjamin B. Warfield," *Pneuma* 1 (Spring 1990): 14-31.

[36]See my book *A Time to Laugh: The Holy Laughter Phenomenon Examined* (Peabody, Mass.: Hendrickson, 1995), pp. 145-78.

[37]Of course, some bodily phenomena could indicate demon possession, but having attended quite a number of Toronto Blessing services, I think I am safe in saying that bodily manifestations caused by demonic forces are the rare exception in these services, not the rule.

[38]The Jews also, for example, wrongly attributed the miracles of Jesus to demons (Jn 7:20; 8:48-52; 10:20-21), implying a belief that demonic supernatural events are possible.

[39]We should be as generous as possible in our definition of heresy. A heretic should *never* be defined as "a person who does not agree with every doctrine I believe in." *Heretic,* in the classic Christian sense of the word, refers to someone who denies or opposes beliefs found in the early creeds of the church, such as the Trinity, the deity of Christ, Christ's atoning death and his bodily resurrection. Thus if a revival preacher teaches that God guarantees materialistic prosperity, this teaching may be false, but it is not heresy in the classic sense. Hence a genuine supernatural event that occurs in such a meeting should not be quickly dismissed as demonic. God may in fact do some miracles or healings through such misguided Christians *despite* their errors.

Chapter 7: Questions About the Occult

[1]According to the survey, 14 percent of the U.S. population feared black cats crossing their path, 12 percent feared walking under a ladder, 9 percent feared Friday the thirteenth, and 5 percent feared breaking a mirror. For a survey of the possible origins of popular superstitions, see Daniel Cohen, *A Natural History of Unnatural Things* (New York: McCall, 1971).

[2]Ronald M. Enroth, "Occult, The," in *Evangelical Dictionary of Theology,* ed. Walter A. Elwell (Grand Rapids, Mich.: Baker Book House, 1984), p. 787.

[3]Ibid.

[4]By "popular media culture" I mean bestselling and influential magazines, news programs, talk shows and so forth. Some Christians define *cult* as any group that opposes or denies historic orthodox Christian beliefs found in the classic Christian creeds. Such a group would be understood by the church fathers as an apostate or heretical group. I would rather use the term *heretical* to refer to this type of group; notwithstanding, we should recognize that many heretical sects also

possess the abusive characteristics found in modern-day media cult groups such as the People's Temple or the Branch Davidians. Hence the broader orthodox-centered understanding of cult and the narrower media understanding of cult definitely overlap, but they are not synonymous.

[5]For a helpful list of occult terms, see "Glossary of Terms," *SCP Journal* 2 (Winter 1980-1981): 7, 9, 11, 13, 15.

[6]I say this is "alleged" because in Scripture no one is able to read minds except God. More likely, psychics who claim telepathy (coined by F. W. Meyers) are "reading" emotions, facial expressions, and general and psychological characteristics. Good guessing also helps. If a crafty person carefully observes a client's reactions (knowing some neurolinguistics, personality types and so on), he or she can often make good guesses at what the client is thinking and feeling, and can change or reinterpret the reading if the client's facial reactions express aversion to it! Genuine cases of telepathy might involve demonic spirits that have observed a person's verbal communication, gestures, reactions and so on, and have somehow communicated this information to the reader.

[7]In the Buddhist tradition the goal of yoga is to obtain *nirvana*, an enlightened "blissful" state where there are allegedly no cravings or ignorance and the human mind is in total control over bodily pleasures and pains. In the Hindu tradition the goal of yoga is to obtain *moksha*, a state of oneness with Brahman, a pantheistic deity. Those who faithfully practice yoga often hope to find or "realize" themselves as "one" with the universe.

[8]See "Astral Projection," CRI Statement 4.058, Christian Research Institute (hereafter CRI), P.O. Box 500, San Juan Capistrano, CA 92693, n.d. Astral projection should be distinguished from near death (NDE) or after death experiences (ADE). Raymond Moody and Elisabeth Kübler-Ross have recorded many instances in which people were clinically dead but came back to life. The people claim to have remained conscious after dying. Some characteristics common to those who claim to have had an ADE include (1) the ability to hear the doctors pronounce them dead and even see their dead bodies, (2) meeting others who had passed away or meeting angelic beings, (3) passing through a tunnel and reaching a bright light that is often associated with ultimate goodness, love or Jesus Christ. Many claim to reach a border or limit that prevents them from going farther. Some have positive experiences, others have negative experiences. But Moody and Kübler-Ross have not always interpreted these people's experiences correctly. They seem to tout a type of universalism in which nobody is judged after death but all are accepted by God or the "great light." But Maurice Rawlings, another thanatologist, affirms that many people have terrible ADES or NDES that point to the reality of hell and judgment after death. These people often seek some type of comfort through prayer or repentance,

or both.

[9]For helpful sources connected with this section, see S. R. Driver, *A Critical and Exegetical Commentary on Deuteronomy*, International Critical Commentary (Edinburgh: T & T Clark, 1895), pp. 221-27; Joanne K. Kuemmerlin-McClean, "Magic," in *ABD*, 4:468-69; David Aune, "Magic," in *ISBE*, 3:214-15; E. P. Graham, "Divination," in *CE*, 5:48-51; M. Gaster, "Divination (Jewish)," in *ERE*, 4:806-11.

[10]Aune, "Magic," 3:218.

[11]See Susan Garrett, *The Demise of the Devil: Magic and the Demonic in Luke's Writings* (Minneapolis: Fortress, 1989), pp. 101-9. According to David Aune ("Magic," 3:218) Greco-Roman magic primarily consisted of protective magic (apotropaic), malevolent (black) magic, love magic aimed at seducing others and revelatory magic. Paul faces the latter of these in Acts 16.

[12]I should also say a word about Dungeons and Dragons and other fantasy games, which are available at local hobby shops. They involve players and a "dragon master" who creates, leads and referees the fantasy. Players can cast spells, perform imaginary magic and rely on many different gods for assistance. Some players get so obsessed with the game that when they lose a beloved fantasy hero, they can actually suffer depression because of it!

[13]The peace symbol is usually said to be an upside-down broken cross of Nero, the anti-Christian Caesar who is remembered as a notorious persecutor of the church. Others claim the peace symbol is a witches' tool depicting a crow's foot. However, the modern peace symbol has little to do with occultism or anti-Christian sentiments. It was designed in 1958 in London as a symbol of opposition to nuclear war. The symbol combines the semaphore signals for the letters *N* (vertical flag) and *D* (two 45-degree-angle flags), signifying the words *nuclear disarmament*. The peace sign of raising two fingers in the shape of a *V* apparently was borrowed from the World War II sign for victory.

[14]Aune, "Magic," 3:214. In ancient Near Eastern cultures magic was "a form of communication involving the supernatural world in which an attempt is made to affect the course of present and/or future events by means of ritual actions (especially ones which involve the symbolic imitation of what the practitioner wants to happen) and/or by means of formula recitations which describe the desired outcome and/or invoke gods, demons, or the spirits believed to be resident in natural substances" (J. A. Scurlock, "Magic (ANE)," in *ABD*, 4:464). For a comprehensive overview of the subject of early magic, see David Aune, "Magic and Early Christianity," in *Aufstieg und Niedergang der Römischen Welt*, ed. Wolfgang Haase (Berlin: Walter de Gruyter, 1980), 2:1507-57.

[15]See Colin Brown and J. Stafford Wright, "Magic, Sorcery, Magi," in *NIDNTT*, 2:552, 556.

[16]Ibid., 2:552-61.

[17]C. E. Arnold, "Magic," in *DPL*, p. 580.

[18]Arnold (ibid., p. 583), for instance, notes that Paul may be battling the magical assumption of capricious "fate" by emphasizing the predestination and election of the church in Ephesians 1. And contrary to the self-serving purposes of magic, Paul instructs Christians to be selfless and to pray according to the will of God (Eph 3:14-19; 5:2). God's power comes through communion with Christ, not incantations (Eph 2:5). Christians must combat the powers that are contrary to Christianity (Eph 4:27; 6:10-18).

[19]The early church fathers claimed that Simon was a type of Gnostic, founding a heretical movement called the Simonians (Justin *Apology* 1.26; Irenaeus *Against Heresies* 1.16; compare *Acts of Peter* 4–18).

[20]In psychic research, *paranormal* refers to phenomena outside the realm of the normal in terms of cause and effect. See "Glossary," *SCP Journal*, p. 15.

[21]See Dan Korem, *Powers: Testing the Psychic and Supernatural* (Downers Grove, Ill.: InterVarsity Press, 1988).

[22]"Subliminal Messages," *CRI Perspective*, CRI, n.d.

[23]For example, "Time of Trouble," in *Thy Kingdom Come*, series 3 (Brooklyn: Watchtower, 1909). For a refutation of numerology, see my book *99 Reasons Why No One Knows When Christ Will Return*, chap. 4.

[24]Arnold, "Magic," p. 582.

[25]For sources and recommended reading material on psychic phenomena, see John Weldon and Clifford Wilson, *Psychic Forces and Occult Shock* (Chattanooga: Global Publishers, 1987); Mark Albrecht and Brooks Alexander, "Biblical Discernment and Parapsychology," *SCP Journal* 2 (Winter 1980-81): 16-28.

[26]Jesus' phrase "the kingdom of God is within you" from Luke 17:21 is often abused by occultists. However, the kingdom of God is not "within you" in the sense that everyone has latent psychic powers. Rather, this verse is saying that the kingdom of God is "among you" or "in your midst" *(entos hymōn)* as the NIV margin reads (see Leon Morris, *The Gospel According to St. Luke: An Introduction and Commentary*, New Testament Commentary [London: Inter-Varsity Press, 1974]; p. 259). I. Howard Marshall writes, "Jesus speaks of men entering the kingdom, not of the kingdom entering men. . . . Jesus is speaking of the presence of the kingdom of God among men, possibly as something within their grasp if they will only take hold of it" (I. Howard Marshall, *The Gospel of Luke: A Commentary on the Greek Text*, New International Greek Testament Commentary [Exeter, U.K.: Paternoster, 1978], p. 655). If Jesus did imply an inward work here, this work would probably refer to Christ's claiming that the religious leaders he was addressing needed to be converted to Christ's message of the kingdom of God before they sought external signs of the kingdom of God.

[27]Albrecht and Alexander, *Biblical Discernment and Parapsychology*, pp.

23-24.

[28]For some good refutations of astrology, consult Charles Strohmer, *What Your Horoscope Doesn't Tell You* (Wheaton, Ill.: Tyndale House, 1988); Andrew Fraknoi, *Sky and Telescope,* August 1989, pp. 146-50; Walter Martin, "Astrology," CRI cassette tape C-005.

[29]Reincarnationists usually claim that Origen (185-254) and some of the other early church fathers taught reincarnation. This is simply not true. Reincarnationists need to produce clear evidence to that effect, and they have failed to do so because there is none! Although Origen believed in the preexistence of the human soul, he did not teach reincarnation. For some good refutations along these lines, see Joseph P. Gudel, Robert M. Bowman and Dan R. Schlesinger, "Reincarnation—Did the Church Suppress It?" *Christian Research Journal,* Summer 1987, pp. 8-10, 12.

[30]Similarly, some might claim that Herod believed Jesus to be the reincarnation of John the Baptist (Mk 6:14-16). It is extremely unlikely that Herod, a Palestinian, believed in the Eastern notion of reincarnation. Even he would have realized that John was alive at the same time Jesus was. Not even reincarnationists believe that the spirit of a person can be the spirit of *another* person when both persons live during the same time. Herod probably believed the animistic notion that the spirit of a person who dies a violent death (that is, John the Baptist) can be controlled by "magicians" (that is, Jesus) to gain more power. But even if Herod did believe in reincarnation, that would not prove that Jesus and his disciples also believed in it.

[31]For a good summary of arguments against reincarnation, see Mark Albrecht, "Reincarnation Versus Resurrection," *Areopagus,* Easter 1991, pp. 18-23.

[32]For an excellent overview and critique of the New Age movement, see Douglas Groothius, *Unmasking the New Age* (Downers Grove, Ill.: Inter-Varsity Press, 1986). Also see the numerous materials available through CRI and Spiritual Counterfeits Project, P.O. Box 2418, Berkeley, CA 94702.

[33]Compare the major New Age tenets in the main text with the tenets of occult philosophy in Brooks Alexander, "Occult Philosophy and Mystical Experience," *SCP Journal,* Winter 1984, pp. 13-19.

[34]New Agers who believe that they create their own reality sometimes might believe that they can do so at the expense of denying objective reality or a core of universal truths and moral beliefs (relativism). In a broad sense, when relativists say there are no absolutes (no objective truths or moral principles to which all should adhere), they must affirm either that their statement is not absolute (hence no one has to or should believe it) or that their statement *is* absolute (which would contradict their claim).

[35]For a refutation of New Age and New World Order conspiracies, see my

book *99 Reasons,* pp. 110-12, 142-47.

[36]I am indebted to Ron Rhodes, my former colleague at CRI. Much of what I have gleaned on the New Age Christ has come from hearing or reading his research or from dialoguing with him. For more information on this subject, consult his book *The Counterfeit Christ of the New Age Movement* (Grand Rapids, Mich.: Baker Book House, 1990).

[37]New Age personalities have promoted a book called the *Life of St. Issa,* allegedly discovered by Nicholas Notovich. It claims that Jesus studied Tibetan Buddhism in the Himalayas during his "missing years" between his childhood and the time he was baptized by John the Baptist. Many New Age advocates believe that Jesus went to India during his missing years and underwent seven degrees of initiation until he *became* the Christ. However, J. Edgar Goodspeed, the late biblical scholar, has shown that although *St. Issa* was reportedly written four years after Christ's crucifixion, it actually relies on the Gospels, Acts and Romans for its source material. These biblical works were written around thirty or more years after Christ's crucifixion. The New Testament seems to contradict the claim that Jesus went East during his missing years (Lk 2:52 [Jesus grew into manhood and studied the Torah]; 4:16 [he went to the synagogue "as was his custom"]; Mk 6:1-6 ["we have known Jesus for years"]. Why didn't the religious leaders ever accuse him of heresy for studying under pantheists when he was supposedly in India? Contrary to New Age beliefs, Jesus was always the Christ (Lk 2:26; Heb 13:8).

[38]For further study on the issue of the historical reliability of Christ and his resurrection, see Gary R. Habermas, *Resurrection of Jesus: An Apologetic* (Grand Rapids, Mich.: Baker Book House, 1980); Paul Barnett, *Is the New Testament Reliable? A Look at the Historical Evidence* (Downers Grove, Ill.: InterVarsity Press, 1986); George Eldon Ladd, *I Believe in the Resurrection of Jesus* (Grand Rapids, Mich.: Eerdmans, 1975); Craig Blomberg, *The Historical Reliability of the Gospels* (Downers Grove, Ill.: InterVarsity Press, 1987); Craig A. Evans, "Jesus in Non-Christian Sources," in *DPL,* pp. 364-68. On a popular level, consult Paul Little, *Know Why You Believe* (Downers Grove, Ill.: InterVarsity Press, 1968), and the various works of Josh McDowell (Here's Life Publishers, P.O. Box 1576, San Bernardino, CA 92402-1576; 1-800-950-4457), including titles such as *More Than a Carpenter* and, more recently, *A Ready Defense* (1990).

[39]For some of my sources, as well as recommended information, see Mark Albrecht and Brooks Alexander, "UFOs: Is Science Fiction Coming True?" *SCP Journal,* August 1977, pp. 12-23; John Weldon and Clifford Wilson, *Psychic Forces and Occult Shock,* pp. 129-47; David Fetcho, "A Sum of Shipwrecked Stars: UFOs and the Logic of Discernment," *SCP Journal,* August 1977, pp. 25-30; William Alnor, "UFO Cults Are Flourishing in New Age Circles," *Christian Research Journal* (reprinted as item DU-005, available at CRI); William Alnor, *UFOs in the New Age* (Grand Rapids,

Mich.: Baker Book House, 1992); Elizabeth L. Hillstrom, *Testing the Spirits* (Downers Grove, Ill.: InterVarsity Press, 1995), pp. 195-209; and UFO information (papers and cassettes) from Hugh Ross, Reasons to Believe, P.O. Box 5978, Pasadena, CA 91107.

[40]A brief examination of Erich von Daniken's *Chariots of the Gods?* is in order because of its pervasive influence. Von Daniken teaches that the "gods" of many of the ancient cultures were actually aliens from other planets who lived and communicated with humans here on earth. He interprets certain drawings from the Incas, Maya and other cultures as pictures of aliens in space suits and spaceships. His books have sold over thirty million copies. His critics have cited many errors in von Daniken's writings (for example, Walter Martin, "Chariots of the Who?" CRI cassette tape C-085; Weldon and Wilson, *Psychic Forces and Occult Shock*, pp. 130-36). Von Daniken has made numerous errors in his calculations, dates and interpretation of drawings or artifacts from early cultures. He claims that the Bible is full of contradictions, but as Weldon and Wilson forcefully demonstrate, it is the teachings of von Daniken that are full of contradictions.

[41]Weldon and Wilson, *Psychic Forces and Occult Shock*, p. 144.

[42]This does not contradict my earlier statement that UFOs sometimes adapt to the culture in which they are seen. There I argued that genuine UFOs seem to be nonphysical. The "chariots of fire" passage only serves to affirm this hypothesis. It is hard for me to accept that a *physically* advanced species from another planet would make their aircraft, or part of their aircraft, look like a horse. Do other planets have horses too?

[43]This does not mean that UFO "aliens" cannot be fallen angels. In fact, I will shortly suggest that "real" ones probably are in the main text.

[44]One calculation gives the assumption that if there were one million planets in the universe whose inhabitants were intelligent enough to fly to other locations of the universe, what are the chances of one ending up on earth? The odds for just one spaceship landing on earth per year could only be possible if *each* of these million planets were to launch ten thousand ships per year. Not only does this number seem excessive for even an advanced civilization to produce, but it does not even approach the numerous UFO sightings every year (Albrecht and Alexander, "UFOs: Is Science Fiction Coming True?" p. 16).

[45]Ibid., pp. 18-20.

[46]John Keel, *Operation Trojan Horse*, p. 44, cited in ibid., p. 19.

[47]See Bob and Gretchen Passantino, "What About Halloween?" Answers in Action, P.O. Box 2067, Costa Mesa, CA 92628. In one legend a man named Jack was so crafty that neither heaven nor hell wanted him, so he wandered about with a lantern ("Jack-o-lantern") looking for a place to stay.

[48]Ibid., p. 3.

[49]For more information on this subject, see John Warwick Montgomery, *Myth, Allegory and the Gospel: An Interpretation of J. R. R. Tolkien, C. S. Lewis, G. K. Chesterton and Charles Williams* (Minneapolis: Bethany Fellowship, 1974).

[50]"Troll Dolls," CRI Statement 3.137, n.d.

[51]Ibid.

[52]I am indebted to Craig Hawkins, former CRI researcher. I sat in on his 1989 occult lectures at Simon Greenleaf School of Law and read his articles: "The Modern World of Witchcraft: Part One," *Christian Research Journal*, Winter/Spring 1990, pp. 9-14; "The Modern World of Witchcraft: Part Two," *Christian Research Journal*, Winter/Spring 1990, pp. 22-27. Some of my source information was derived from his research. Also helpful was some information "straight from the horse's mouth" on the Internet.

[53]The mother goddess and the horned god are called by many names. Below is a list of some of the most common ones:

Mother Goddess	Horned God
Aphrodite	Adonis
Artemis	Apollo
Astarte	Dionysius
Sophia	Eros
Cybel	Hades
Diana	Horus
Gaia	Odin
Isis	Osiris
Kali	Pan
Venus	Thor

[54]Witches do not ride in the air on broomsticks. Brooms were (and occasionally still are) ridden in ceremonies to help encourage grain growth, but the participants do not fly in the air!

[55]Somewhat dated, but still one of the best introductions to Satanism remains Craig Hawkins's "The Many Faces of Satanism," *Forward*, Fall 1986, pp. 17-22.

[56]Ibid., p. 19.

[57]See Gretchen and Bob Passantino and Jon Trott, "Satan's Sideshow," *Cornerstone* 18, no. 90; Jon Trott, "Satanic Panic," *Cornerstone* 20, no. 95; Jon Trott and Mike Hertenstein, "Selling Satan," *Cornerstone* 21, no. 98; David G. Bromley, "Satanism: The New Cult Scare," conference paper presented at the Institute for the Study of American Religion (P.O. Box 90709, Santa Barbara, CA 93190-0709), May 1991; "Does Satanic/Sadistic

Ritual Abuse Exist?" http://web.canlink.com/ocrt/ra_none.htm.

[58]Kenneth Lanning, "Satanic, Occult, Ritualistic Crime: A Law Enforcement Perspective," *The Police Chief* 56; citation from Bromley, "Satanism: The New Cult Scare," p. 17.

[59]Helpful materials along these lines are found in Douglas Groothius, *Confronting the New Age* (Downers Grove, Ill.: InterVarsity Press, 1989); Hawkins, "The Modern World of Witchcraft: Part Two"; Hawkins, "Witnessing to Witches," *Christian Research Journal*, Summer 1990, item no. DW-180 available through CRI; "Witnessing to Occultists," *CRI Perspective*, CRI.

Scripture Index

Genesis
1–3, *85*
1–15, *186*
1:1, *21*, *152*, *157*,
  159
1:2, *193*
1:2-10, *194*
1:21, *92*
1:26-27, *158*
1:31, *57*, *59*, *86*, *194*
2, *81*
3, *59*, *84*, *85*, *89*,
  90, *157*, *177*, *195*
3:1, *91*, *177*, *193*
3:5, *90*
3:14, *89*
3:14-15, *84*, *87*, *91*,
  193
3:24, *18*, *26*
4, *60*, *120*
5:3-4, *60*
5:17-18, *65*
5:24, *22*
6, *23*, *59*, *60*, *61*,
  63, *64*, *65*, *66*, *67*,
  68, *72*, *74*, *98*,
  161, *162*, *173*,
  178, *185*, *187*, *191*
6–9, *187*
6:1-4, *60*, *66*
6:1-5, *64*, *161*
6:2, *61*, *63*, *186*
6:4, *187*
6:4-5, *65*
6:5, *65*
6:5–7:23, *187*
6:5-7, *67*
6:5-22, *60*
6:17, *66*
7:19, *67*
9:6, *66*
10, *37*
10:1-5, *181*
10:6-20, *181*
10:8, *186*
10:8-9, *66*
10:9-12, *182*

10:21-31, *181*
16:7-13, *30*
16:11, *45*
18, *22*, *23*, *178*
18:2, *178*
18:2-22, *64*
18:16, *178*
18:16-33, *178*
19:1, *178*
19:10-11, *20*
19:11, *43*
19:23-24, *180*
20, *118*
22:11-18, *30*
24:7, *41*, *180*
28:12, *18*, *20*, *41*
31:11-13, *46*
31:19, *145*
32:3, *18*
32:24-31, *30*
41:14-16, *153*
46:27, *37*
48:15-16, *30*
50:20, *105*

Exodus
1, *37*
2:20, *158*
3, *30*, *41*
3:2, *30*
3:2-6, *31*
3:14, *159*
4:22, *61*
7, *97*
7:11, *145*, *150*
7:11-12, *139*
7:11-13, *145*
7:22, *139*
8:6-19, *189*
8:7, *139*
8:10, *145*
8:18-19, *139*
14:19, *42*
20:5, *127*
20:5-6, *128*
21:28, *91*
22:17, *145*, *150*
23:20-21, *30*
25:10-22, *26*
25:17-22, *70*
30:23, *179*
32:30-34, *180*
32:33, *180*
33:20-23, *30*
34:13-14, *149*

Leviticus
16:6-22, *98*
16:8, *98*
17:7, *54*, *77*, *147*
18:21, *145*
19:19, *63*
19:26, *145*
19:26-31, *150*
19:31, *127*, *146*
20:6, *150*
20:15, *91*
20:16, *63*
20:27, *150*

Numbers
5:11-31, *65*
11:16, *37*
13, *187*
13:26-30, *67*
13:31-33, *68*
13:32-24, *68*
13:32-33, *66*
13:33, *187*
13:33-34, *67*
13:34, *67*
16:31-34, *127*
19:11-16, *56*
20:16, *30*
22:22, *93*
22:31-35, *40*
22:32, *93*
23:23, *145*
33:55, *110*

Deuteronomy
2:10-11, *66*
2:10-12, *66*
2:20-21, *66*
3:11, *66*
4:10, *128*
6:4, *159*
7:3, *63*
13:1-3, *139*
13:13, *97*
14:1, *61*, *185*, *186*
14:1-2, *186*
18, *142*
18:9-12, *69*
18:9-13, *135*, *145*
18:10, *145*, *150*
18:10-12, *127*, *168*
18:11, *146*
18:14, *147*
22:9, *63*
28–30, *128*

29:29, *28*, *88*, *154*
32:8, *37*, *59*, *62*
32:8-9, *125*
32:10, *197*
32:16-17, *147*
32:17, *53*, *77*
33:2, *24*, *32*

Joshua
5:13, *31*
6:2, *31*
7:24, *127*

Judges
2:1-5, *30*
6:11-24, *30*
9:23, *43*, *57*
9:37, *145*
13:3-5, *45*
13:21-22, *30*
17:5, *145*
19:22, *97*
20:13, *97*

1 Samuel
2:12, *97*
10:27, *97*
11:2, *197*
15:29, *121*
16–23, *116*
16:14, *43*, *55*, *56*,
  57, *124*, *131*
16:14-23, *75*
16:23, *43*, *124*
17:4, *67*
18:10, *129*
18:10-11, *116*
28:3-11, *146*
28:8-16, *69*
28:12, *188*
28:15, *188*
29:4, *93*

2 Samuel
1–5, *188*
7:14, *61*
9:23, *93*
14:17, *180*
14:17-20, *20*
19:27, *20*
20:1, *97*
21:16, *66*
21:16-22, *66*
22:5, *97*
24:16, *30*, *43*

24:26, *180*

1 Kings
1:2-3, *99*
1:6, *99*
1:16, *99*
5:18, *93*
7:29-36, *26*
8:27, *30*
8:39, *99*
13:18, *40*
18:28, *116*
19:3-7, *41*
19:5, *180*
19:5-8, *45*
21:10-13, *97*
22:19-22, *27, 192*
22:22, *43*

2 Kings
1:3, *180*
1:3-4, *40*
1:15, *180*
2, *155, 161*
2:11, *161*
6:15-17, *42*
6:15-18, *113*
6:17, *17*
17:17, *145*
18:35, *125*
19:35, *43, 180*
21:6, *145*
22:3, *198*
22:6, *43*
22:16, *118*
22:23-38, *43*
23:4, *149*
23:10, *145*
23:24, *150*

2 Chronicles
4:4, *178*
11:15, *54, 77, 102*
15:2, *124*
33:6, *145, 146, 147, 150*
36, *95*

Ezra
1:21, *179*

Nehemiah
9:6, *21, 24*

Job
1, *18, 44, 57, 62, 82*
1—2, *84, 93, 95, 96, 98, 100, 101, 105, 115, 182, 186, 192*
1:5-6, *125*
1:6, *59, 62, 192*
1:12, *100*
1:15, *100*
1:16, *100*
1:17, *100*
1:18-19, *100*
2, *109*
2:1, *59, 62*
2:6, *100*
2:7, *115, 116*
2:7-8, *100*
3:8, *92*
4:15-16, *19*
4:18-19, *21*
5:1, *36*
9:13, *92*
11:17, *82*
15:8, *27*
15:15, *21*
17:16, *198*
18:14, *95*
20:8, *68*
25:2-3, *32*
26:5, *68*
26:11, *118*
26:12, *92*
26:13, *92*
28, *101*
33:23, *40*
38:4-7, *21*
38:7, *20, 22, 59, 62*
38:17, *198*
38:32, *82*
40—41, *92, 193*
41, *193*
42:9-10, *120*

Psalms
2:7, *61*
18:11, *26*
18:15, *118*
28:1, *82*
29:1, *38*
30:3, *82*
31:5, *121*
33:8, *35*
34:5-7, *35*
34:8, *49*

34:18, *136*
38:21, *93*
51:10, *136*
58:1, *27*
58:6, *146*
68:17, *32*
71:13, *93*
72:9, *91*
74:14, *92*
78:49, *43*
87:4, *92*
88:10-11, *68*
89:5-7, *24*
89:6-9, *27*
89:10, *92*
89:19, *61*
90:11, *35*
91:6, *53*
91:11, *49*
96:5, *53*
103:7, *118*
103:17, *127*
103:20, *20*
103:20-21, *38*
104:4, *177*
104:26, *92*
105:9, *118*
106:36-38, *116*
106:37, *53, 77*
107:18, *198*
109:6, *93*
109:12, *127*
135:5, *57*
139, *35*
139:15, *196*
148:1-2, *38*
148:2, *24, 28*
148:2-5, *21*

Proverbs
2:18, *68*
6:24, *192*
14:12, *169*
16:9, *105*
16:18, *136*
19:21, *105*
25:28, *147*
30:15, *184*
30:19, *193*

Ecclesiastes
5:6, *18*

Isaiah
2:6, *145*

3:3-20, *145*
6, *26, 161*
6:2, *22*
6:2-3, *21*
8:17, *198*
8:19, *146*
8:20, *146*
11, *103*
11:1-5, *121*
11:5, *121*
11:6, *145*
13:21, *53, 54, 98*
14, *80, 82, 83, 87, 190, 191*
14:3, *82*
14:9, *68*
14:12, *80, 81, 82, 83, 185, 190, 191*
14:13-15, *80*
14:14, *82*
19:1, *26*
19:3, *146*
19:14, *136*
22:22, *119*
24:21, *112*
24:21-22, *125*
26:14, *68*
26:16, *145*
27:1, *92*
29:4, *146*
30:6, *178*
30:7, *92*
34:12, *53*
34:14, *54, 70, 98*
41:10, *21*
41:26, *154*
43:10, *158*
43:10-11, *159*
44:23, *196*
45:7, *57*
46:9-10, *99*
47:9-12, *146*
47:13, *145*
47:13-14, *153*
49:23, *91*
51:9-10, *92*
52:7, *122*
55:10-11, *118*
57:3, *145*
59:14-19, *121*
61:1, *108*
61:3, *136*
65:3, *53*
65:4, *146*

Jeremiah
3:9, *149*
7:31, *145*
8:17, *145*
10:2, *153*
14:14, *145*
19:6, *145*
23:18, *27*
27:9, *145*
29:10, *123*
29:11-13, *158*
32:35, *145*
37:16, *82*
50:39, *54*

Ezekiel
1, *161*
1:10, *26, 178*
1:13, *178*
3:14, *189*
8:1-3, *189*
9, *22*
9:1-11, *43*
9:4, *183*
10:12-14, *22, 178*
13:6-23, *145*
13:18-20, *146*
21:21, *146*
21:21-26, *145*
23:24, *110*
25—32, *81*
26—28, *81*
28, *80, 82, 87, 185*
28:2, *80*
28:11-19, *80*
28:13, *80, 81*
28:15, *81*
28:16, *178*
29:3-5, *92*
31, *81*
31:14, *82*
32:2-10, *92*
32:20-28, *66*
33:8-11, *171*
37:1, *189*

Daniel
1—6, *95*
1:17-20, *153*
2:2, *145, 146, 153*
2:10, *146*
2:27, *146*
2:27-28, *99*

2:27-30, *153*
3:8-29, *42*
3:25, *42, 59, 62*
3:28, *182*
4, *82*
4:13, *20, 27, 28*
4:13-26, *43*
4:17, *20, 27, 28*
4:23, *28*
6, *36, 55, 124*
6:22, *18, 42, 49*
7:8, *87*
7:9-10, *46*
7:10, *32, 47*
7:20, *87*
8:10, *71, 73, 87*
8:13, *73*
8:16, *28*
8:24, *73*
9:21, *28*
10, *125, 136, 189*
10:1-13, *125*
10:10, *49*
10:13, *26, 28, 29, 37, 38, 49, 72, 113, 125, 136*
10:20, *49, 113, 125*
10:20-21, *37, 72*
10:21, *26, 37*
12:1, *26, 37*
12:3, *73*
12:7-13, *46*

Hosea
1:10, *61*
4:12, *136*
4:12-14, *149*
9:7-8, *95*
12:2-4, *30*

Amos
9:2-4, *30*

Obadiah
4, *82*

Jonah
3:2-4, *108*

Micah
3:6-11, *145*
5:8, *122*
5:11, *145*
7:17, *91*

Nahum
1:15, *97*

Zechariah
1:3, *124*
1:8, *41*
1:10-12, *23*
1:11-13, *30*
2:3-5, *46*
3:1, *95, 180*
3:1-2, *93, 117*
3:1-4, *82, 84, 192*
3:2, *180*
5:9, *22, 23*
9:11, *82*
10:2, *145*
13:1-4, *93, 115*
13:2, *75*
14:5, *27*

Malachi
3:5, *145, 150*
3:7, *124*

Matthew
1:18-25, *44*
1:20, *41*
1:23, *159*
2:13, *41, 44*
2:19-20, *41*
2:19-21, *45*
4, *85, 124*
4:1, *94, 115*
4:1-11, *17*
4:3, *95*
4:5-6, *45*
4:8-9, *100*
4:10, *39, 93*
4:11, *45*
5:3, *55, 135*
6:10, *49*
6:13, *94*
7:7-10, *137*
7:15-20, *76*
7:16-20, *131*
7:21, *157*
7:21-23, *132*
7:22, *53, 72*
8:2, *29*
8:12, *171*
8:16, *55, 78, 128, 196*
8:28, *129*
8:28-29, *51*
8:28-34, *78, 128*

8:29, *103*
8:31, *53, 72*
8:32, *127*
9:18, *29*
9:32-34, *75, 78, 128*
9:33, *127*
9:34, *53*
10:1, *119*
10:18, *35*
10:20, *117*
10:28, *78*
10:29-31, *35*
11:27, *159*
12:22, *78, 135*
12:22-23, *75*
12:22-32, *75*
12:24, *52, 72, 99*
12:25-27, *99*
12:28, *52, 59, 75, 189*
12:28-29, *149*
12:29, *76*
12:32, *104*
12:40, *196*
12:43, *56, 74, 98*
12:43-45, *128*
13:19, *94*
13:25, *95*
13:38-41, *115*
13:39-42, *46*
13:43, *73*
14:26, *68*
14:33, *29*
15:1-20, *198*
15:21, *127, 135*
15:21-28, *75*
16, *106*
16:16-17, *159*
16:18, *119*
16:19, *118, 119, 120*
16:21-23, *105*
16:22, *118*
16:23, *106*
16:27, *45, 46*
17:14, *116*
17:14-21, *75, 78, 128*
17:21, *124, 134*
18:10, *34, 35, 36, 49*
18:10-13, *35*
18:15-20, *120*
18:18, *118, 198*
18:20, *38*
19:4-6, *90*
20:20, *29*

22:30, *25, 63*
23:13, *198*
24:4-5, *76*
24:9-13, *73*
24:13, *123*
24:20, *139*
24:23-27, *76*
24:31, *45, 47*
24:36, *46, 154*
25:31, *27, 45*
25:41, *55, 80, 112*
25:46, *58, 104*
26:53, *32, 45*
26:63-64, *159*
26:67, *110*
28:2, *18, 20*
28:2-7, *44*
28:3, *22*
28:16, *29*
28:18, *72, 118, 149*
28:19, *77*

Mark
1, *18*
1:13, *45*
1:21-24, *129*
1:23, *55, 103*
1:23-24, *74*
1:24, *51, 56*
1:24-27, *56*
1:25, *126, 134*
1:25-28, *75*
1:34, *51, 53, 56, 72, 74, 78, 118, 128*
1:39, *74*
3:11-12, *51, 74, 118*
3:14, *127*
3:22, *52, 99*
3:22-27, *127*
3:24, *71, 119*
3:25-27, *111*
3:26, *71*
3:27, *76, 119, 145*
3:29, *104*
4:15, *115*
4:39-41, *118*
5:1-4, *57*
5:1-5, *129*
5:1-13, *73*
5:1-20, *56, 75, 78*
5:2-3, *56*
5:2-5, *116*
5:3-4, *116*
5:6, *56*

5:13, *56, 199*
5:15, *116*
6:1-6, *206*
6:14-16, *205*
6:49, *68*
7:24-30, *75, 117, 127, 135*
7:25-30, *135*
7:26, *56*
7:29-30, *75*
8:32-33, *118*
8:38, *45*
9:1-10, *69*
9:14-29, *75, 78*
9:17-25, *55*
9:18-22, *129*
9:25, *56, 127, 134*
9:25-26, *135*
9:28-29, *153*
9:29, *124, 134*
9:33, *78*
9:42-50, *171*
10:17-23, *132*
11:23, *118*
12:25, *23*
12:38-40, *104*
13:26, *45, 46*
13:27, *45*
13:32, *46*
13:36-42, *45*
14:62, *45, 46*
14:65, *110*
16:3-4, *20*
16:5, *22, 44*
16:8, *127*
16:9, *75*
16:15, *122*
16:17, *117, 134*

Luke
1:11, *38*
1:11-19, *28*
1:11-20, *44*
1:17, *155*
1:26-38, *44*
2:8-13, *44*
2:9, *20*
2:13-14, *38*
2:13-15, *20*
2:14, *49*
2:21, *44*
2:26, *206*
2:52, *206*
4:2, *133*
4:5-7, *94*

4:31-37, *118*
4:33, *129*
4:33-34, *129*
4:33-36, *74*
4:35-36, *118*
4:36, *127*
6:46, *132*
7:21, *78, 128*
8:2, *75*
8:12, *94*
8:26-33, *75*
8:26-39, *78*
8:28, *56*
8:30, *72*
8:31, *60, 111*
8:31-32, *56*
8:34-37, *75*
9:1, *117, 119, 127, 134*
9:26, *27, 45*
9:28-33, *69*
9:37-43, *75, 78*
9:41-42, *129*
9:49, *52*
9:52, *18*
9:55, *118*
10:17, *117, 127*
10:17-18, *59*
10:18, *73, 75, 76, 84, 85, 86, 93, 190*
10:20, *117, 196*
11:14-15, *78*
11:15, *99*
11:17-22, *101*
11:20, *52, 75, 189*
11:21, *76, 95*
11:24-26, *55, 128*
11:46-48, *74*
11:52, *120*
12:8-9, *45, 46*
13:3, *132*
13:10-17, *75, 116, 128*
13:11-16, *133*
13:16, *115*
15:7, *20, 38*
15:10, *20, 49*
16:19-31, *69, 171, 188*
16:23, *42*
17:3, *198*
17:21, *204*
20:36, *19*
21:36, *124*
22:3, *93, 131*

22:3-5, *105*
22:31-32, *84, 100, 101, 115*
22:43, *41, 45*
22:53, *54*
23:39-43, *25*
23:40-41, *198*
23:43, *107, 108*
23:46, *107, 108, 197*
24:4, *49*
24:4-5, *20, 22*
24:4-7, *44* –
24:39, *68*
24:49, *153*

John
1:1-3, *21, 77, 118, 152*
1:1-14, *159*
1:12, *169*
1:14, *118*
1:18, *178*
1:21, *155*
1:51, *20*
3:1-8, *153*
3:3-8, *155*
3:16, *77, 122, 158, 171*
3:16-18, *169*
3:19-21, *54*
4:1-4, *56*
4:24, *178*
4:25-26, *159*
5:18, *159*
5:21, *108*
5:28-29, *25, 155, 180*
7:20, *116, 201*
7:37-39, *155*
8:24-58, *159*
8:44, *56, 85, 90, 94, 95, 115, 171*
8:48-52, *116, 201*
8:53-59, *31*
9:34-38, *198*
10:10, *171*
10:20-21, *116, 201*
10:28-30, *123*
10:30, *159*
10:36, *159*
11:1-6, *108*
11:14, *108*
11:17, *108*
11:43-44, *180*
12:31, *75, 84, 94,*

101
12:31-32, *85*
13:2, *105, 115*
13:27, *93*
14:6, *24, 29, 159*
14:6-14, *39*
14:13-14, *137*
14:30, *94*
15:1-5, *131*
16:5-10, *85*
16:30, *101*
16:33, *122*
17:1, *153*
17:15, *94*
20:11-12, *44*
20:22-23, *120*

Acts
1, *46, 75*
1:9, *107*
1:9-11, *108, 153*
1:10, *22*
1:10-11, *22*
1:11, *49*
1:24-26, *147*
2, *107*
2:2-4, *153*
2:4, *137, 153*
2:17-23, *59*
2:23, *105*
2:27, *196*
2:34, *137*
2:37-42, *120*
2:38, *132*
2:38-39, *153*
2:47, *120*
3:12, *153*
3:18, *105*
3:19, *120, 132*
4:7, *118*
4:8, *135*
4:11-12, *120*
4:12, *135, 159*
4:31, *153*
5, *115*
5:3, *93*   -
5:3-4, *131, 153*
5:7-11, *42*
5:16, *56, 78, 127*
5:19, *20, 49*
7:14, *181*
7:30-38, *30*
7:53, *24, 41*
8:5-12, *75*
8:7, *56, 78, 127*

8:9-24, *132*
8:18-24, *153*
8:19-24, *150*
8:20-24, *120*
8:26, *41*
9:3-8, *109*
10, *41*
10:3-4, *20*
10:3-5, *40*
10:3-6, *40*
10:10, *144*
10:30, *22*
10:38, *75, 94, 101*
10:44, *41*
11:26, *197*
12:3-15, *36*
12:5-11, *20*
12:7, *41*
12:7-8, *40*
12:15, *35*
12:21-23, *43*
12:23, *20*
13:4-11, *129*
13:4-12, *147, 168*
13:6-12, *117*
13:10, *94, 115*
13:13, *109*
14:3, *153*
14:16, *101*
14:19, *110*
16, *203*
16:9, *69*
16:16, *154*
16:16-18, *56, 117, 129*
16:16-19, *144, 147*
16:18, *127, 135*
16:31, *122*
17:11, *77*
17:18, *77*
17:25-28, *171*
17:30, *101*
18:2, *189*
19:11-12, *117, 135*
19:12, *127, 135*
19:12-13, *56*
19:13, *52*
19:13-19, *149*
19:13-20, *148, 149*
19:15, *114, 149*
19:16, *57, 74, 129*
19:17-20, *135*
20:28-35, *151*
20:29-30, *76*
22:17, *109*

23:5, *109*
23:9, *20*
26:17, *93*
26:18, *101*
27:23, *20*
27:23-25, *40*

Romans
1:3-4, *108*
1:28, *104*
3:23, *157, 169*
3:23-26, *123*
4:1, *108*
5:8, *169, 171*
5:12-19, *90*
6:12-18, *122*
6:23, *123, 169*
8:9, *153*
8:9-11, *131*
8:11, *108*
8:18-23, *111*
8:19-23, *103*
8:26, *200*
8:28, *37, 105, 110, 123*
8:38, *71, 72, 116, 185*
8:38-39, *24, 119*
8:39, *72*
10:7, *196*
10:9-10, *122, 132, 169*
10:15, *122*
11:8, *136*
13:1-3, *71*
13:12, *54*
14:9-11, *192*
14:23, *137, 157*
16:17-18, *151*
16:20, *93, 100, 111*

1 Corinthians
1:1-2, *39*
1:1-9, *138*
1:18, *123*
1:30, *131*
2:1, *109*
2:4, *199*
2:4-5, *110*
2:6, *72*
2:6-8, *105*
2:8, *72*
3:11-15, *27*
3:16, *138*
4:9, *185*

4:11, *110*
5:1-5, *115*
5:5, *93, 132*
6:3, *24, 112, 185*
6:19, *131*
6:19-20, *138*
7:5, *93, 115, 125*
7:7, *109*
8:1-5, *21, 29, 53*
10:1-22, *77*
10:6-11, *195*
10:10, *116*
10:11, *178*
10:12, *17*
10:20, *77*
10:20-21, *53, 73, 147*
11, *25*
11:10, *25, 49*
12, *153*
12:3, *129*
12:4, *134*
12:10, *198*
12:13, *131, 138, 155*
13:1, *49*
13:8-13, *137*
14:2, *137, 200*
14:4, *137*
14:14-15, *137*
14:15, *124*
14:26-33, *138*
14:39, *137*
14:40, *138*
15:1-3, *76, 159*
15:1-8, *122*
15:2-3, *169*
15:12-57, *25*
15:20-26, *90, 155*
15:22, *108*
15:24, *71*
15:24-25, *72*
15:24-28, *103*
15:45-56, *90*
15:51-57, *119*
16:13, *121*

2 Corinthians
2, *115*
2:6-11, *124*
2:11, *93*
2:14, *108*
4:4, *94, 100, 115, 125, 192*
5:4-8, *69*
5:7, *114*

5:8, *25*
5:10, *27*
6:7, *122*
6:14, *54, 97*
6:14-15, *97*
10:1, *109*
10:4-5, *121*
11:1-14, *77*
11:1-15, *109*
11:2-14, *115*
11:14, *90, 190*
11:16-33, *109*
11:23—12:9, *114*
12:2, *110, 195*
12:2-4, *144*
12:7, *109, 110, 115, 133*
12:7-10, *105*
12:8, *110*
12:9, *110*
12:12, *199*

Galatians
1:8-9, *40, 41, 76*
3:1, *150*
3:5, *199*
3:19, *24, 41*
4:3, *188*
4:8, *21, 53, 95, 158*
4:8-11, *188*
4:9, *119, 188*
4:13-14, *109, 197*
5:19-21, *132, 147, 168*
5:20, *150*
6:11, *109*

Ephesians
1, *204*
1:3, *73*
1:7, *118*
1:10, *103, 122*
1:13, *123*
1:13-14, *123*
1:19-20, *24*
1:19-23, *149*
1:20-22, *107*
1:21, *71, 72, 189*
1:21-22, *49*
2:1-9, *123*
2:2, *82, 99, 100, 101, 107*
2:2-4, *125*
2:2-5, *149*
2:5, *204*

2:6, *73*
2:8-9, *77, 122*
2:14-18, *122*
3:10, *20, 71, 99, 105, 122*
3:14-19, *204*
4:8, *106, 107*
4:8-10, *149*
4:9, *196*
4:15, *168*
4:24, *122*
4:25, *121*
4:25-27, *115*
4:26-27, *192*
4:27, *94, 116, 149, 204*
4:30, *123*
5:2, *204*
5:9, *121, 122*
5:18, *123*
5:18-20, *124, 153*
5:26, *123*
6:10-12, *71*
6:10-13, *121*
6:10-18, *116, 120, 134, 149, 204*
6:11-12, *55, 57, 107, 113*
6:12, *54, 71, 82, 99, 101, 121, 189*
6:14-17, *121*
6:16, *94*
6:18, *124*

Philippians
1:11, *122*
1:21-23, *25*
1:21-24, *69*
2:9-11, *24, 118, 132*
2:10, *192*
2:10-11, *72, 103*
2:15, *73*
4:6, *124*
4:6-8, *100*
4:8, *114*

Colossians
1:12-13, *54*
1:13, *131*
1:15-16, *21, 57*
1:15-18, *118, 152, 157*
1:16, *24, 71, 72, 189*
1:20, *57, 103*
2:8, *188*

2:9-10, *72*
2:10, *24, 49, 71*
2:13-15, *189*
2:14-15, *85, 107*
2:15, *71, 72, 106, 107, 108, 118, 119, 189, 196*
2:16-23, *189*
2:18, *29, 39, 188*
2:20, *188*
4:2-4, *124*

1 Thessalonians
1:5, *199*
2:18, *115*
3:2-5, *123*
3:5, *95, 116*
3:13, *20, 27*
4:16, *29, 180*
4:16-18, *25*
5:4-5, *54*
5:6, *121, 147*
5:8, *147*
5:17, *124*
5:21, *77*

2 Thessalonians
1:7, *46, 49*
1:7-10, *49*
2, *111*
2:1-12, *116*
2:3, *73*
2:3-4, *87*
2:8, *118*
2:9, *115*
2:9-12, *139*
3:3, *94*

1 Timothy
1:20, *93, 116, 132*
2:1-3, *124*
2:5, *19, 24, 29, 39, 159*
3:2-7, *124*
3:6, *85, 86, 125*
3:6-7, *115, 192*
3:7, *86*
3:16, *49, 108*
4:1, *73, 76*
4:1-5, *56, 116*
4:1-6, *56*
4:2, *104*
5:13-15, *124*
5:14, *86*
5:15, *93, 115*

5:21, *26, 45*
5:21-22, *27*
6:12, *123*

2 Timothy
1:7, *55, 135*
2:1, *121*
2:3, *121*
2:4, *121*
2:25-26, *171*
2:26, *86, 94*
3:8, *139*
3:13, *152*
4:2, *198*
4:7, *123*

Titus
2:2, *147*
2:4, *147*
2:6, *147*
2:8, *192*
2:13, *77*
3:5, *155*

Hebrews
1, *177*
1:2, *157*
1:3-14, *24*
1:4-6, *177*
1:6, *24, 29*
1:7, *177*
1:8, *77*
1:8-13, *177*
1:14, *19, 22, 24, 35, 38, 41*
2:2, *24, 41*
2:5-8, *24*
2:13, *198*
2:13-14, *85*
2:14, *90, 94, 101, 107, 118, 119*
2:14-17, *85*
2:16, *103*
3:12-14, *123*
4:13, *35*
5:12, *188*
6:4-5, *111*
6:4-6, *104*
6:5, *75*
6:18, *121*
7:12-25, *41*
8:7-13, *41*
9:27, *155*
10:1-10, *41*
11, *122*

12:20, *91*
12:22, *32*
13:2, *22*
13:5, *123*
13:8, *206*

James
1:13-16, *132*
2:17-26, *122*
2:19, *56, 72, 192*
3:1, *104*
3:11-12, *131*
3:14, *115*
4:7, *120*
4:7-8, *124*
4:8, *121*
4:17, *157*
5:4, *28*

1 Peter
1:10-12, *20, 105*
1:13, *147*
1:25, *123*
2:10-11, *40*
2:24, *122*
3:4, *136*
3:7, *137*
3:18, *108*
3:18-19, *108*
3:19, *106, 108,*
  197
3:19-21, *60*
3:22, *24, 108*
4:7, *147*
5:8, *94, 95, 112,*
  115

2 Peter
2, *152*
2:4, *60, 62, 72, 99,*
  108, 111, 178
2:10-11, *24*
2:10-12, *118*
3:9, *112*
3:10-12, *188*
3:16, *77*

1 John
1:5-7, *54*
1:8, *122*
1:9, *122*

1:9—2:6, *133*
1:10, *122*
2:1-2, *122*
2:13-14, *94*
2:14, *124*
2:19, *132*
2:22-23, *159*
2:29, *122*
3:4, *157*
3:8, *85, 94, 101, 145*
3:8-12, *115*
3:10, *115*
3:11-15, *85*
3:12, *94, 115*
4:1, *55*
4:1-6, *40, 76, 129*
4:4, *78, 100, 112,*
  118, 122, 131,
  134, 145, 169
5:1, *155*
5:4-5, *122*
5:13, *123*
5:14-15, *137*
5:16-18, *132*
5:17, *157*
5:18, *131*
5:18-19, *100, 122*
5:19, *94, 115, 125*

Jude
6, *20, 55, 56, 60,*
  62, 63, 72, 111,
  178
8-10, *40, 118*
9, *26, 28, 117*
11, *62*
13, *73*
14, *20, 32*
14-16, *46*
20, *124*

Revelation
1, *182*
1:1, *41, 46*
1:17, *107*
1:18, *119, 120*
1:20, *37*
2:1, *37*
2:5, *132*
2:8, *37*
2:9, *115*

2:10, *94, 115*
2:12, *37*
2:13, *189*
2:18, *37, 159*
3:1, *37*
3:7, *37, 120*
3:9, *115*
3:14, *37*
4, *26, 161*
4:1, *185*
4:1-3, *144*
4:6-8, *178*
4:8, *21*
4:8-11, *17*
5:1-7, *24*
5:2, *183*
5:11-12, *49*
5:11-13, *32*
5:11-14, *29*
5:13, *179*
7, *46*
7:1, *20*
8, *46*
8:2, *28*
8:4, *36*
9, *43*
9:1, *42, 60, 73, 82,*
  116, 191
9:11, *116*
9:12, *195*
9:15, *46*
9:20, *53, 77*
9:21, *150*
10, *22, 182*
10:1, *183*
11:3-7, *42*
11:12, *180*
11:15, *180*
12, *58, 59, 73, 84,*
  86, 92, 102, 115,
  123, 185, 191, 194
12:1-3, *54*
12:3, *73*
12:4, *73*
12:4-5, *73*
12:5, *115*
12:7, *49, 55, 73*
12:7-8, *74*
12:7-9, *26, 28, 113*
12:7-11, *108*
12:9, *58, 73, 84, 89,*

93, 101, 107, 115,
  177
12:9-11, *84, 85, 192*
12:10, *84, 115*
12:10-12, *73*
12:11, *100, 118*
12:12, *56, 111, 115*
12:13-17, *115*
13, *87, 111*
13:1-4, *112*
13:2, *110*
13:8, *105*
13:11, *139*
14:10, *20, 27*
14:11, *171*
14:14-16, *47*
14:14-20, *45, 46*
15:6, *22*
16, *46*
16:12-15, *115*
16:13, *56, 57, 139*
16:13-14, *116*
16:17, *115, 195*
17, *190*
17—18, *112*
18:2, *54, 56, 98,*
  197
18:23, *150*
19, *118*
19:9-10, *29*
19:10, *39*
19:11-14, *31*
19:14-21, *46*
19:19—20:2, *111*
20, *84, 103, 112*
20:1-3, *47*
20:1-4, *85*
20:2, *84, 89, 93*
20:4, *25*
20:4-6, *155*
20:10, *85, 111, 171*
20:10-15, *104*
20:11-15, *25, 155*
21, *84*
21:8, *147, 150*
22:8-9, *20*
22:14-15, *147*
22:15, *150*